Effective Leadership, Management and Supervision in Health and Social Care

SAGE was founded in 1965 by Sara Miller McCune to support the dissemination of usable knowledge by publishing innovative and high-quality research and teaching content. Today, we publish over 900 journals, including those of more than 400 learned societies, more than 800 new books per year, and a growing range of library products including archives, data, case studies, reports, and video. SAGE remains majority-owned by our founder, and after Sara's lifetime will become owned by a charitable trust that secures our continued independence.

Los Angeles | London | New Delhi | Singapore | Washington DC | Melbourne

Effective Leadership, Management and Supervision in Health and Social Care

RICHARD FIELD and KEITH BROWN

2nd Edition

SAGE | LearningMatters

Learning Matters
An imprint of SAGE Publications Ltd
1 Oliver's Yard
55 City Road
London EC1Y 1SP

SAGE Publications Inc.
2455 Teller Road
Thousand Oaks, California 91320

SAGE Publications India Pvt Ltd
B 1/I 1 Mohan Cooperative Industrial Area
Mathura Road
New Delhi 110 044

SAGE Asia-Pacific Pte Ltd
3 Church Street
#10–04 Samsung Hub
Singapore 049483

Editor: Kate Wharton
Development editor: Lauren Simpson
Production controller: Chris Marke
Project management: Deer Park Productions
Marketing manager: Tamara Navaratnam
Cover design: Wendy Scott
Printed and bound by CPI Group (UK) Ltd,
Croydon, CR0 4YY

First edition published in 2010 by Learning Matters Ltd
Second edition published in 2016 by Learning Matters,
an imprint of SAGE

Library of Congress Control Number: 2016950579

British Library Cataloguing in Publication Data

A catalogue record for this book is available from the
British Library

ISBN: 978-1-4739-7197-4
ISBN: 978-1-4739-7198-1 (pbk)

At SAGE we take sustainability seriously. Most of our products are printed in the UK using FSC papers and boards.
When we print overseas we ensure sustainable papers are used as measured by the PREPS grading system.
We undertake an annual audit to monitor our sustainability.

Contents

About the authors

Professor Keith Brown holds academic and professional qualifications in social work, nursing, teaching and management. He has worked in the education and training field for over 25 years, in both universities and local authorities, and is currently Director of the National Centre for Post-Qualifying Social Work and Professional Practice and Director of the Institute of Health and Social Care Integration, at Bournemouth University.

Dr Catherine Driscoll has worked in the NHS in both mental health and community settings, in the voluntary and community sector and, for the last 20 years, in Local Authorities. She was the Director for Adult and Community Services in Dorset County Council before moving to her current role of Director of Children, Families and Communities for Worcestershire in June 2016. She has a PhD from the School of Public Policy at The University of Birmingham.

Dr Lee-Ann Fenge is Deputy Director of the National Centre for Post-Qualifying Social Work and Professional Practice at Bournemouth University. She is a qualified social worker, and has worked in settings with both adults and children. Her research interests concern inclusive and creative research methodologies for engaging with seldom heard groups, and she has undertaken a number of projects in collaboration with the voluntary sector. She teaches around the topics of leadership and supervision, and has led a number of evaluations of current health and social work practice linked to integration and new ways of working.

Richard Field is director of Learning Means Ltd, a consultancy specialising in management and leadership development in the public and voluntary sectors. Richard is a Visiting Fellow of Bournemouth University working within the Institute of Health and Social Care Integration and is also associate of the Office for Public Management (OPM). Richard is a qualified Executive Coach and a licenced user of a range of psychometric instruments. Previous experience includes working as a local authority accountant and as a university programme manager.

Jane Holroyd is director of Jane Holroyd Consultancy, a consultancy specialising in leadership development in the public sector. Jane is a Visiting Fellow of Bournemouth University and has over 25 years' experience working in senior leadership roles within the NHS, both acute and primary care sectors. She has a proven track record in complex change management and service redesign. Jane is passionate about the development of leadership through the development of individuals with programmes that are based in the reality of the public sector and that focus on making a real difference to front line services. To this end she has developed and delivered a Self-leadership: Building Personal Resilience and Relationships that work within Health and Social Care programme at Masters Level. Jane is a trained executive coach and is currently contracted with Macmillan Cancer Services. She is a Henley Business School prize winner.

Emily Rosenorn-Lanng is a researcher at The National Centre for Post Qualifying Social Work and Professional Practice, Bournemouth University. She has worked in Social Research for over 10 years, undertaking projects throughout the health, social care, tourism, and heritage sectors, specializing in bespoke research methodologies, data handling and analysis. Emily provides research consultancy to national partners and has supported practitioners across the health and social care sector to undertake Service Improvement Projects.

Dr Sue Ross is currently the Service Director for Children's Social Care in Bournemouth and a Visiting Fellow of Bournemouth University. She is a registered social worker with over 40 years' experience in adult and children's services in the NHS and in local authorities and has held Director and Chief Executive roles in Scotland, Wales and England. She is a Trustee of a national voluntary organization providing services for people with learning disabilities, Independent Chair of South Tyneside's Adult Safeguarding Board and has authored and chaired a number of Serious Case Reviews and Service Reviews. She is a qualified and experienced coach and mentor with the Institute of Leadership and Management.

Foreword

This second edition has been written as a direct result of our desire to put into print our latest thoughts, aspirations and desires to support and facilitate high quality leadership, management and supervision in Health and Social Care.

It is our view that much of the current material supporting leadership, management and supervision is not specific enough to deal with the unique challenges of operating in the Health and Social Care field. This is the reason why we wanted to revise this text to help and support all those professionals who aspire to lead, manage and supervise staff within the Health and Social Care sector.

This second edition retains and updates those parts of the successful first edition that remain relevant and important to leadership and management practice, to which material addressing new and emerging challenges facing leaders and managers has been added. Specifically, this text now covers leading in an integrated environment, commissioning and self-leadership each of which is either new or now more significant to health and social care than when the first edition was written. This new editorial also acts as a generic overview of the SAGE/Learning Matters Post-Qualifying Leadership and Management series of handbooks, and the various chapters in this text provide a summary and introduction to the themes contained within the wider series.

It is our sincere desire that the text meets these needs and helps to promote and support the most effective leadership, management and supervision of our vital health and social care services.

Keith Brown
Director of the National Centre for Post-Qualifying Social Work and Professional Practice and
Director of the Institute of Health and Social Care Integration

Acknowledgements

The second edition of this text has been greatly enriched through the inclusion of knowledge, experience, insight and expertise from a wide range of contributors including senior leaders, lecturers, consultants and researchers, each with many years of experience working in health and social care.

Introduction

Purpose and approach

This book seeks to offer a practical introduction to effective leadership, management and supervision in health and social care. It is designed for those leading, managing and supervising teams and services in health and social care and is equally applicable to those working for commissioning organisations, commissioning support units or health and social care providers, including internal business units. It is therefore relevant to a wide range of health and social care professionals including doctors, nurses, social workers, senior practitioners and those from allied health professions.

As well as being relevant for those exercising leadership, management and supervision as part of a wider professional role this text is also aimed at those specialising in management and administration within Clinical Commissioning Groups (CCGs) general practices, health trusts, clinics etc. This book attempts to capture as concisely as possible the key dimensions, issues, models and skills needed to lead and manage a team or service.

It will be of interest to those on undergraduate programmes that feature leadership, management or supervision, post-qualifying courses forming part of a Leadership and Management pathway or those on other post-qualifying pathways. It may also be used to support in-house induction and introductory programmes for managers.

We have taken a particular approach to this second edition that has a number of dimensions:

- We have deliberately focused on a number of key areas of activity you need to manage to lead a team efficiently and effectively.

- We have adopted an approach that encourages you to critically analyse performance and plan for improvement.

- We signpost many additional texts and materials that will support you in developing into the best leader or manager that you can become. In particular, many of the chapters form a valuable insight into leadership issues covered in more depth within the SAGE/Learning Matters Leadership and Management series of handbooks.

- We have provided reflection points to help you reach judgements about your leadership and current team performance and to plan improvements.

- We believe that our health and social care value base means that leaders must be participative, so engaging your team in the management of services is a common theme throughout.

- We have broken this text into 11 chapters each of which starts with a set of outcomes, includes examples and case material intended to illustrate leadership, management and supervision in practice and, with the exception of Chapter 1, each concludes with lay learning points.

In Chapter 1 we offer our view of the current and likely future context for health and social care leadership and management. As part of this we identify a number of key environmental drivers, resultant pressures and associated challenges facing leaders and managers, all of which has informed our choice of content.

One of the new features of the health and social care landscape to emerge since the first edition of this text is the drive to more fully integrate health and social care, a development reflected in the content of the second chapter entitled Leading for integration, and in Chapter 9, Integration through effective change leadership.

Chapter 3 focuses on another new topic, self-leadership which we see as essential to equipping leaders to operate in the new and much more challenging environment. This leads naturally into Chapter 4 which looks at how leaders can develop their style of leadership.

Chapter 5 addresses supervision which remains a key part of leadership practice in the helping professions.

Chapter 6 is a welcome contribution from Dr Sue Ross, a senior experienced health and social care manager who shares her thoughts about leading successful teams in health and social care.

The next two chapters, 7 and 8 address planning and budgeting, both of which are key to successful operation. Since the first edition the health and care sector has adopted commissioning and it is important to understand what this means and how it is evolving. Chapter 7 therefore also includes an introduction to commissioning along with material concerning strategic thinking which we argue is more important than the preparation of traditional strategy documents.

Dr Catherine Driscoll, another experienced senior social care manager thoughtfully considers in Chapter 9 how health and social care integration can be pursued through effective change leadership.

In Chapter 10 the case is made for impact evaluation of leadership programmes and a process by which this can be completed, is outlined.

The final chapter, 11, is a summary of key theoretical perspectives that explain how our understanding of leadership and management has developed over the years and continues to evolve.

Editors' views about leadership, management, supervision and personal development

As editors of this text we are aware that our personal beliefs and shared values impact on how we write and edit this text. We acknowledge that these beliefs are not universally held and that each person approaching this text has their own experiences, views and beliefs that will influence how accepting or challenging they are of the content. We believe that:

- What leaders do (management) and how they do it (leadership) are vital to good quality care.

- Supervision is a core management function in health and social care and a fundamental leadership activity.

- Devolved management and distributed leadership are essential to effective organisations.

- Each person needs to develop their own authentic approach to management and leadership informed by a mix of experience and theory.

- All development activity should be an opportunity for both personal and organisational growth leading to better outcomes for patients, service users, staff and other stakeholders.

- Challenge and support are necessary for effective development.

- Individuals should be encouraged to critically reflect on their experience and theory – constantly striving to develop practice.

- The fast changing pace of health and social care coupled with acute time pressure means that leaders and managers need to be able to dip into specific areas of learning within text books that address current needs or those they anticipate having in the near future.

These beliefs have significantly influenced the structure, chapter length, writing style, reflection prompts and the level of challenge and support featured in the content.

Most importantly we believe that all health and social care professionals need to lead the services they are responsible for with the service user/client/patient at the very heart of their efforts. At times of pressure, be it resource or capacity, it is often easy to focus in on the organisation or sector that you are responsible for sometimes at the expense of the 'end user'.

Health and social care professionals ultimately exist to make a difference to citizens of society in their moments of crisis/need. We owe it to both our professionals, society at large and most importantly those whom me work with (our patients and service users) to make sure we efficiently lead, manage and supervise in order to deliver the very best health and social care services.

We hope that this book will help you and your team in supervision and while working as a team to solve problems, deliver and improve services.

Chapter 1
Context

Keith Brown and Richard Field

CHAPTER OUTCOMES

As a result of completing this chapter you will:

- Be aware of key features of the current health and social care context within which leadership, management and supervision are practised.

- Appreciate some of the key pressures experienced by managers working within health and social care.

- Understand what, in our view, are the key challenges facing those leading and managing health and social care over the next five years.

- Understand how our sense of the environment, pressures and challenges has influenced the focus of this text.

This chapter starts with a brief overview of the current context within which leadership and management in health and social care is practised and how this might shift over the next five years. A summary of key pressures and challenges facing leaders and managers are identified and implications outlined. The chapter concludes with an explanation of the editors' responses within this text.

Overview of the current and likely future context

The public sector in general and health and social care, in particular, is facing what is probably the most difficult time in its long history and it is easy to paint a dark picture of the future. Within the next five to ten years, difficult conversations need to be had, decisions made and actions taken, if we are to avoid the collapse of health and social care services as we know them.

However, another view is that this as a period of unparalleled opportunity, a time when we can really think about what good health and social care looks like and challenge long-held assumptions, traditions and practices. We believe we will look back at the period 2008 to 2020 and see this as a pivotal point in the history of health and social care – the time that an old, broken paradigm was abandoned and a new, better one emerged.

A journey is underway which will see immense change; a different deal between the state, individuals and communities, greater individual and community self-help, more equal relationships between practitioners, service users and patients, a reduced and different role for the state and for those working in the helping professions.

This period is, and will remain, potentially difficult for those leading, featuring as it does considerable uncertainty and turbulence. Already we are seeing transformation at organisation level or at least waves of change, new initiatives – some of which work immediately, some work but only after considerable revision while others need to be abandoned. We are reassessing the value of what health and social care profession-als have been doing for many years. Personal and professional beliefs and values are being challenged leading some managers to question whether they are still attracted to health and social care. We are seeing a shift is sources of power, status and reward.

The current context for health and social care features a significant number of forces that are driving this transformation, including:

Demand for services

The need for health and social care is increasing, particularly for the older population. The United Kingdom had a population of 65.1 million in 2015 (ONS). In 2016, 11.4 million people are over the age of 65 (Age UK, 2016: 3), a figure that is expected to rise to 16 million by 2033 (Age UK, 2016: 3) this includes around 1.7 million aged 85+, a figure that is expected to double by 2039 (Age UK, 2016: 3). Life expectancy at the age of 65 currently stands at 85.9 and 83.4 for women and men, respectively (Age UK, 2016: 7) and it is estimated that 20 per cent of people cur-rently in the UK will see their 100th birthday (Age UK, 2016: 3).

Approximately 4 million older people in the UK have a limiting longstanding illness (Age UK, 2016: 8), the additional cost of which by 2018 is likely to be £5 billion pa (Age UK, 2016: 8), a financial cost that will rise much further given that the number of older people with these conditions is expected to rise to 6.25 million by 2030.

There are a number of prevalent conditions that are a particular challenge to the health system including the number of people that are overweight or obese, have diabetes and/ or are living with dementia. The NHS England Business Plan 2016/17 reported that 'the prevalence of Type 2 diabetes has been rising fast, driven by obesity; the number of people diagnosed with this condition is projected to grow from 2.7 million in 2013 to 4.6 million in 2030. In addition, a further 5 million people are estimated to be at a high risk of developing Type 2 diabetes'. (NHS England, 2016: 21)

By 2025 the number of people with dementia is expected to have risen to 1.14 million, compared to 850,000 in 2014 (Age UK, 2016: 12). Currently, dementia costs the UK around £26 billion per annum on dementia care.

The consequences of changes in the population are many, for example since 2004/5 there has been a significant increase in the number of admissions to hospital for people aged 60–74 by 2014/15 – up by 51.1 per cent, the corresponding figure for those aged 75+ is an increase of 58.4 per cent. In 2012/13 the cost of the 2,211,228 emergency admissions to hospital involving the over 65s was estimated to be £3.4 billion (Age UK, 2016: 8).

The impact on social care is significant but somewhat less visible, due in part to how it operates which is very different to health, for example prior to the recent introduction of the national eligibility threshold local authorities could determine how serious social care needed to become before the local authority would offer support. It is not surprising that years of demand and resource pressure had by 2012, resulted in eligibility criteria set at substantial or critical (85 per cent and 2 per cent of local authorities respectively) (Age UK, 2016: 14).

When the level of need and demand is growing and resources are constant or fail to keep pace there is inevitably an increase in 'unmet need'. It is estimated that 900,000 older people with care related needs do not receive any formal support, this is around 33 per cent of those that should (Age UK, 2016: 14).

Resources

Increases in need and demand come at a time when the health and social care system is facing financial difficulty. The Five Year Forward View published in 2014 made reference to a funding gap of £30 billion a year by 2020/21 (NHS, 2014). The NHS England 2016/17 Business Plan opined that a 'very significant financial challenge' remains but suggests that the Spending Review settlement in November 2015 was a 'credible basis on which to address the gap'. This headlines for the 2015 settlement included a £10 billion real terms increase in health funding between 2014/15 and 2020/21, front loaded so that £6 billion occurs before the end of 2016/17, a 'strong funding settlement for social care' and £22 billion of efficiency savings in health (DH and HM Treasury, 2015). The strong funding settlement for social care included new powers to raise Council Tax by up to 2 per cent for social care (Adult Social Care Precept) and continuation of the Better Care Fund. However, a joint paper from the Nuffield Trust, The Health Foundation and the Kings Fund suggest that this additional funding will fail to close the social care funding gap which they estimate will be between £2.8 billion and £3.5 billion in 2019/20. (Nuffield Trust, Health Foundation and King's Fund, 2015: 8).

The NHS England 2016/17 Business Plan (NHS, 2016) reported demand on Accident and Emergency Departments, Emergency Ambulances, NHS 111 service and general practice continue to rise which reflects in part increases in the population generally and amongst the elderly in particular. Recent reported problems with the primary care system particularly with regard to accessing GPs, the out-of-hours service, closures of walk-in centres and the introduction of the NHS 111 telephone service appear to be confusing patients causing many to attend Accident and Emergency rooms for ailments that could and should be treated elsewhere. The 2015

Conservative pledge to create a seven-day service, followed by a serious industrial dispute involving junior doctors together with significant shortages of specialist staff such as paramedics and GPs are extremely problematic, prompting fundamental questions to be asked such as who does what in primary care. Difficulty in finding an adequate number of staff is reflected in massive and increased use of agency and contract staff which is very costly. A King's Fund report published in July 2016 reported that, based on unaudited figures, there was an aggregate deficit of £1.85 billion for NHS providers and commissioners in 2015/16 – a threefold increase on 2014/15. The authors suggest that the recent 'relatively strong performance by mental health and community services providers may have been delivered at the expense of cuts in staff and risks to patient care'. They go on to state that the 'scale of the aggregate deficit makes it clear that the overspending is largely not attributable to mismanagement in individual organisations – instead it signifies a health system buckling under the strain of huge financial and operational pressures' (Dunn, P, et al, 2016).

Adult social care finance is in a poor state with ADASS reporting funding reductions of £4.6bn over the last five years (31 per cent in real terms) (ADASS, 2016: 7). In 2016/17 however, there was a small planned cash increase of 1.2 per cent in spending across the country due in large part to the introduction of the Adult Social Care Precept. This average masks individual changes in spending of between +20 per cent to -13 per cent (ADASS, 2016). The financial future is more difficult to predict due in part to the push towards integration accompanied by Better Care Funding, decisions about future levels of Adult Social Care Precept, retention of business rates by local authorities etc. In combination, these changes will affect the total amount of money in the system with local authorities affected to different degrees due to local circumstances and decisions by elected members.

A lack of suitable care accommodation continues to delay discharge from acute hospitals, causing the cost of care to be higher than it need be and reducing acute capacity for other patients. Over the last few years, there has been a concerted attempt to move care back into the community, supporting people to live in their own homes as long as possible. The number of older people going into residential care is stable despite rising numbers of the elderly (Age UK, 2016: 14). The capacity of local authorities to fund residential care is very limited which means that increasingly those seeking this will need to self-fund or be funded by third parties. Home care, for which demand is increasing as a consequence of older people staying in the community longer, also faces significant financial challenges including finding and retaining paid carers, squeezed margins caused by a combination of the national living wage and low declared hourly rates by commissioners. Just under 6,400 older people were affected by providers ceasing to trade within the last six months (ADASS, 2016). A further 4,400 were being cared for by providers who had decided to hand back council funded contracts in the same period (ASASS, 2016).

The future financial situation for health and social care is very uncertain given the result of the EU referendum, as evidenced by Chancellor Osborne's announcement on

1 July that the Government had abandoned the target of achieving a budget surplus by 2020. While this might normally have been a welcome announcement and perhaps an indicator of an easing of financial pressure the contrary is true, as it was in response to 'clear signs' of shock following the vote.

It is highly likely that the health and social care sector will continue to operate in a difficult financial climate. While it may well be the case that more money will be available, and this might match or slightly exceed the amount needed to meet inflation increases, it is highly unlikely to be sufficient. Demands for greater economy and efficiency will continue, while at the same time the scope for realising this is reducing. A point will soon be reached where financial deficits will grow, taxes may have to increase, deep cuts may be made or more radical ways found to deliver the outcomes wanted by communities.

Changes to pensions, including the age at which payments start, will prove problematic for individuals who are physically or mentally unable to work in their later years and will, therefore, be forced to run down savings as they wait for pensionable age. As a result, the capacity to self-fund care later in the life will reduce, particularly where the person is remaining in their own home. This may well lead to more significant health and social care needs arising earlier than would otherwise be the case, thus increasing demand on the state sector.

Legal, political and professional

Since 2010, there have been a number of key political and professional developments in health and social care notably the Health and Social Care Act 2012 and the Care Act 2014, the former of which reorganised the health system, in particular introducing Clinical Commissioning Groups. The Care Act 2014 clarified responsibilities and standardised aspects of how social care takes place.

Over the last 30 years or so, much local authority direct service provision has reduced, and in many cases is now close to zero. Over the years, compulsory competitive tendering, outsourcing, creation of social enterprises and various 'arms-length' arrangements have been used to reduce internal provision. In health, there have been similar movements towards using the private sector but these are more modest and there remains significant internal provision. Commissioning, which should not be confused with outsourcing, is currently the main role played by public sector organisations with provision increasingly seen to be a private or voluntary sector matter. The capacity to deliver, therefore, increasingly rests with organisations that are subject both to commercial and public sector environmental factors.

Integration of health and social care has been encouraged and supported with significant funding managed via the Better Care Fund. The voluntary and community sector which suffered significant reductions in state funding during the recession is now seen as a significant resource to the statutory sector and a way of bringing citizens into the care system as assets. The last few years has seen great efforts made to give patients greater involvement, freedom and flexibility in their treatment and care, examples of which include the choose and book system and personal health budgets in health and direct payments and personal budgets in social care. At the same time, patients in particular are being encouraged to take greater responsibility for their own health and well-being through for example self-management of conditions which together with social prescribing are potentially important ways of producing better health and social care outcomes for patients and clients whilst at the same time reducing demands on the primary care system. Developments in commissioning are proceeding in the same direction; recognising that health and care outcomes can often be realised through a variety of means, of which providing a service is only one. There is renewed interest in prevention and more importantly well-being, nudging citizen behaviour such that the onset of conditions is avoided or at least delayed. Increasingly, health and social care organisations are seeing individuals and the communities in which they live as assets – initially as a way of replacing state funded resources for example through the use of volunteers. This largely deficit approach is part of a more significant movement towards asset-based commissioning where practitioners and service users collaborate as equal partners to co-identify the assets in a community, the outcomes desired and the chosen way of meeting these including individual and community self-help, supported as needed by state resources.

There are a number of implications associated with these drivers – greater numbers of people living for longer with more advanced health and social care needs which, to a considerable extent, will be met in the community, delivered by the lowest possible paid members of staff or by volunteers. This poses a number of questions about the quality and consistency of care for much of this will be done unobserved and unmonitored. There are currently 3.5 million people over the age of 65 who live alone, within which are two million, aged 75 and above (Age UK, 2016: 23). The level and range of risks to which these older, frail and often confused patients is exposed is considerable and increasing, with financial scamming added to physical, mental and emotional abuse along with high levels of malnutrition.

Indeed, current research undertaken by the National Centre for Post Qualifying Social Work and Professional Practice suggests that financial scamming of vulnerable citizens is far more widespread than previously thought and that its impact on the health and welfare of its victims is very significant (Olivier et al, 2016).

In order to manage the scale of the problem and issues, health and social care services will need to move away from 'silo' mentalities and work even more closely together to meet the needs and protect the vulnerable. This will require clear leadership to challenge and change ways of working that put the interests of citizens at the forefront, not the agency.

Opportunities

It is easy to see the various drivers negatively, that they will forever harm our way of life; that we will never have it so good again, to coin a phrase. However, this view suggests that currently, everything we have by way of services or support is perfect, that the real needs of individuals are met and all of this occurs in a cost effective manner. The truth of the matter is that many of the services traditionally provided have not worked, or at least has not worked as well as they might. The large deficit approach, whereby professionals determine needs on behalf of individuals or groups and then respond to these by designing, funding and running a service is myopic and needs to end. This approach successfully turns patients and service users into passive recipients that become increasingly dependent on provided services. A radical rethink is underway, with a growing realisation that individuals and communities have assets that they could contribute to achieving the outcomes that are important to them, with an associated shift for the role of the state in supporting individuals to engage in the commissioning process. This will bring hitherto un-thought-of resources into the commissioning process and allow state resource to be better utilised in helping individuals and the community achieve desired outcomes. Being active in contributing to achieving outcomes for self and others is of itself beneficial.

Key pressures

The current context exerts considerable pressure on the health and social care system and of course those that lead and manage health and social care organisations or services. In our work with individuals and organisations we are acutely aware of the pressure that many managers and their staff feel, associated with:

- Trying to meet the needs of an ever-increasing and demanding population.

- Managing demand, which in practice is often a euphemism for withdrawing services.

- Working with limited if not diminishing resources.

- Trying to improve outcomes and performance.

- Maintaining safe services for service users, patients and carers.

- Implementing significant change in the way in which public services operate – for example – the introduction of commissioning, integrating health and social care and wider collaboration.

- Understanding and demonstrating the impact of services and other activities to ensure best use of resources.

- Reaching a new and increasingly equal relationship between practitioners, service users and the community.

- Pushing of responsibility and tasks down to the lowest level that they can reasonably be expected to be discharged and dealing with staff who previously were performing but may now fail to perform.

- Dealing with high levels of contradiction, uncertainty, novelty and complexity.

Challenges

Many challenges flow from this combined pressure, including the need to:

- Acquire new knowledge, master new skills or apply old skills to new contexts.

- Develop new ways of leading, managing and supervising staff and agency workers who are fewer in number, may work largely from home or at least hot-desk and generally appear more stressed.

- Be innovative and take risks within organisations that rarely have an appetite for risk.

- Ensure that staff and agency workers at all levels have access to development.

- Build and maintain effective relationships with an increasingly diverse set of stakeholders.

- Function with lower levels of supervision, wider spans of control, and for many, greater workloads.

- Maintain services today while preparing for an ever more uncertain future.

- Exercise sound professional judgement when under pressure.

Our response

The second edition of this text is intentionally focused on a number of the key challenges facing leaders and managers. In addition to key topics from the first edition such as self-awareness, supervision, planning and budget management readers are introduced to a number of new areas including:

- Self-leadership which can make a significant contribution to our ability to make a sound professional judgement when under stress.

- Commissioning and how this might change over the next few years.

- Strategic thinking which will be increasingly important to tackling wicked issues and preparing for the future.

- Integration of health and social care and the potential implications for leadership.

- Evaluation with a particular focus on leadership programmes.

- Change and team leadership.

We passionately believe that the challenges can only be met by creative, thoughtful and inspired leadership – leadership that is not simply focused on meeting budget challenges and organisational priorities, but one where creative solutions are thought through, removing professional and organisational silo's so that all our efforts are focused on the end user – the patient, service user or client.

Of interest here, is that various parts of the health and social care system use different words to simply describe people – patients, customers, service users, clients to name a few. Of course, the person at the centre, whatever they are called by the 'system' simply wants appropriate care and support. They are less interested in who provides it, but rather that it is available. Further integration is surely both inevitable and necessary and this will be a major leadership challenge if not the major leadership challenge in the coming years.

To this end we trust this new edition provides a valuable resource and inspiration to the delivery of an even more effective health and social care system, and yes, we want to emphasise effective rather than simply efficient.

Chapter 2
Leading for integration

Lee-Ann Fenge

CHAPTER OUTCOMES

As a result of completing this chapter you will:

- Understand the background context to leading integrated services.
- Be able to identify enablers and barriers of leading an integrated approach to service development and delivery.
- Understand how to develop effective system leadership.
- Be able to contribute to integrated planning processes.
- Understand the importance of effective communication in leading effective integrated services.

Introduction

This chapter will highlight the key features associated with leading integrated services, focusing on what leaders need to know and what leaders can do to develop integrated care provision. As well as exploring key themes linked to developing integrated service provision, key resources will be explored to help you develop your own leadership style within the context of integrated care. This is relevant to all involved in integrated provision as integrated leadership occurs at all levels in the hierarchy and is not something only done by Chief Executives and Directors. The position a person occupies will influence what they actually do and how they lead in an integrated way.

To begin with, the chapter will highlight key leadership theory providing a backdrop to discussion of leadership across health and social care provision. Over time, theories around leadership have changed and developed as key approaches have come into fashion and have then been replaced by new ways of thinking. Part of this is driven by the fluctuating demands placed on leaders and the types of behaviours they are required to demonstrate in response to the dynamic socio/political context in which organisations operate. Early approaches to leadership focused on individual characteristics which made people great leaders, the most significant being trait theories. These approaches have recently gained new impetus through an interest in 'visionary or charismatic' leaders (Zacarro, 2007), and an understanding of traits as an integrated set of cognitive abilities, social capabilities and dispositional tendencies. For example, traits may be linked to extraversion, openness, creativity and problem. However, there has been little research evidence supporting trait approaches to problem solving (Barling et al, 2011).

Later theories of leadership have focused on the situational context of leadership, originally developed by Hersey and Blanchard (1969). This concerns the relationship between the leader and the followers, and requires that leaders match their style and approach to the abilities and commitment of their followers. More recently, leadership theory has focused around notions of transformational leadership (Burns, 1978), and the importance of the leaders ability to influence and motivate how others see themselves (Mumford, 2010). Burns (1978) described two types of leadership: transactional and transformational. Transactional leadership involves a series of exchanges between leaders and followers, whereas transformational leadership involves the leader in understanding and supporting the needs of followers. This approach has been used to explore leadership within the NHS and local government through research using a Transformational Leadership Questionnaire, which found that an engaging style of leadership and shared process with staff positively influenced staff productivity (Alimo-Metcalf and Alban-Metcalf, 2001).

The notion of authentic leadership is a more recent approach to understanding leadership (Avolio and Gardner 2005), although there is no one single definition of authentic leadership. Northouse (2010: 206) suggests that authentic leadership can be viewed from three perspectives: intrapersonal, developmental and interpersonal.

- Intrapersonal definition – relates to the leaders self-knowledge and self-concept, and relates to positive psychological capabilities such as self-awareness, integrity and transparency.

- Developmental definition – this relates to something which can be nurtured rather than a fixed trait.

- Interpersonal definition – the reciprocal relationships which exist between the leader and followers.

As authentic leadership is still a developing area for research, it remains unclear how it operates within organisational contexts, but it can be related to the ability of the leader to learn to be more authentic in their approach over time. You may identify elements of 'authentic' leadership in your own leadership style including in the relationships and communication methods you employ with colleagues and stakeholders. This may have a powerful influence on the development of trust and collaboration, and reflects the balance you adopt between command and collaboration.

You may already be familiar with some of the different approaches to leadership mentioned above, but the aim of this chapter is to explore leadership in the context of integrated care. This means moving away from traditional approaches to leadership to embrace new ways of leading organisational change. Curiosity, connectivity and coaching capability have been identified as the most significant traits of effective leadership in the current health and social care environment of integrated services (Fillingham and Weir, 2014). Creative leadership solutions can be nurtured to sustain new approaches to collaborative working, developing new roles and seamless person-centred provision through effective system leadership.

The context of integrated care

Integrated Care is central to government policy in developing an effective approach to delivering the health and social care needs for the future population, and 'integrated care' approaches are seen as the best hope for a sustainable NHS in the future (Goodwin et al, 2013). This is part of a global approach to improving health and social care for a growing global ageing population, particularly for those ageing with long-term and/or multiple health problems (European Observatory, 2012). A core part of the vision laid out in the *NHS Five Year Forward View* (2014) involves acute hospitals becoming more closely integrated with other forms of care. However, in practice what this actually means can be contentious. Does this mean the integration of acute services with community health services, or with mental health services, or social care services or a combination of all? This may depend who you are talking to, and will certainly vary depending on location/geography.

'Integrated care' is a term which has many definitions and meanings and this in itself can lead to difficulties in interpreting what it is and how it is led. This will also exert an influence on stakeholder involvement and their commitment to the development of new ways of working. According to Armitage et al. (2009) 'integrated care' has some 175 definitions and concepts related to it, and this lack of clear definition or understanding can make it difficult to achieve agreed goals and consensus across different disciplines and agencies.

REFLECTION POINT 2.1

Think about the meanings associated with the term 'integrated care' within your own area of practice. Is there a common definition used, or is it defined and understood differently by different professionals and stakeholders? For example, you could ask colleagues what the term 'integrated care' means to them and compare their responses.

Do doctors, nurses, OTs, social workers, physiotherapists, district nurses, domiciliary care, volunteers and service users/patients have the same understanding of integrated care?

What does integrated care mean? At its heart is a commitment to 'joined' up services to provide improved person-centred provision. This is reflected in the definition of integrated care offered by National Voices (2013: 4) that 'Integrated care means person-centred coordinated care'.

In a report for *Monitor* Frontier Economics gives the following working definition of integrated care 'around the smoothness with which a patient or their representatives or carers can navigate the NHS and social care systems in order to meet their needs' (2012: 15).

Table 2.1 Knowledge and skills framework (Fillingham and Weir, 2014)

What skills and knowledge do you need to do this?

Technical know-how

- Service design.
- Governance arrangements.
- Innovative contracting and financial mechanisms.
- Technological 'savvy'.

Improvement know-how

- Systems thinking.
- Improvement science.
- Large-scale change.

Personal effectiveness

- Interpersonal skills and behaviours.
- Coaching ability.
- A visionary and participative style.

This is new territory for many health and social care leaders and one which has been identified as requiring new and different ways of working. This is summed up by Fillingham and Wier (2014: 3) who suggest that 'Leading across complex inter-dependent systems of care is a new and different role that needs to be undertaken alongside the already difficult task of leading successful institutions'.

A project led by and the King's Fund and the AQuA (the Advancing Quality Alliance) has developed a framework for the knowledge and skills needed for successful leadership across integrated systems (Fillingham and Weir, 2014: 17). See Table 2.1.

Creating a shared vision

A key challenge for those leading integrated care is to create a shared vision across a number of key stakeholders. This is more than a mission statement and reflects specific goals which can be clearly expressed and evaluated. It is important that this vision is co-produced with key stakeholders (including users of services/patients and carers) as well as all partners involved in the development and delivery of integrated provision. It is therefore not a top down approach but involves all stakeholders in co-creating a shared vision across different levels of a project or organisation. This shared vision statement should motivate and inspire people to work together to make the vision a reality.

Another way of thinking about this is to see the integrated system as a wider 'community of practice' (Wenger, 1998). Individual perspectives and actions therefore form part of a wider integrated system which can be grounded by a shared vision statement. Your role as a leader of integrated provision is therefore to:

- Articulate a clear shared vision with clear outcomes which can be effectively evaluated.

- Achieve shared understanding and a shared sense of purpose and direction for integrated services and new ways of working.

- Overcome resistant attitudes and gain commitment from stakeholders.

- Overcome barriers to progress and maintain momentum.

As you lead integrated provision it is important to formulate a shared vision and this includes engaging the commitment of others during a process of change. It is important to be mindful of processes which can influence organisations during periods of change and reorganisation.

Marshak (2006) identifies six processes which can operate in organisations during periods of change. This may help you consider key elements as you lead a process of reflection and refining of vision framing and articulation.

Table 2.2 Six processes involved in leading change through integration (adapted from Covert Processes at Work (Marshak, 2006))

Reasons – Rational and analytical logics – the underpinning policy directive towards integrated care and service provision

Politics – Individual and group interests – in terms of integrated care this cuts across health and social care boundaries, and includes the private, voluntary sector as well as other key stakeholders including volunteers, users of services, patients and carers

Inspirations – Visionary aspirations and how these are captured within the wider culture of integrated provision

Emotions – affective reactions and feelings to the change in practice resulting from integrated care – it is important that these are acknowledged as unexpressed emotion or discontent can be driven underground

Mindsets – Guiding beliefs and assumptions – can relate to underpinning philosophy and beliefs of different professional groups which might enable a shared vision of person-centred provision, or silos of professional jurisdiction and practice. Mental models are "deeply ingrained assumptions, generalizations, or even pictures or images that influence how we understand the world and how we take action" (Senge, 1990, p. 8). It is important to understand how these might act as a barrier to change.

Psychodynamics – any change can lead to anxiety and unconscious processes within the workforce. It is important that these concerns are listened to and addressed.

As you lead the development of a shared vision for integrated care, it is helpful to explore the approach of different stakeholders within this process. This is important as part of your role as a leader of integrated care is to:

- Build trust and collaboration.

- Facilitate shared decision making.

- Harmonise change across structures, processes and patterns to achieve the shared vision of integration.

The Social Identity Theory of Leadership (Archer and Cameron, 2013) can be a useful way of exploring the importance of collaborative leadership within integrated provision.

As part of this it is useful to explore pattern mapping, and how aspirations, relationships, decision making, power and conflict contribute to the development of a clear vision for integrated provision.

Stakeholder mapping can be a useful method of exploring stakeholders' conflicting aspirations and demands. It can assist you in identifying different stakeholder expectations and power and helps in establishing priorities and outcome measures. It can also help you identify opinion leaders.

It is focused on two main areas:

- How motivated the stakeholder is to impress their vision or expectations on the process and the exercise of power.

- The extent to which the stakeholder has power to impose its wants.

It can be useful to use a matrix similar to the one proposed by Johnson et al (2008) to explore stakeholder approaches.

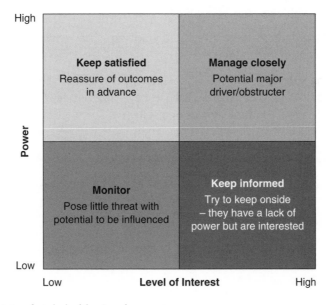

Figure 2.1 Matrix of stakeholder involvement

Using this framework of stakeholder involvement it may be helpful to consider the following questions for each group of stakeholders you work with.

- What matters to these people in terms of developing integrated care and service provision?

- What are the points of interdependence?

- What conflict is possible?

As you may be working with a range of key stakeholders during the visioning process it might be worth exploring how 'creative tools' might help to facilitate this process.

- Develop a visual poster/sheet to identify key outcomes/values.

- Work in small groups (especially when working with a large group of people).

Examples:

- The National Voices Scheme has developed a number of 'I Statements' as a narrative of what service users/patients want from integrated collaborative provision. For example the 'I' statements for communication are:
  - I tell my story once.
  - I am listened to about what works for me, in my life.
  - I am always kept informed about what the next steps will be.
  - The professionals involved with my care talk to each other.
  - We all work as a team. I always know who is coordinating my care.
  - I have one first point of contact. They understand both me and my condition(s). I can go to them with questions at any time.
- Using visual methods to share integrated visioning – see www.coastalwestsussexccg. nhs.uk/our-vision-for-integrated-care.
- Story boarding – this is a narrative technique that offers an effective way to explore the interactions and experiences that individuals have. You can develop a story board with key stakeholders to illustrate a process or a system.

Benefits, enablers and barriers

The following section explores the benefits, enablers and barriers of leading integrated care.

Benefits of integrated care

The benefits of integrated care according to Frontier Economics (2012) include:

- Improved quality.

- Improved patient experience.

- Improved clinical outcomes, which could include improved admission and re-admission rates.

- Improved patient safety.

- Improved cost efficiency.

Enablers for integrated care

Enablers for integrated care, developed from the work of Alltimes, G. and Varnam, R. (2012: 13) include:

- A shared vision of the case for change between GPs, local authorities, and other partners.
- Strong, courageous and persevering leadership, particularly from local professionals.
- Sufficient time spent building relationships, developing a shared culture and govern-ance between organisations.
- Involvement of people and communities as key partners in designing services.
- Iroactive provision of information and support to help people make decisions about their own care.
- Sharing information between all providers involved in an integrated journey of care.
- Joint commissioning between health and social care based on shared vision and budgets.
- Using flexible funding models and innovating around existing incentives.
- Alignment of governance procedures, staff management and training.
- Leadership investment in supporting behavioural change and shared ambitions within providers.
- Responsiveness to feedback of frontline staff.
- Strong commissioners prepared to follow through on a vision to integrate around the needs of patients.
- Sharing of activity and performance data between commissioners and providers.
- Anticipation and mitigation of side effects of service changes, such as initial 'double-running' of service.

Barriers

The Health and Social Care Act 2012 established the sector regulator Monitor to exercise a duty to 'exercise its functions with a view to enabling the provision of healthcare services provided for the purposes of the NHS to be provided in an inte-grated way'. The Frontier Economics (2012) report identifies that there are a number of different types of barrier to integrated care. These include:

- Quality of IT and communication systems: inter-operability.

- Operating procedures between health and social care: lack of procedures can lead to delays and gaps in the pathway.

- Transfer of funds from one institution to another and tariff concerns.

- Risk aversion.

- Service users choosing alternative providers.

- Governance: lack of clarity about responsibility.

- Clinical practice: lack of consensus and unwillingness to transfer patients from one part of the system to another.

- Cultural differences: differences in management style, willingness to share information and resources.

However, when considering the barriers within any specific context it is useful to reflect upon the barriers within a context that takes account of the different types of care and how barriers vary across them, i.e. there may be different barriers in terms of whether provision concerns planned or unplanned provision, or concerns management of complex ongoing care pathways such as cancer or mental health.

REFLECTION POINT **2.2**

Think of your own experience of integrated services and consider the leadership styles and approaches you have experienced or witnessed, and the impact of these on integrated services provision.

Effective system leadership

Improvement methods can create a common language and approach that help connect leaders across professional and organisational boundaries. At the core of this is an approach to develop 'system leaders'. A systems-thinking perspective recognises that learning needs will emerge and change over time. Leaders must be comfortable working across often blurred boundaries (Fillingham and Weir, 2014). Change should be grounded in improvement methods which encourage learning by doing, using small tests of change to identify what works best for a particular community, whilst being forever mindful of the cultural aspects of change. This moves away from previous technical models of leadership. This different approach of systems leadership requires leaders who can 'command and collaborate' (Ibarra, 2012). This requires the ability to move out of silos which prevent collaboration across agencies, to embrace collaborative ways of working which tap into the knowledge and ideas of other key stakeholders. This combines two previous 'rhetorics' about leadership that had variously described it as either decisive 'command' focused leadership or collaborative and inclusive leadership focused on flexibility and innovation.

According to Better Care guidance (The Better Care Fund, 2015: 8), when leading whole system outcomes it is also useful to consider alignment with the three areas of impact that are central to Better Care:

- Improved experiences of care.

- Improved outcomes in terms of changes to people's health and wellbeing.

- Better use of resources.

A systems approach to leadership is most effective when it is underpinned by a common vision and a set of ideals focused on the needs and ambitions of a particular community. This raises the importance of an authentic dialogue with the local community and effective mechanisms to tap into the needs of the local community. There is a synergy here to an approach which is underpinned by 'co-production' with users of services, patients and carers.

According to the Social Care Institute of Excellence (SCIE) co-production is based on an underpinning philosophy of equality where everyone is valued as having assets to bring to the process (SCIE, 2015).

A number of resources are available to help leaders develop co-produced system outcomes and the following examples might be worth considering:

- SCIE How to do co-production www.scie.org.uk/publications/guides/guide51/how-to-do-coproduction/index.asp

- North West London Tool Kit www.healthiernorthwestlondon.nhs.uk/bettercare/integratedcare

---

REFLECTION POINT 2.3

Developing effective system leadership requires leaders who can comfortably work across blurred boundaries. The following five questions comprise a framework for reflecting on your experience of system leadership in the workplace:

1 *Think about the specific context of integrated care provision you are involved in leading and developing. Reflect upon the Knowledge and Skills Framework in Table 2.1 and consider what skills and knowledge you need to do this?*

2 *What are the benefits of moving towards integrated provision in your practice area? What might these be in terms of your own leadership role, the organisation you work in, the wider culture of care, and finally the benefits for users of services/patients and/or carers?*

REFLECTION POINT **2.3** *(CONT.)*

3 *What 'enablers' for integrated care can you identify in your context of practice? What implications might this have for your own leadership of integrated systems?*

4 *What 'barriers' to leading integrated care can you identify within your own context of practice? What implications might this have for your own leadership of integrated systems?*

5 *How might you lead an approach to integrated service provision which is underpinned by a commitment to 'co-production' with users of services, patients and carers? What approaches might you adopt to ensure an authentic engagement with the views of these key stakeholders?*

The following example gives further insight into how one area has adopted a system leadership approach to integrated care.

Example: Manchester City Council (2013a) Living Longer Living Better

Living longer, living better: an integrated care blueprint demonstrates the evolution of new leadership roles and the need for a clear and cohesive system leadership. The overarching body responsible for this is the health and wellbeing board. Supporting the health and wellbeing board is an executive health and wellbeing group, chaired by the City Council chief executive. Supporting these two groups has been a new leadership construct which emerged from the team that developed the blueprint document in 2013. This has been dubbed the City Wide Leadership Group.

A key area of development has concerned developing a reframed governance arrangement, and the emergence of new relationships and a new leadership style. This approach is described by Dr Mike Eeckelaers, Chair, Central Manchester Clinical Commissioning Group (CCG) (Fillingham and Weir, 2014: 32)

'As Chair of the CCG, which is a membership organisation, I know that I have to draw people together and work towards a consensus. That fits well with my preferred personal style and I aim to carry that approach forward into our wider partnership work. We know that we can achieve far more for our patients and the people of Manchester by working collaboratively with others than we possibly can on our own'.

The approach within this example has been a distributed approach to leadership through system leadership at multiple levels within the system working effectively across boundaries, influencing and persuading others to deliver common goals (West et al, 2014). This systems leadership approach distributed throughout the system has worked alongside a strong organisational leadership approach.

Resilience

Resilience has been described as 'the capacity to recover from and adjust to adverse situations' (Northouse, 2010: 219). According to Kanter (2013) resilience is an essential characteristic for successful leaders, and this is particularly relevant for those grappling with dynamic system changes as leaders of integrated care provision. Kanter's approach describes resilience as building on the cornerstones of confidence through:

- Accountability (taking responsibility and showing remorse).

- Collaboration (supporting others in reaching a common goal).

- Initiative (focusing on positive steps and improvements).

Effective leaders of sustainable change are highly resilient. This resilience means that they are able to respond to new and ever-changing realities. However, resilience is not just an individual characteristic but thrives on a sense of community, and in terms of leading integrated provision this relates to the wider organisational and systems culture surrounding integration. Snyder (2013) suggests that a resilient leader who has a mindset which is focused on a growth, performs significantly better on difficult and challenging tasks.

Resilience can be developed and it is suggested that leadership programmes that strengthen positive psychological resources support participants to develop confidence and resilience in times of change (Shannon and Van Dam, 2013).

However, some theorists suggest that it is important to see resilience within a broader social framework, critiquing traditional models of resilience which place responsibility for resilience purely on individual psychological adaption. For example, Considine, Hollingdale and Neville (2015: 218) counter this individualistic approach by suggesting that it is equally important to explore the wider socio-political context of the resilience within the workplace. The defining principle of social resilience is 'to promote ways in which a social environment can be developed or enhanced in order to support and assist individuals and groups'. When applied to leading integrated provision, this suggests that it is important to promote ways in which the wider integrated environment can be developed or enhanced such as building on the assets and strengths within the wider integrated culture of care. This can be achieved by mapping the strengths and assets within the integrated system guided by four key principles:

- Reframing thinking, goals and outcomes identifying champions to drive change.

- Recognising the assets available to achieve the change (individual, organisational, cultural and physical resources available).

- Mobilising assets for a defined vision/purpose to develop systemic action across organisational boundaries.

- Co-producing outcomes – building on the assets of key stakeholders.

Linked to developing resilience is the concept of Self Leadership, and the way in which we understand ourselves through our relationships with others. This relates to developing social awareness and enhanced communication skills, and an ability to use our own personal resources to best advantage as we lead others. For in depth reading about Self Leadership please see Holroyd and Brown's (2014) text on 'Self Leadership: Building Personal Resilience and Relationships that work within Health and Social Care'.

Mechanisms for handling conflict

The development of integrated provision can lead to feelings of unease as individuals and agencies grapple with new ways of working, and traditional ways of working and cultures of practice are challenged. Changing systems of practice can provoke a range of reactions in people, and as a result individuals may become defensive and obstructive. Any approach to developing system leadership needs to tackle obstruction and conflict, and explore effective means of airing conflicts whether they be individual, professional or inter-organisational.

It is important to understand that conflict is a subjective experience, and means different things to different people. Some people are more comfortable with conflict than others, and some people thrive on conflict. Research suggests that a lack vision and shared philosophy within integrated care provision can lead to conflict, and that as a result 'without a shared understanding of aims and objectives, partnerships may struggle to develop a sense of purpose' (Cameron, A. et al, 2012: 11). It is essential that those developing integrated systems are able to manage conflict effectively and quickly. A number of learning resources are freely available to help support conflict management, and it is worth researching which approach best meets your needs as a system leader.

NHS Institute – managing conflict

www.institute.nhs.uk/quality_and_service_improvement_tools/quality_and_service_improvement_tools/human_dimensions_-_managing_conflict.html

The importance of measuring impact

As the march towards the integration of services continues it is important to develop increased understanding about what works and why. However, there is some suggestion that a lack of evidence-based impact information can hinder understanding of how to best integrate health systems within different contexts and for different desired outcomes (Armitage et al, 2009). They suggest that this requires:

- Clear methods for monitoring success and failure of integrated systems.

- Tools to measure integration outcomes including cost-effectiveness.

- Case studies that document processes, principles, and challenges in planning and implementing integrated care within different contexts.

- Comparative analyses of different approaches to integration.

Any such evaluation framework also needs to work at three levels by identifying the growth and development of key leaders in the system; assessing the progress in effective team-working across organisational boundaries; and most critically of all, assessing the progress towards improved outcomes for patients, citizens and tax payers. It is also important to adopt measures that align with the main elements of a national, regional or local strategy concerning integration.

It may be worth exploring what tools exist that you can draw upon and this might include:

How to ...understand and measure impact – Better Care Fund 2015 available from:

www.england.nhs.uk/wp-content/uploads/2015/06/bcf-user-guide-04.pdf.pdf

The House of Care model – a co-ordinated service delivery model available from:

www.kingsfund.org.uk/publications/delivering-better-services-people-long-term-conditions

The Integration of Health and Social Care – the Torbay approach, available from

www.kingsfund.org.uk/publications/integrating-health-and-social-care-torbay

Key learning points

Government policy is focused on the increased integration of health and social care provision, and this requires a new approach to systems leadership. Key elements of a systems leadership approach include the need to:

- Create a shared vision across a number of key stakeholders to build trust and shared decision making.

- Lead 'joined' up services to provide improved person-centred provision.

- Be comfortable working across blurred boundaries whilst supporting the development of collaborative ways of working across complex interdependent systems of care.

- Utilise a 'command and collaborate' approach to leadership which embraces collaborative ways of working which tap into the knowledge and ideas of other key stakeholders. This might also be described as a visionary and participative approach.

- Recognise the strengths and assets available within the wider integrated system to achieve the change and development.

- Demonstrate resilience by adapting and responding to new and ever-changing realities of integrated provision.

- Use appropriate improvement and evaluation methods to reflect back on the outcomes identified as part of the shared visioning process.

It is important to move beyond individualistic approaches to leadership, to understand the wider cultural, social and political dimensions which influence the organisational context of integrated health and social care provision. These systems are in a constant state of flux and change and therefore require resilient leaders who can both navigate through turbulent waters, whilst collaboratively harnessing the strengths of the wider system to reach a shared vision. There is a need for continual review of outcomes and the most appropriate measurements of impact to ensure that shared visions are developed and sustained in the future.

Chapter 3
Self-leadership

Jane Holroyd and Keith Brown

CHAPTER OUTCOMES

As a result of completing this chapter you will:

- Appreciate the important value of self-leadership.

- Understand how fundamental a better state of mind is and how it is a natural human capability available to us all.

- Realise that the old 'command and control' models of management no longer work.

- Recognise the importance of devolved models as providing the foundations for self-leadership to flourish.

- Appreciate how we can observe moment-by-moment through self-observation impact in the now, and through self-regulation, the ability to suspend a natural urge to judge and presume – being comfortable with knowing nothing and therefore being open to seeing what really is.

- Be able to realise the importance of your 'why' – your purpose, the reason you go to work.

- Understand the vital role self-compassion plays in being compassionate.

- Grasp the importance of our natural abilities to build rapport, social awareness and create relationships with the many different generations present within the workforce.

- Understand how integral trust is to effective communication as the cornerstone of working in effective teams.

Self-leadership is quintessential for effective management, leadership and supervision. It is about everyone whatever their role at whatever level. It not only relates to self but the management and interaction of others. In this chapter therefore will be an exploration of self-leadership as a concept with this term defined, together with an examination of proposed vital foundations and associated facets. State of mind for example, as a construct is integral to all that we do in the name of effectiveness.

The value of self-leadership

In 2013, Royles (2013) stated that the Francis report (an inquiry into the Mid Staffordshire NHS Foundation Trust) would be the biggest leadership challenge the NHS had faced to date. Singularly defining in its history as a moment in time were we could see Goleman et al's (2013: 75) pacesetting gone wrong. A dissonant leadership style of being distracted by targets in a 'do it because I say so model' which negated the central business, the why and the raison d'être of the NHS, implicitly the provision of healthcare with an operating framework of 'do no harm'.

In social work, other catastrophic events such as the death of Victoria Climbié and Peter Connelly and the Rotherham abuse scandal punctuate that leadership across organisational boundaries has struggled to protect.

What created such apparent blindness, the kind referred to by Heffernan (2011) as 'wilful'; a legal term which describes a knowing, a knowledge of something being wrong but somehow believing there is no point saying, surely someone else would have said, and furthermore it is someone else's responsibility not mine? What creates this systemic 'blindness' in individuals; and what would truly prevent it from happening on any scale again?

The crux of this question and the reciprocal answer lies in a conceptual paradigm shift in leadership development. The antidote is a change in focus. No longer can it be about individuals with the title of manager or leader, it needs to include every individual taking the accountability within and across boundaries and responsibilities for the results.

But what real paradigm shift has occurred and most importantly what shift in leadership development has taken place to ensure it does not happen again? With budget expenditure of £1,515 per manager per year spent on leadership development within the public sector (McBain et al, 2012) why has the leadership gap been left so wanting? To ensure balance, it is appropriate however, to stress that it is not simply a disease of the NHS or social care sectors, for you only need to look at the banking world and financial services, to see that something is missing.

Leadership development has however, often been a top-down initiative rather than a bottom up necessity. A focus on command and control and an emphasis on leaders rather than leadership has resulted in systemic failings within organisations. Torres (2013) emphasises that leadership development across all sectors has failed to produce the great leaders required for today's new flattened structures, adaptability and innovation requirements.

Northouse's (2013) definition of leadership as being, 'a process whereby an individual influences a group of individuals to achieve a common goal' – potentially hints at the problem. For when we make leadership about certain individuals within organisations we ultimately provide the mechanism of abdication for everyone else, 'it's not my job', 'I just come to do the work', 'I don't get paid to' and with it, responsibility and accountability can be lost. This disconnection potentially creates gaping holes between the top and the bottom with transparency replaced with silos of those who seem to know the plan and those who don't but who are trying to make sense of it all. The consequence, assumptions run riot as people disconnect and a lack of trust becomes the prevailing legacy.

But why self-leadership?

Why self-leadership?

No one defining leadership theory or model

An historical and quick overview of leadership theories soon reveals a preoccupation with the 'hero' myth that 'great leaders' are born, the trait camp, which was quickly followed (when the research did not add up) to concentrating on imitating behaviours, what leaders do, the simplistic flaws then replaced with a preoccupation in the situation and contingent theories. Again, when the research evidence showed the yawning gaps, the 'followers' become the flavour of the moment with servant leadership and transformational models. No solution found, created combinations of theories which remain the current distraction. A preoccupation solely with tools and techniques which fail the shop floor test of reality; the individual therefore needs a different template which starts with getting out of their own limited thinking, working instead from a place of clarity in each moment, better matched to meet the daily demands.

Important to the concept of leadership is starting with self, and as Mary Oliver (2003) says the only person you can save, or change is yourself. You can influence people to change but ultimately the only person that you can change is yourself.

The journey – the only life that you could save

Individuals create cultures not organisations and therefore this is where we need to start. Mary Oliver in her poem called 'The Journey' describes 'the only life that you could save' or change as being your own (Oliver, 2003). This concept of starting with 'self' – Oliver poignantly depicts the moment someone decides to change as a sense of a realisation, a rising up inside, something uncomfortable but necessary. It is this awareness, this innate wisdom that we have often tuned out, we override, we've lost touch with as we meander through life's journey, distracted by the busy of constantly doing rather than simply being.

> One day you finally knew
>
> what you had to do, and began,
>
> though the voices around you
>
> kept shouting
>
> their bad advice –
>
> though the whole house began to tremble
>
> and you felt the old tug

at your ankles

'Mend my life!'

each voice cried

But you didn't stop.

The change she talks about is transformational, an understanding of both the need, and want to take a different path. It is this real sense of listening to self and of getting back in touch with, having a strong inner intelligence of what is right for us and like any change it captures the uncomfortableness, and the pull of other individuals wanting the status quo to remain. The infected need to 'advise'.

Self-leadership focuses on an 'inside out' solution involving everyone not simply the leader by title; it fits neatly with the reduced and dispersed structures which exposes the dated hierarchical command and control approach to leadership, which has sheltered bullying and 'group think'. It is about improving the quality of thinking within the moment of interactions. We are not taught about, or made aware of our thinking, but as Rock (2007: 288) would state, 'what we achieve at work is driven by what we think'.

But explicitly what is self-leadership?

What is self-leadership?

Self-leadership is not a new concept for it was developed by Charles Manz in 1983 and later further refined with Christopher Neck to mean 'a process of influencing self' (Neck and Manz, 2010: 4). Self-leadership therefore is about influencing ourselves first and foremost to generate the very best version of our 'self' to bring to each intervention, implicitly to be responsible for the impact we have on others and ourselves. It is an ability to engender the best in individuals in any circumstances for the ultimate outcome of providing better services. Most importantly it is about everyone and not simply the individual with the title of manager or leader. It is about achieving full potential, crucially when needed, to accomplish whatever the tasks and challenges might be. It relates to an individual changing their behaviour as a result of a better state or presence of mind. Explicitly self-leadership is:

> *The ability to bring out the best in individuals in any circumstances for the ultimate outcome of providing better services.*

> (Holroyd, 2015: 24)

Indeed, self-leadership is a concept of its time, more pertinent now than ever before and is contingent upon four foundations. These four foundations are fundamental to individual and organisational success and like the foundations of a house are vital to keeping a building upright; these foundations therefore are integral to self-leadership and include:

- State of mind.

- Everyone counts.

- Devolved structures.

- Evaluating impact.

If we examine each of these in turn, the first of all the foundations and the most important is state of mind.

1. State of mind

A better state of mind is at the very centre of self-leadership and is the missing element that inextricably impacts the outward discernible results of leadership. Banks (1998: 3) would refer to it as the 'missing link', Kline (2009: 21) as 'a way of being in the world' and Siegel (2010: 109) as 'the inner sanctuary of clarity'. Such clarity of mind has a direct correlation with the potential in the moment to act rather than react – to interact from the best possible state. This better state of mind is a human capability available to us all.

Self-leadership is about tapping into this innate wisdom, a natural internal resilience of human potential; creating essentially perspective when it counts, reducing the impact of overwhelm, a better quality of thinking – a better state of mind. Professionals with the ability to react with flexibility at those key moments, in practice being able to assess with wisdom, experiential tacit knowledge, the kind rooted in real world practice. It allows staff to 'tap into' being their best (the purpose and the reason they come to work) and reduces the destructive risk and impact of poor quality thinking which can manifest as; collusion, victimhood, blaming, negative catastrophising, moaning, martyrdom and all manner of fears and limiting beliefs.

Individuals under pressure can become victims of unconscious and unhelpful habitual thinking processes, reinforced through repetitive stressors keeping the amygdala in an active, or hair trigger reactive state. This unhealthy turmoil can be countered by a reciprocal inbuilt system of re-balance and the ability to calm down such mental reactivity called introceptive awareness (Farb et al, 2012).

Do you know your current state of mind? Are you sabotaging yourself and what do you keep telling yourself? These are all questions which relate to our state of mind and the perceived reality of the world in our heads.

Adaptability is an essential characteristic of leadership behaviour, understanding therefore when our state of mind is clear or unhelpful is about this adaptability and is integral to self-leadership. State of mind includes the ability to be fully present, to respect the individual in front of you, to be capable of 'extreme listening' (Pransky, 2011: 112) not listening to reply but to understand completely, conscious listening. In doing so to exercise respect, the unconditional type of respect – tuning in to identify what is felt, to be curious enough to listen beyond the words (Holroyd, 2015).

All important aspects of exercising compassion, getting out of our own way to be fully there for someone else. Relating in this way McGonigal (2013) suggests that the science is very compelling, and that human connection and compassion ironically contributes to an inbuilt stress resilience. This links to well-being. Being in a better state of mind is about positive well-being, Neill (2013: 67) would remind that it is part of our natural 'factory settings' an 'innate mental health'. However, human beings adversely impact their state of mind through excessive worrying, ruminating, procrastinating and tuning into rather than out of stress. Tuning out, or seeing stress as McGonigal advises as 'helpful' creates the biology of courage…and is so doing generates 'resilience'.

Every single individual has this capacity of a better state of mind, it isn't exclusive to leaders, we all have an innate ability in every interaction to impact in a different way no matter what stressors we are under. This vital uniform potential is why everyone needs to count – leadership cannot therefore be exclusive to single individuals.

2. Everyone counts

The degree and continuous nature of change and transitions require that every person has to count. As the subtitle of a King's Fund (2011) document sums this up 'No more heroes' and the Leadership Qualities Framework for Adult Social Care (2013) states 'Leadership starts with me'. It is about everyone (Holroyd, 2015).

Relying on a few individuals in the 'hero' mythology that was better historically suited to meet the needs of a different time we can see the loss of the potential, of the greater many. The degree and magnitude of change required to bring about true integration across boundaries of differing authorities and organisations means that everyone at every level needs to own the collective alignment of the direction of travel. The Centre for Creative Leadership in conjunction with The King's Fund (2014a, 2014b) have identified this essential pre-requisite for any healthcare organisation to be successful in the current climate.

If leadership is not everyone's business, there is a potential to abdicate responsibility declaring instead that it is someone else's responsibility up there in the organisation with accountability, and true commitment being lost. Leadership is often discussed as a way of influencing and motivating others into action. This inference suggests that individuals do not already have this innate ability to be self-motivated, it requires some other to create this, in what Wilfred Bion in Jon Stokes's chapter suggests, is potentially 'dependency' (Stokes, 1994: 21). In this model the leader looks after individuals protecting them, for example, from the harsh messages within the environment, change, re-structuring – this 'pathological' form of dependency however, potentially inhibits growth and development and more specifically who is anyone to make an assumption that someone is not able to cope.

Indeed, Ham et al (2016: 4) identify the vital strategy of transforming the delivery of health and social care 'from within' – identifying the importance of leadership at every level. Doing it 'to' models, and precluding individuals in a top-down approach loses the buy in to the shared endeavour, the essential hearts and minds of change. Self-leadership is a platform for promoting not only that everyone counts, but also everyone needs to exercise self-leadership in all that they do. This is not an exclusive concept for practitioners (health and social work and care) but to the users of all services as a joint commitment.

Furthermore, Drew Dudley (2010) would say that we have made leadership bigger than what it should be, that leadership instead, needs to be about moments of impact. Making it bigger makes people believe that they cannot lead. At times within organisations the sense of overwhelm is palpable, yet we all have the potential to choose the impact we have with the person in front of us. It is about these moments that we can really make a difference and this explicitly is an individual choice. It is not a contrived or prescribed way to be, but a genuine choice.

It is not about everyone leading or no one leading, it is instead collective moments of leadership enacted within each decision made – the choices exercised knowing the impact you want to make within any given situation. It is influencing ourselves to achieve this through self-leadership and fundamentally through a better state of mind.

Getting individuals to respond in every moment in this way means changing the focus away from someone else's responsibility to one were true ownership is part of every interaction. Self-leadership is therefore both how we influence self and others to act and react in a given moment with a clear mind, no matter what the demands of the environment might be.

It provides a safeguard in terms of the quality of interactions. For individuals who self-lead are able to tune in and appreciate when their thinking may be less effective, for example, when stressed, tired, emotional and missing seeing what is in front of them, an awareness and an ability to change in the moment their reaction, and therefore the overall outcome. It stops individual's abdicating responsibility for how they do things, and most importantly how they relate to others. It is inclusive not exclusive. In order however, for everyone to be able to exercise self-leadership requires devolved structures really truly allowing leadership being enacted right at the very front of services in each interaction.

3. Devolved structures

The past and current preparation for leaders has been based on a redundant and flawed hierarchical model (of command and control), which can perpetuate an 'us and them' inference (Zheltoukhova, 2014: 6) rather than an emphasis upon collective models centred on systemic frontline leadership. Indeed, the NHS Confederation (2014) suggest that 'there is evidence from the NHS and other industries, including the oil industry, that top-down command and control cultures, are the worst kind of culture for quality and safety' (Holroyd, 2015).

It is advanced that to deal with huge disruptive changes such as true integration requires a totally fresh approach to ensure that everyone is both engaged and owning the responsibility for getting the right results to create a 'culture of genuine engagement' (Alimo-Metcalfe and Alban-Metcalfe, 2011:11).

The devolved models of distributed, dispersed and shared approaches instead allow for self-leadership to flourish and frontline ownership to occur. All these concepts accept the sharing of power and a move away from relying on single units of leadership prevalent within top-down models (Thorpe et al, 2011). Mumford (2012) describes, distributed leadership as 'leadership where responsibilities are not held by one person, but instead are held by multiple individuals' with professional roles lending themselves well to distributed leadership (Thorpe et al, 2011). A shared endeavour, working on a project or area together and having a say is vital for facilitating this approach. Translating a vision or key objectives into a defined 'shared endeavour' ensures a buy in from those creating the endeavour, and in the translation and making sense process, something that will work in the practical world of the frontline.

Dispersed methods closely resemble an informal or emergent approach where individuals lead themselves and are responsible for their own management and coordination. Instead of a traditional leader-follower model there is a reciprocal power relationship, the power is pooled between leaders and followers. The focus is on the process of leadership rather than on individual leaders.

The final shared model of leadership is similar to distributed and dispersed but would be more about 'horizontal leadership beyond organisations' (Grint, 2010). An example, would be a network working collaboratively within a partnership agreement. This allows leadership to occur beyond the usual line accountability structures.

Being explicit about collaboration and what is expected of all individuals as part of developing an inclusive shared endeavour is at the heart of success within these structures. It relies on those with the title of manager understanding and letting go of any needs to control of being fully supportive of engagement and being instead the facilitators, the conductors, the educators and the developers.

Being strategic is often the phrase used to differentiate the board room from the operational end, letting go of this exclusive and potentially disinhibiting inference is vital; for being strategic is about spotting in the chaos of everything what we should concentrate on. With better self-leadership, a better state of mind, individuals at all levels are able to identify what matters and collaboratively establish, the focus, Bion's (1994: 25) 'primary task' what we are here to achieve. Keeping focused on an agreed shared endeavour with the primary task clearly at the centre, the purpose and not wavering or becoming distracted when it gets tough, is what self-leadership is about.

Integrated leadership development also becomes key as individuals exercising self-leadership work together to establish shared endeavours; agreed outputs and outcomes which fit the organisations priorities. Key to such development requires the accountability of evaluation, examining what difference has been made, what has been the explicit impact of providing leadership development.

4. Evaluating impact

To prevent cycles of legacy problems of expensive leadership training (often borrowed from elsewhere), resulting in little impact at the 'front end' (and therefore disillusionment) and further expenditure, assessment and specifically evaluation is crucial. This is the 'so what difference' has this made to the operational front end.

Extensive experience in evaluating the impact of professional leadership programmes (Keen et al, 2013) show real behavioural changes and changes in practice which supports a new emphasis on self-leadership which allows leadership to be everyone's business not the few with the title. Evaluation and evaluating impact is integral to quality assurance and continuous improvement. Getting feedback is a fundamental part of the learning and development process. Indeed, evaluating effectiveness has a dedicated chapter within this text to demonstrate and showcase how essential it is in leadership and management development to evaluate impact.

Just as the four foundations therefore provide the fundamental underpinnings to self-leadership the next eight facets form the building blocks (Holroyd, 2015).

The facets of self-leadership

The facets are identified under two broad headings:

- Leading self.

- Leading others.

This captures the very nature of self-leadership that it is both about self and others.

The facets of leading self are discussed in more detail in Holroyd (2015) – *Self-Leadership and Personal Resilience in Health and Social Care*. Facets are the building blocks of self-leadership. Creating the very best version of our self. They are therefore mentioned here briefly as including the following:

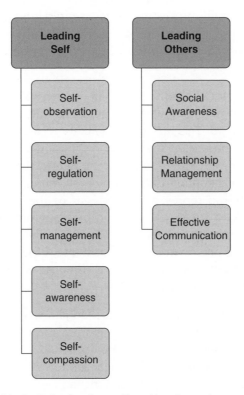

Figure 3.1 Self-leadership includes leading self and leading others

Leading self

Self-observation

It is in De Mello's (1990: 47) terms, the 'I' looking at 'me', this important helicopter view of noticing in the moment what is really happening. It is not a technique but simply about suspending judgement resisting our brains natural compulsion to judge and assess (an unconscious activity played out before we are consciously aware), to evaluate, to over-analyse, to make up our minds too quickly.

This very natural propensity to jump to the solution before really 'seeing' what is wholly in front of us and therefore unearthing a better option is why self-observation is key. Being mindful of how we are in any given moment, are we jumping to an assumption in this interaction? Are we looking at this with fresh eyes or a predictive, automatic assumption lens? Awareness in the moment through self-observation is therefore vital.

Self-observation therefore provides a moment-by-moment appreciation of our state of mind. A tuned in awareness and ability to connect with a sensed appreciation of our quality of thinking.

Self-regulation

Eisenberg et al (2011: 263) would describe self-regulation as part of 'effortful control' and 'the ability to wilfully or voluntarily inhibit, activate, or change (modulate) attention and behaviour, as well as executive functioning tasks of planning, detecting errors, and integrating information relevant to selecting behaviour'.

Self-regulation is therefore linked to our ability to control and regulate our attention to really focus on something when we need to, and to behave in a certain way even if we don't want to. This includes the ability to manage our emotions. It is described as effortful because it uses a significant amount of energy in the form of glucose and oxygen, not stored in the brain, indeed the brain uses 20 per cent of the total energy consumption of the body even though it only weighs approximately 3lbs (1.5kgs) and represents 2 per cent of the total body weight. This invariably means that we are at risk of the unconscious automatic processes of our brain which take less glucose and oxygen controlling what we do, this is especially true when we are tired and/or stressed. Kahneman (2011) describes this as system one, the thinking fast automatic unconscious response where we develop impressions, patterns, intuitions and biases.

In order to help to suspend our unconscious judgements and any potential associated biases it is important to appreciate and prevent habitual ways of thinking through self-regulation. This may be about purposefully resisting the urge to judge and instead be comfortable with not knowing, John Keats in a letter to his brothers described this concept as being 'negative capabilities':

'I mean Negative Capability, *that is when a man is capable of being in uncertainties, mysteries, doubts, without any irritable reaching after fact and reason'.*

(John Keats, 1817)

This comfortableness with not knowing would allow instead someone to generate a hypothesis, to ask a better question, for example, what information is missing, what question could I ask, what does this mean to me, what do I already know, what assumptions might be underlying this? To be curious, remembering that you cannot be curious and angry at the same time, allows a better state and frame of mind for seeing something you may have missed. Using this approach allows the emotional heat to be removed, and with it a potential brain hijack, the type which causes you to say when you come out of a heated meeting, 'Oh I wished I'd said that', incapable through the moment of the red mist to see clearly.

Self-management

Self-management is closely related to the management of our emotions and self-regulation. Self-management is about developing a consistent sense of self, being mindful of arriving at work with the influences from home bleeding into our daily life. Some people would say they are able to go home, touch the gate post and forget all about work; but many more cannot do the reverse.

What does this mean in reality, it can result in a constant regurgitation of thought, of preoccupation and therefore less resources to be effective. This residual attention deficit impedes peak performance. Indeed, as Glei (2013: 69) states 'In a world filled with distraction, attention is our competitive advantage'. This is the ability to keep focused on what really matters and to stop getting hooked emotionally, for this sabotages productivity. Being in the right state of mind and exercising self-leadership will prevent this from occurring.

An important feature of self-management is the management of self-confidence. Confidence is an integral part of resilience and when coaching one of the most complained deficits by individuals is 'I need more confidence'. This links to self-beliefs and potential limiting beliefs, a story we keep telling ourselves if I had more confidence then I could:

- Say such and such…
- Challenge him/her.
- Go to that meeting.
- Present well.
- Go for promotion.
- Say what I think.

So self-management has a crucial role to play and is linked closely with self-awareness.

Self-awareness

This concept is discussed elsewhere within this text however, self-awareness is a vital facet of self-leadership and a building block for a better state of mind. It is not just the awareness of self in terms of knowing myself but also a felt sense in the moment of being able to tune in and really connect with what is occurring, connecting with feelings and their impact upon thought.

An important feature of self-awareness is captured by Sinek's (2009: 37) 'Golden Circle' and the very important centre circle of 'Why' – the purpose, our beliefs, our values, our passions, the why we go to work. Sinek proposes that most individuals communicate from the outside in, the what we do, presenting the facts and the figures rather than the inside out, explicitly what we really stand for, tuning in to peoples' feelings and connecting on what is a transformational level were individuals are more likely to follow, be loyal, work for the same cause and beliefs. Someone's 'why' might be about quality, providing the best service in every interaction they may have. It may be about developing others, staff, clients through every opportunity and focusing on the belief that individuals have the resources within to enact change.

The crucial feature of the Golden Circle is that he aligns this with the human brain, the tenets of biology. Implicitly the centre of the circle, the 'Why' and the 'How' align with the limbic area – the emotional centre, the part of the brain which has no capacity for language but is able to feel whether something is right and the, 'What' with the neocortex where we logically think and process language. He stresses the importance of tuning into your 'Why' and in so doing attract others to do the same.

Organisations can easily become institutions when they lose touch with their 'Why' and fail to enact their 'Why' in everything they do. We see this in doctors' surgeries and other front facing industries were individuals/customers/service users are ignored whilst they stand at reception desks waiting whilst staff often talk to each other, as though they are not there, or continue to type away never giving the human being in front of them a second glance. To be ignored in this way is a felt sense and something the 'Why' of Sinek's circle would feel. That is the important piece, everyone knows how it feels to be ignored, even for a short period of time, and no matter really what is said after, the felt sense can leave a residual ripple of disconnection.

Figure 3.2 reminds us that 'why' needs to be at the centre of all we do, the purpose, what really matters to individuals, teams and organisations.

Self-leadership is very much about tuning into the 'Why' and enacting this in all that we do. The importance of 'Why' and self-awareness is linked to another very important construct of self-compassion.

Self-compassion

Exercising self-compassion is absolutely required in order to be compassionate to others. As Brown (2012: 75) suggests that when we can exercise self-compassion

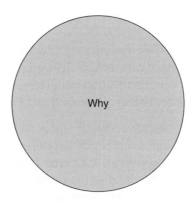

Figure 3.2 The Golden Circle – The Why (Sinek, 2009:37)

by being 'gentle with ourselves', we are 'more likely to reach out, connect and experience empathy' and be able to be compassionate towards others. Neff (2011) describes three important components of self-compassion as being *self-kindness*, *common humanity* and *mindfulness*.

Self-kindness is the ability to stop the psychological harm we do to ourselves in our own heads; the cruel internal dialogue beatings – 'you failed because you're useless, you're not smart, you're not worthy, you're not lovable, not competent'.

Common humanity is the recognition of the 'common human experience – the acknowledgement of the interconnected nature of our lives' (Neff, 2011: 61). It links with Lencioni's (2016) concept of 'humility' a pre-requisite of an ideal team player and which he describes – 'humility isn't thinking less of yourself, but thinking of yourself less' (Lencioni, 2016: 158).

Mindfulness she describes as the 'clear seeing and non-judgmental acceptance of what's occurring in the present moment' (Neff, 2011: 80).

Taking time to pause in the day and instead of reaching for our mobile phones to search for messages or the internet when we have to wait in a queue or fill a space in time, to instead pause and take a moment to get back in touch, to tune in, reconnect. This is about improving our state of mind rather than to be constantly hooked in. We were not designed to be on all the time – defaulting back to our natural factory settings of taking moments to re-charge.

Self-compassion is about helping others to do the same and this links to the next section in relation to leading others.

Leading others

Self-leadership is always about others and not simply about self. There are three important facets of leading others: social awareness, relationship management and effective communication. The first of the three, social awareness, is not always a natural ability but is the important capability of tuning into others.

Social awareness

An essential component of social awareness is the ability to tune in and exercise empathy, to allow us to connect with others. It is a crucial part of creating better working relationships, team cohesion through appropriately addressing conflict and in so doing improving team effectiveness (Pavlovich and Krahnke, 2014).

Social awareness isn't about acquiescing to please everyone it is about building relationships based on good rapport. Rapport however, doesn't mean you need to agree – it is about creating opportunities for better communication. It is not about manipulating someone to do something – it is really about getting out of our own way and instead allowing a very natural process to take place. 'Primal empathy' is this process and is the brain's inborn ability to make a real connection to anticipate through 'mirror neurones' what someone is likely to feel and do (Ramachandran, 2011). It is a key safety feature within groups to be able to anticipate what an individual will do, whether they are friend or foe.

Getting out of our own way, stopping judgements, being an empty vessel in order to tune in is how we access this important and natural ability. An ability which is so crucial to the facets of relationship management and communication.

Relationship management

Relationship management is integral to the success of any individual, team or organisation and is vital to leadership, management and supervision. Relationship management always stems from and out of, better self-management and being in the best state of mind. Individuals don't leave organisations; they frequently leave because of a relationship break down which can often be with their manager.

Working on self-first can therefore change, for the better, perceptions of, and relationships with others and is always so very crucial to relationship management. An important and growing awareness is the significance of diversity as a necessary ingredient of successful teams and great leadership (Torres, 2013). The Chartered Institute of Personnel and Development (CIPD, 2015) reminds of the vital role of the next generation – and how the very different generations need to work together, to better understand each other in order to maximise all the contributions. It is recognised that many more people will be working longer past the normal bounds of retirement and as a result there will be a number of different generations present within the established workforce.

Different generations provide a great diversity prospect but also with it some potential challenges. Relationship management and understanding the potential differing needs of the generations is a very useful adjunct. The diagram below captures the different generations.

There is a different psychodynamic across the generations with differing needs and aspirations. A great deal of research has been carried out to understand the Y Generation as

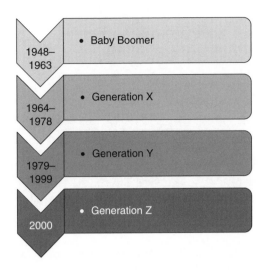

Figure 3.3 Diversity across the generations in the workforce – the impact of the Y Generation
Copyright – awaiting answer to query

they were seen as the future workforce. What we know from the CIPD (2015) report is that these individuals are more goal and achievement orientated and want to be considered for career advancement perhaps before their older colleagues feel they are ready. They come to work to learn and seek a more pronounced work–life balance. Perhaps they saw their parents concentrating on working to earn and devoting too many hours. They prioritise support and importantly function best when they are provided with clear objectives, regular one-to-one feedback with a coaching style of leadership.

They will follow rules if they understand why, and might need additional support with communicating, team working and their confidence. Further development in areas such as writing skills, analysis, self-awareness and emotional intelligence are all advised by the CIPD (2015). The best mentors for the Y Generation are the baby boomers.

Getting the communication right with this group and any other group is crucial to effective working environment.

Effective communication

Effective communication includes all aspects from what is not said, the non-verbal aspect, to the verbal language patterns (the specific words chosen) the tone, timbre, volume, the accent, hepatics, posture everything we give away. One of the most important elements of effective communication is how we listen. Being listened to creates a real quality of communication.

Listening to understand rather than to reply was the essence of Stephen Covey's (2004) seven habits of highly effective people. Bommelje (2013) would agree that to really understand we need to listen; to always be clear what the listener's purpose is to be willing to really connect. Listening is a fundamental part of Patrick Lencioni's

Figure 3.4 Five dysfunctions of a team (Lencioni (2005: 6))

© Lencioni, 2005. Overcoming the Five Dysfunctions of a Team: A field guide for leaders, managers and facilitators. Wiley

(2005) antidote to the five dysfunctions of a team which starts with the vital role of trust, see diagram below.

Trust is such a fundamental concept that without it any progression is lost, and with it, an underlying fear of conflict, a lack of commitment and an avoidance of account-ability with the outcome that planned results are not achieved. Lencioni (2005) would advocate that in terms of trust you go there first and that 'no quality or characteristic is more important than trust' (Lencioni, 2005: 13). Brown (2012) would agree and like Lencioni believes this stems from an important concept of vulnerability. People can think being vulnerable is weak but it is a vital ingredient to making individuals feel able and safe to share. Before anything, trust must therefore be established.

Teams who fear conflict can create conflict as any tensions are not appropriately addressed. Lencioni would suggest getting the undiscussables on the table allowing individuals to express what these might be otherwise people say 'yes' in the meeting only to walk out of the room with 'no' in their heads. This creates a lack of buy in with accountability lost and with it the results.

Self-leadership is an integral concept to systemic leadership and leading others.

Self-leadership is the subject of another text in this series; Self-Leadership and Personal Resilience in Health and Social Care.

Key learning points

- Self-leadership is of significant potential value in today's complex, chaotic and ever changing environments.
- State of mind, everyone counting, devolved environments and evaluating impact are important and fundamental aspects of self-leadership.

- Self-leadership is not only about self but implicitly and most importantly about the effective management of others.

- Starting with self and suspending our natural ability and propensity to judge and assume gives way to an ability to tap into our natural human potential to really be in the now; to see what is fundamentally in front of us and to enact our 'why' – our purpose and values.

- Building relationships based on effective communication, of being vulnerable enough to produce a binding trust creating the necessary base to discuss the undiscussables, to establish commitment, accountability and achieve the right results is all that self-leadership is.

Chapter 4

Developing your leadership style

Richard Field

CHAPTER OUTCOMES

As a result of completing this chapter you will:

- Understand the importance of self-awareness and the centrality of this to effective leadership.
- Have further developed your awareness of self.
- Have further developed your capacity to understand and value difference.
- Have identified ways in which you might adapt your behaviour in order to relate to those around you.
- Be able to articulate your approach to leadership.

Introduction

Forming and sustaining productive relationships with those we work with irrespective of role and status is at the heart of effective leadership. As leaders we need to be able to relate to a range of people, recognising and valuing their individuality in terms of personality, interests, needs and preferences. This ability to relate requires both awareness of self and of others. Within this chapter, you will find a number of reflection points and activities, each of which is intended to prompt self-audit and reflection.

This chapter is informed by the following assumptions that:

1. In order to be effective, we need to be able to relate to a diverse range of people from within and outside our organisations.

2. As individuals, we share certain similarities but at the same time differ and are unique.

3. We all have natural preferences – just as we are left or right handed we have ways of seeing, interpreting and responding to the world around us.

4. Our natural preferences are reflected in our behaviours.

5. While our natural preferences serve us well in many circumstances, there are times when we need to behave 'unnaturally'.

6. Many of us can and do behave 'unnaturally' when required.

7. We are more likely to be successful when our natural preferences fit the situation we face, and less so when they do not.

8. We can all learn to be effective in a wider range of situations by developing our range of behaviours.

9. We all have a choice about *what* we do and *how* we behave.

10. We need to take individual responsibility for our behaviour and associated outcomes.

Relating to individuals

At the heart of effective leadership is an ability to work effectively with others. This is not optional; it is essential.

In the course of a single day, most of us have 360-degree interactions with our managers, those who report to us, colleagues and people outside of the organisation. One of the challenges we each face therefore is how to work with a wide range of people, some of whom we experience as being different, which can be a potential source of benefit and joy but is all too often puzzling, frustrating and difficult.

Transactions form the basis of most management activity i.e. 'in return for this I want that', enforced largely through reward and sanction. However, if these are the only sources of power used by a leader or manager they will soon encounter situations where their ability to influence is much diminished. Management and leadership increasingly occur in situations where reward and sanction are inappropriate or inadequate; other forms of influence need to be deployed. The effective leader understands that each person they seek to influence is different and the approach adopted needs to reflect this individuality.

REFLECTION POINT 4.1

Take a few moments to think of someone who at some point in a working relationship you experienced as being different from you. At what point did you first notice this difference and did you view this positively or negatively? What specifically did you notice about them as being different? Have you noticed this with other people?

Did the point at which you noticed a difference occur early in your relationship or emerge later? Often, the difference is most keenly felt when a relationship has not yet properly formed or where there is a problem or stressful situation.

Points of difference can negatively or positively affect a relationship. Negative effects can occur where a difference is noticed but neither understood nor valued. When difference is understood, valued and contributes to a relationship the outcome can be very positive.

CASE STUDY 4.1

John and Jane

When John is given a task he likes to be clear about what is required, when it has to be completed by and what the output should look like. John is reluctant to start working on a task until he has what he considers to be sufficient guidance. John has a preference for procedures, seeking these when given a task and in turn giving them when he asks a sub-ordinate to complete a task.

Jane, who is John's line manager prefers to give staff as much freedom as she can, tends not to interfere in how a task is done and provides little guidance unless asked. Jane has a preference for options and likes working for someone who lets her 'get on with it', in turn granting the same freedom to her subordinates.

John and Jane mismatch in terms of whether they prefer procedures or options; a difference that is quite common and can be a source of frustration and impatience between two people. Figure 4.1 shows the typical responses of people mismatching in this way.

Where a person has a strong preference, like Jane has for freedom regarding how she undertakes tasks, they are likely to encounter lots of people who they experience

	Manager provides considerable direction	**Manager provides very little direction**
Report requires considerable direction	*Match* Manager's style coincides with the direct report's requirements	*Mismatch* 'Why doesn't my manager tell me exactly what they want me to do?' (Report) 'Why can't my member of staff use their initiative? — I am fed up with spoon-feeding them.' (Manager)
Report requires considerable freedom	*Mismatch* 'Why can't my manager just let me get on with it? I don't like being micro-managed.' (Report) 'Why does my member of staff question why something has to be done or how I want it done?' (Manager)	*Match* Manager's style coincides with direct report's requirements

Figure 4.1 Mismatch example

as having the opposite preference, which in Jane's case is procedural. It follows that some of the problems we have with those we experience as different are not so much due to their behaviour but to our own preferences.

In mismatch situations, rather than continuing to think of other people as being different from you, try asking yourself 'how do I differ from them'? This can significantly affect how we perceive difference.

If you know your natural tendency is to offer minimal instruction and find that some staff have difficulty with this, you can choose to behave differently by providing greater detail when you allocate a task. This should minimise anxiety for those staff with a procedural preference and avoid the need for you to provide additional guidance later. At the same time, it might be helpful to continue giving less guidance to those people who need more freedom. This ability to flex behaviour according to task, context and personality is highly desirable.

Awareness of difference often leads to recognising that this adds something to, rather than detracts from, a relationship. It is a mark of emotional intelligence that we can progress from recognising difference, to valuing it, harnessing it and finally, seeking it. Understanding, valuing and working effectively with those we experience as being different is vital to personal and organisational success.

Developing this understanding is a lifetime's work. Consciously or not, you will have already started this work and this section should help you consolidate this and prompt new insights and learning.

Dee Hock, former Chief Executive of Visa International, captures this perfectly:

> *The first and paramount responsibility of anyone who purports to manage is to manage self: one's own integrity, character, ethics, knowledge, wisdom, temperament, words and acts. It is a complex, unending, incredibly difficult, oft-shunned task. We spend little time and rarely excel at management of self, precisely because it is so much more difficult than prescribing and controlling the behaviour of others. However, without management of self no one is fit for authority, no matter how much they acquire, for the more they acquire, the more dangerous they become. It is the management of self that should occupy 50% of our time and the best of our ability.*

> (Hock, D., 2000, paragraph 15)

Leaders achieve their ends through those they work with and as a consequence their ability to build and sustain relationships is of paramount importance. Daniel Goleman (1998) advances the view that the primordial task of leaders is to drive the collective emotions of the organisation, thus requiring emotional intelligence.

The ability to work effectively with diverse colleagues is becoming increasingly important and requires us to sense how others might be, understand how we might be affecting a situation and diagnose how we might modify our actions should we so choose. At the heart of this is a need for self-awareness.

Relating in groups and teams

Within employing organisations, we belong to work, project and management teams or groups comprising colleagues within the same service, organisation or sector. Increasingly, we work alongside people who use our services and their representatives, politicians, volunteers, staff of other agencies, suppliers, community groups, etc.

Leaders and managers need to be able to:

- Move in and out of groups and teams with ease.
- Collaborate with those from other professions, agencies or sectors.
- Work in novel, complex and uncertain contexts.
- Deal with diverse problems.

When working as a team we need access to a range of experience, knowledge and skills appropriate to the context and challenges faced. Increasingly, the operating environment demands a high level of team diversity as reflected in different personalities, professional backgrounds, varying attitudes to risk, etc. Such diversity extends the range of problems that the team will be able to tackle and increases the likelihood of productive conflict and innovation. The greater the complexity and the rate of change in the environment in which the team operates, the greater the need for diversity within the team.

However, a high level of team member diversity is accompanied by the significant challenge of learning how to work together effectively. The potential for misunderstanding, disagreement and plain 'not getting along' are high in these circumstances. Teams with relatively low levels of diversity can be expected to form more quickly, reach agreement more readily and be easier to manage. As levels of diversity increase, relationships between members are likely to become more difficult to the point where, without emotional intelligence, the effectiveness of the team is likely to decrease.

When working in groups and teams, there are therefore two major challenges; how to achieve the task and how to work with each other. Frequently, team members make the mistake of focusing only on tasks which may work while the task is progressing well and in a way that meets the needs, interests and preferences of every member. However, life is rarely this easy and at some point, difficulty is likely to be experienced either with the task and/or how we relate to each other. With luck, the team will include someone with natural facilitation skills, or be led by a charismatic leader who is able to resolve such issues. Without this luck, it will be up to team members to resolve any problems at the point at which they occur, something which is difficult if earlier attention has not been paid to process and how team members work with each other.

Team members can, therefore, choose either to consciously work on process and relationships from the outset of team formation, or react to relationship problems as and when they occur.

Whatever the choice, team members need to work productively with those they experience as different, which involves them:

- Understanding themselves and what they bring to a team.

- Appreciating how others might be and valuing what they bring.

- Developing a range of behaviours that will help team members work effectively with each other.

To an extent, this range of behaviours has to be learnt; some are less natural and require a certain effort. While it might be possible for a person working with others to make all the adjustments necessary for the relationship to work, this can be both demanding and unfair. Where three or more people are working together it is highly unlikely that all the required adjustments can be made by one person. Ideally, everyone involved in a team should be able to flex behaviour so the degree of adjustment made by each person is consequently lower and less demanding. Individual team members can also develop an ability to intervene when two people are in unproductive conflict. This ability is possessed by many people, however, the knowledge of this is often largely unconscious and could frequently be developed further.

This sub-section ends with an opportunity to reflect on your experience of flexing your behaviour.

ACTIVITY 4.1

Identify a time when you have modified your approach to a situation as it unfolds.

- *What was the situation?*
- *Who was involved?*
- *What were you trying to achieve?*
- *How did your approach change?*
- *What prompted you to change your approach and why?*
- *Was the change of approach successful?*
- *What have you learnt as a result?*

Flexibility, outcome clarity, awareness and motivation (FOAM)

For many people, leading appears to be a largely unconscious set of skills in which they are quite successful. It is highly unlikely that you could have got this far in your career without being able to read situations and change the way you behave in response. At the heart of this ability is emotional intelligence, defined by Daniel Goleman as 'how leaders handle themselves and their relationships' (Goleman, 1998: 6).

An effective leader prepares for each situation they face, selecting an approach they believe will deliver the intended outcomes while being prepared to adjust their behaviour as the situation unfolds. Selection and adjustment are related skills that require FOAM, each aspect of which is explored below.

Flexibility – an ability to select and deploy a range of approaches in a situation

A person who can only behave one way will occasionally be successful but more often will experience difficulty and perhaps failure. A one-size-fits-all approach to dealing with situations is limiting, and effective leaders are able to select an approach from a range available to them and deploy this with skill. Deciding how to approach a particular situation is an important skill, as is an ability to change or flex the chosen approach as the situation unfolds.

CASE STUDY 4.2

Susan's situation

Susan has to give difficult feedback to a colleague who she knows quite well and expects will be upset and possibly angry. Accordingly, she has decided on an approach and pre-pared thoroughly.

However, a little way into the conversation it appears to Susan that her colleague is not taking the feedback seriously, in which case the intended outcome of the conversation is unlikely to be realised. Susan's approach so far has been calm and gentle; her judgement, however, is that she is failing to convey the seriousness of the situation. Susan is aware that she is beginning to lose control of the situation and is becoming irritated and tense, which based on previous experience can lead to her becoming aggressive. Thankfully, Susan has access to a range of approaches to giving feedback and switches to one which is more appropriate to her colleague's reaction.

Access to a range of approaches to situations can be developed through formal education, training, coaching, observation, reading, etc. The rest of this book will help you understand different approaches to many aspects of management and leadership; however, this represents just a start, for personal development should continue for the rest of your career if not the remainder of your life.

Outcomes – an ability to developed well-formed outcomes

For any situation, there are a set of outcomes that can be pursued and which drive how we behave and the energy we will commit to a line of action. In many situations, there is an immediate and obvious outcome that can become the sole focus of our attention, perhaps to the detriment of other less obvious ones.

CASE STUDY 4.3

Susan's situation (continued)

Returning to Susan's situation, her initial concern is that the 'Person receiving the feed-back understands it and commits to acting in the way Susan wants in future'.

This immediate and obvious outcome comprises a number of smaller outcomes, which it is useful to specify. In addition, there are other outcomes regarding how Susan wants to experience the conversation and the impact she would like this to have on the longer-term relationship. Susan actually wants:

- *The person receiving feedback to:*
  - *Accept it;*
  - *Understand what they need to do in future;*
  - *Feel they can change their behaviour;*
  - *Want to change their behaviour;*
- *To be seen to be fair and developmental.*
- *The conversation to be positive, to be heard and respected.*
- *The future relationship to be enhanced rather than damaged as a result of how the feedback conversation progresses.*

Having a full range of outcomes in mind helps Susan plan and monitor the feedback conversation.

Awareness – of self and others

Understanding ourselves is the first step in developing our ability to work effectively with others.

There are a considerable number of frameworks or theories that can help us understand how we and others behave; enable us to anticipate how we are likely to react and behave in certain circumstances and offer insights as to productive ways of behaving in these situations.

These theories vary from relatively simple ideas such as whether someone prefers procedures or seeks options through to the more complex theories of personality such as the Myers-Briggs Type Indicator (MBTI). Four such frameworks that are explored later in this chapter are:

- Metaprograms, habits or filters.
- Timelines.
- MBTI.
- Maps of the world.

Motivation – to achieve the desired outcomes

While the ability to be aware, flexible and understand desired outcomes is extremely important, this is only of value if the person is motivated to act. It is possible for someone to be involved in a situation where they sense what is happening, understand this is unlikely to lead to their desired outcomes and know how to correct the situation and yet fail to act. Motivation to act is highly important to leadership.

Figure 4.2 indicates the impact of any missing or weak parts of FOAM.

Flexibility	Outcome clarity	Awareness	Motivation	Implication
X	✓	✓	✓	Inability to act when you know what is wrong.
✓	X	✓	✓	Uneasiness about how a situation is developing without knowing why.
✓	✓	X	✓	Carrying on regardless, unaware that intended outcomes are at risk.
✓	✓	✓	X	Knowing what you want to achieve, seeing that it is going wrong, and knowing what needs to be done to correct it but failing to act

Figure 4.2 FOAM

The remainder of this chapter focuses on awareness of self and others.

Awareness of self and others
Metaprograms, habits or filters

Neurolinguistic programming (NLP) identifies a considerable number of metaprograms or habits that are thought to affect how we behave (O'Connor and Seymour, 2003). The earlier example of procedures and options is a metaprogram and a further four are offered below. When looking at these it is helpful to identify:

- Which of these best describes your preferred habit; and

- Someone you know who appears to have the opposite habit.

It is important to recognise that all of these habits are potentially valuable and each of us needs to consider how best to respond to people who exhibit habits that are different to our own.

Towards and away

Many people are motivated towards outcomes they value and want and are more likely to embrace change if they understand the benefits and can see the attractiveness of what is being proposed. Other people tend to be motivated more to avoid what they do not like and for them, change is more likely to be embraced when they understand why the current state is considered undesirable and are assured that risks associated with the change have been identified and will be managed.

General and specific

Whenever we communicate, we make a series of choices about what we include and how we express it; one aspect of that which is particularly apparent when problem solving concerns the level at which something is described. A manager calling a meeting may state that they are concerned by something that they have chosen to label 'staff sickness'. When discussing this issue the manager may find some colleagues offer contributions such as 'I think the real issue here is staff morale, not sickness', or perhaps 'I think this is a wider problem with society', both of which are examples of thinking more generally or 'chunking up' an issue. Other individuals tend to the opposite habit, which is to be more specific with typical contributions being along the lines of 'I think the real problem is actually long-term sickness', or perhaps '... long-term sickness in "A" team'. These individuals tend to see things in more specific terms and 'chunk down' issues.

Difference and similarity

Some people develop their understanding of an issue or problem by spotting and removing apparent inconsistencies or contradictions in what they are being told. They may spot apparent inconsistencies or differences within a conversation, between two or more speakers, by comparison with what they understood previously, etc. Contributions such as 'I thought this morning you said that there were no circumstances when you would... but you just said that...' is a typical contribution of someone who tends to understand by eliminating 'difference'. People with a 'difference' habit can appear a little critical and their questions interpreted as challenging. Other people have a tendency to learn by spotting similarity between comments made by different people and/or by the same person over time. Contributions such as 'Is this another example of the poor leadership behaviour that you were talking about this morning?' are typical of someone who has a similarity habit. People with this habit tend to appear positive both in terms of what they say and their body language.

Internal and external

Ask a person 'how do you know if you have done a good piece of work?' and you will tend to get one of two typical responses. With the first response people indicate that they will know they have done a good job when someone tells them, for example during their annual appraisal, via customer feedback or more generally, comments made by others. This type of response suggests the person may be exter-nally referenced, getting their standards from other people and for them, it is likely to be important that they receive feedback, recognition and praise without which they may be uncertain of how well they are performing. The second type of response is 'I just know when I have done a good job' and is typical of someone who has a strong sense of their own internal set of standards. Such internally referenced people tend to have less need for feedback and may reject the comments of others if they do not accept the standards of that person.

REFLECTION POINT **4.2**

Taking one of these metaprograms, identify a situation when you are aware of both habits being involved (e.g. where you exhibited a 'towards' habit and another person an 'away' habit).

- *What impact did these different habits have?*

- *How did you feel?*

- *To what extent if any did your habit cause you to behave in a way that was unhelpful?*

- *Would it have been possible to behave in a way that better matched the habit of the other person?*

Timelines

It is suggested that each of us has one of two attitudes to time, either being time con-scious and concerned about timekeeping, an attitude often referred to as being *through time*; or, relatively unaware of time, an attitude often referred to as being *in time*.

These attitudes to time can be quite marked and are often a source of irritation between individuals. Those with a 'through time' disposition tend to be punctual, if not early for meetings and can get irritated by someone who is late, perhaps viewing them as being disorganised, inconsiderate or downright rude. People with an 'in time' orientation may view those that do not share this preference as being time obsessed and sometimes rude as their need to avoid being late for their next meeting means they inappropriately curtail their current conversation or 'clock watch'.

Those of us with a 'through time' preference would do well to consider the behaviour of 'in time' people differently. A more positive view is that 'in time' people are 'in the moment' giving their full attention to what they are currently doing; if as a consequence they are slightly late for their next appointment or commitment does it really matter?

Others of us with a preference for being 'in time' would do well to question whether the behaviour of 'through time' people helps ensure that planned actions occur when desired and that best use is made of the time of everyone concerned. While the natural habits of 'through time' and 'in time' people may be a strong influence on our managerial or leadership style it is possible to learn how to behave differently thereby improving personal performance.

Suzi's time problem

Suzi is a trainer with a through time preference and a tendency to get irritated by participants who turn up after the planned start time for a session. Suzi likes to start her sessions promptly as this is what she has planned and because a number of other like-preferenced people have turned up early or at least on time. When Suzi started as a trainer, if a participant was late she used to interpret this as rudeness, an inability to plan their life, etc. to which she used to respond by either:

1) Ignoring them when they did arrive.

2) Acknowledging their presence but not bringing them up to date.

After one or two difficult incidents Suzi realised that the reason for arriving after the start time might be outside of the person's control and, in any case, pursuing either of her usual responses is unlikely to facilitate the learning of latecomers and may mean that they are not able to contribute fully to the learning of others.

A third option which is less natural to Suzi, but more appropriate, is to greet participants who arrive after the start time warmly, ensure they are comfortable and bring them up to date as soon as practicable.

Myers-Briggs Type Indicator (MBTI)

There are a number of more sophisticated models that help us explain how we differ and which form the basis of psychometric instruments used for personal development; one such example is the MBTI (Reinhold, 2010).

The MBTI is a well-established instrument that helps individuals understand their own and others' personality preferences. MBTI helps individuals realise the benefits of diversity and develop effective ways of working with those they experience as different. Used with teams MBTI stimulates awareness of overall team type and enables strengths and potential development needs to be identified. In particular, MBTI helps participants develop effective approaches to communication, problem-solving, change and conflict management.

At the heart of MBTI are four dimensions, presented below as questions.

- Where do you prefer to focus your attention? How are you energised? (Extroversion or Introversion)

- What kind of information do you prefer to pay attention to? How do you acquire information? (Sensing or Intuition)

- How do you prefer to make decisions? (Thinking or Feeling)

- Which lifestyle do you prefer? (Judging or Perceiving)

(MBTI, 2007, Step 1)

In respect of each dimension a person has a preference, for example, extroversion (E) or introversion (I), and the instrument reports the preference along with the clarity with which this is reported.

There are 16 possible combinations of letters, each of which possessing typical characteristics associated with the preference reported for each dimension and the interaction between them. MBTI can be completed in two levels or steps. Step 1 results in the identification of a four-letter type such as ENTJ (Extroverted, Intuitive, Thinking and Judging). MBTI Step 2 results in more detailed feedback in respect of 20 facets that make up the four dimensions. Step 2 provides a much richer picture of preference and therefore can make a more significant contribution to developing self-awareness.

Maps of the world

The fourth framework or idea is that each one of us carries with us a 'map of the world' through which we make sense of what is going on around us, we use it to reach decisions and it guides our behaviour. This map covers all aspects of our lives including at work, our understanding of patient/user needs, how our organisation works, how we should behave, etc.

Our individual maps which differ significantly should constantly evolve to include material derived from family life, schooling, friends, our first and subsequent jobs, particular events, training and general experience, etc. For many people, the development or revision of their maps is largely unconscious and the subsequent use of these is unquestioning.

ACTIVITY 4.2

As a simple illustration of a map try to identify seven ways a manager can motivate their staff. Look at your responses and sift them into those that are a form of reward and those that involve punishment.

Typically, managers working in a public service organisation tend to offer ideas involving reward rather than punishment. Now taking the reward responses divide these into two further categories, those that:

- *involve monetary incentives, cars, perks and any other extrinsic rewards; and those that*

- *concern the nature of the work, e.g. interesting tasks, empowerment, support, praise, training and other intrinsic rewards.*

Managers with a public service background are more likely to offer reward responses and within this intrinsic examples, as this tends to be their experience of being managed and seeing others managed, possibly reinforced through internal training programmes. Equipped with this map of the world, a manager faced with a member of staff who they consider needs motivating is likely to automatically turn to intrinsic rewards. If the map is strong, the likelihood that the manager will explore options for using extrinsic rewards or punishment will be low.

Individual maps can significantly affect our behaviour and the likelihood of personal and organisational success as illustrated by David's tale.

CASE STUDY *4.5*

David's tale

David is a middle manager aged 47 who is frustrated at his inability to progress within his organisation. David consistently receives positive feedback and his annual appraisals indicate no areas where his performance could be improved. David's line manager encourages him to go for promotion on a regular basis. David is considered to be a hard worker and prides himself on his flexibility, punctuality and excellent sickness record. With regard to promotion, David believes that experience and proven competence should determine promotion decisions.

In the last three years, David has applied for three promotions, each time being short-listed and interviewed yet failing to get the post. On two occasions posts were awarded to external applicants and on the third occasion the post was given to a much younger internal candidate; none of these managers possessed the same experience as David. He is beginning to talk about being discriminated against on the basis of his age.

The only feedback David has received regarding his recent applications is that his CV could be updated and that when being interviewed he should offer more detailed examples of how he would approach particular situations. He has been told that on each occasion the successful applicant did a better interview on the day.

Early in his career David had considerable success when going for promotion and considers himself to be good at job interviews.

(Continued)

55

David's map	New material – not yet assimilated in David's map	Implications
Employees should be honest, punctual, work hard, volunteer for new duties and seek development.	Recruitment/promotion are based on interview performance on the day, not prior job performance.	If David is to be successful he needs to:
Success comes to those who are experienced, have shown they can perform and deserve it. Interviews are an opportunity to show that you have performed in the past and will be able to in the future.	The application form is the basis for short-listing and the interview alone is the basis for appointment decision. There is a need for the panel to tick all the boxes – so candidates should prepare carefully and 'play the game'.	i) let go of the belief that 'interview success should be based on experience and proven competence' and replace this with 'success goes to those that interview well';
		ii) challenge his view that he is being discriminated against;
		iii) confront his inability to perform at interview and learn how to 'play the new game'.

Significant influences on David's map are:

- *His father who had very strong views about how people should behave at work and be rewarded.*

- *A line manager whose views were broadly consistent with the views of David's father.*

- *Early recruitment/promotion experiences over the first 15 years of working life – David was first time successful in four job applications early in his career.*

- *The interpretation of recent interview experiences arising from conversations with peer colleagues of a similar age and similar interview experiences.*

Recognising the required change in his map is painful to David, causing him to wonder about the relevance of his values, challenging him as to whether he should change his behaviour and surfacing a need to develop interview competence. David has a number of choices including:

- *Continuing with his existing map, applying for jobs as now in the hope that sooner or later he will be part of a group of applicants where everyone else is worse at interviewing.*

- *Continuing with his existing map, cease applying for promotion and accept his career is over.*

- *Changing his map, developing interviewing skills and continuing to apply for jobs.*

While maps are personal to the individual concerned the maps of team members are likely to share common features. A team of accountants, for example working for a public service organisation, will typically find that the professional territory of their individual maps is similar. The part of their maps that covers how their organisation works is also likely to be shared and similar in certain respects to other groups in the same organisation.

Working on an inter-professional, inter-organisational or inter-sectoral basis poses many challenges including coping with the diversity of maps held by those involved. Working with this diversity is easier where the different maps are recognised and shared early in the relationship.

However well developed our maps are, there will be occasions when these fail to help us understand a situation we face. Such map 'failure' arises for a number of reasons, including:

- Changes in the external environment that are novel and not covered by our map.

- The age of our maps, which for many senior managers contain material that is over 30 years old.

- Content within our maps that has never been challenged until a particular point in our lives is reached.

Change is often a time when our map of the world is tested and some of the difficulty experienced with major change is the need for maps to be re-drawn. If we are unaware of the importance and content of our maps this re-drawing can be quite a slow and painful process.

As individuals, we have a simple choice:

- Seek to understand our maps, recognising that while these are potentially invaluable they are probably not the only way of thinking about an issue and might need to change. Just as maps shape our thinking, they also limit it. Proactive map-making can be a real spur to creativity as it affords an opportunity to play with different ways of looking at a situation.

- Fail to engage with our maps, allowing these to unconsciously influence our actions until a point is reached when they no longer seem appropriate and we experience having them being re-drawn for us. This approach tends to make us more reactive to change and we are likely to find the process more painful.

Statement of personal leadership

Whenever a new manager, leader or supervisor is appointed there follows a settling in period during which they learn about their new context, role and the staff that they have acquired. For the staff this is a period of discovering what sort of person they will be working for, recognising that they might be quite different from their predecessor in terms of what and how they delegate, the sort of relationship they seek with their staff and how they want 'things done round here'. Inevitably people in power influence the culture or the 'way we do things round here' (Deal and Kennedy 1982). Relatively aware managers, leaders or supervisors have an understanding of:

- The culture of the team and/or organisation they have inherited.

- Whether they need or want to cause a shift in culture.

- How their natural behaviour may impact on the current and intended future culture.

- The personal drivers of their behaviour such as personality type, attitude to risk.

- How they need to manage their behaviour.

The settling in period or 'coming together process' between new managers and their teams can take some time during which productivity may be affected, stress levels might increase and potentially damage is done to future relationships. Each team member will have a combination of one-to-one and shared exchanges and experiences with the new leader, all of which they will interpret through their own filters and maps of the world. Over time each team member will develop an understanding of how their leader leads, to an extent similar to how others see this, yet differing in certain respects. In the current work environment, the ability to form effective working relationships at speed is vital and the coming together process needs to be completed quickly. One way of speeding up this process is for the leader to disclose at the outset details of how they like to lead rather than letting this emerge over time. This could perhaps be a topic for the first team meeting and then reinforced during subsequent one-to-one conversations.

Kouzes and Posner (2002: 44) make the case for being a credible leader and the importance of both 'having a voice' and 'giving voice'. They former requires self-understanding of the values and beliefs that are important to you along with the principles that guide your action. Giving voice requires finding a way of communicating this in an authentic way that is comfortable to you. In order to develop a leadership philosophy that can be shared Kouzes and Posner (2002: 88) advocate writing a 'credo memo' which is in effect a Statement of Personal Leadership. As well as being shared with direct reports and colleagues such a statement could inform the content of a CV and inform responses to interview questions. It also provides evidence that a person has thought about themselves and their leadership. The form and content of such a personal statement will rightly vary from person to person and may include content that reveals:

- What is important to you such as values or beliefs, for example, the need to 'put customers first'.

- What you are seeking from staff, for example, a commitment to listening and responding to what service users are seeking.

- How you like to delegate, for example using a range of approaches that fit the maturity of the individual.

- The extent to which you like to direct and support staff, for example, a preference to have coaching conversations as far as possible but willing to be directive when necessary.

- What you can expect from staff, making reference perhaps to the need for a willingness to work flexibly.

- 'Buttons' others should avoid pushing such as surprises – 'if anything looks like it is going wrong please tell me at the earliest opportunity'.

- What you can expect from me, for example, fairness, support.

- If appropriate, a reference to a leadership model that is central to your practice such as perhaps Hersey and Blanchard's theory of situational leadership (1993).

There is a considerable risk that these statements are little more than a set of clichés or behavioural aspirations which may be presented in too romantic a way, be unrealistic in the context and, or lack congruence. Poorly developed and poorly articulated statements of personal leadership are likely to be met with a degree of scepticism if not cynicism which makes how these are pitched, vital.

Setting your stall out this way takes a degree of bravery and must be accompanied by a commitment to 'live the statement' as any variation from this will be quickly spotted. It is advisable to review every aspect of a statement asking three questions.

- To what extent is this true of my practice?

- Could I evidence this to others if asked?

- Is this appropriate in the current context?

It is advisable to practice delivery of this statement to ensure familiarity with the content and that you are able to present this with congruence.

ACTIVITY 4.3

Imagine you have been recently appointed as team leader and are about to meet the whole team for the first time. Conscious you don't get a second chance to make a first impression... what would you say about the way you prefer to lead in less than 10 minutes?

Key learning points

- Arguably it does not matter which of the ways of looking at difference you use. What is important is to develop awareness of self, and an ability to anticipate how others might be, using this understanding to inform your behaviour.

- For some people, metaprograms prove useful while others prefer timelines or perhaps MBTI. Remember that these are only a few of the models that are available and it may be worth extending your map of the world to include other popular models, addressing for example learning styles and team roles.

- An ability to work with a wide range of people is essential for successful leadership. Particularly in novel, complex and uncertain times, diversity is of considerable value; the difference you experience in another person may ultimately be the difference between success and failure.

- High levels of diversity demand high levels of emotional intelligence, without which there may be unproductive conflict, dysfunctional behaviour and a failure to benefit from the specific contributions of people who differ in some respects.

- Understanding what you believe in and how you prefer to lead is vital to effective practice. Sharing this openly when working with or supervising others can speed up the process of establishing productive relationships. Preparing a Statement of Personal Leadership can help individuals find and give voice to their leadership and become credible.

Chapter 5
Supervision

Lee-Ann Fenge and Richard Field

CHAPTER OUTCOMES

As a result of completing this chapter you will:

- Be able to define supervision and explain the potential benefits this brings to staff, patients, and service users as well as to the organisation.

- Understand different approaches and strategies that can be used when supervising.

- Be familiar with and able to use an effective supervision model.

- Understand and be able to prompt critical reflection in supervisees.

What is supervision and what are the potential benefits?

Generally, supervision can be defined as being the action or process of directing and observing what someone does or how something is done.

Whilst supervision is a feature of all employment the extent, frequency, depth, formality and style varies significantly. Whenever a manager asks a member of staff to undertake a task they need to decide how much instruction to give and if, when and how to monitor progress. The level of instruction and monitoring should reflect the importance of the task, the level of skill possessed and maturity of the person to whom the task has been given.

In practice, the level, nature and quality of supervision will also reflect legal, professional, organisational requirements and the personalities of those involved.

Outside of the helping and caring professions, supervisory practice tends to be patchy, often being limited to staff who are in training, is ad hoc rather than planned and routine, focused on task completion, prompted by performance problems and undertaken without a 'supervision contract'.

In the helping and caring professions, however, supervision is very different, being more structured, formal, reflective and embedded. There are a variety of supervision definitions for these professions that reflect the backgrounds of those involved and variety of contexts within which they practice. The British Association of Social Workers (2012: 7) defines supervision as being:

'A regular, planned, accountable process, which must provide a supportive environment for reflecting on practice and making well-informed decisions using professional judgment and discretion.

Hawkins and Shohet (2012: 5) consider supervision to be:

'A joint endeavor in which a practitioner with the help of a supervisor, attends to their clients, themselves as part of their client–practitioner relationship and the wider systemic context, and by so doing improves the quality of their work, transforms their client relationships, continuously develops themselves, their practice and the wider profession'.

Certain key words or phrases in these two definitions are essential to understanding effective supervision. Firstly, it should be a regular and planned process for which the Social Work Reform Partners (2014: 12) issue guidance regarding frequency and duration. Secondly, supervision is an accountable process involving a degree of challenge for supervisees for which a supportive environment is required. Finally, reflection is key to ensuring the breadth and depth of learning that is critical in the helping and caring professions.

Whilst a majority of supervision occurs between employees working within the same organisation, there are a few situations where supervision is given by someone outside the organisation. An example of this is coach supervision where the necessary knowledge, skill and experience to supervise might not exist within an organisation. Supervision in its widest sense extends beyond one-to-one, regular meetings to include, for example, telephone or corridor conversations that have a supervisory quality. Supervision can also be conducted on a peer basis or within groups led by a formal supervisor.

The focus of this chapter is supervision in one-to-one meetings conducted where supervisor and supervisee are in a line management relationship.

Supervision offers a number of potential benefits to at least four different stakeholder groups, as summarised in Table 5.1.

How does supervision compare to coaching and other helping disciplines?

Supervision is part of a cluster of helping disciplines that are similar in some respects yet differ in others. This cluster includes coaching, mentoring, counselling and therapy as well as supervision, each discipline informed by different schools of thought, models and practice. In line management, supervision and coaching are encountered

Table 5.1 Benefits of supervision by stakeholder

For the supervisee	For the supervisor	For patients, service users and carers	Organisation
Insight about their professional practice and organisational performance.	Mutual learning.	Experience well-informed decision making.	Improved staff retention and reduced levels of staff absence.
Developing competence, confidence and capacity.	Having an opportunity to reflect on their own learning and share this with others.	Reassurance that professionals are being regularly challenged and supported to provide the best possible care.	Reassurance that professional standards are being upheld.
Understanding what they do well, could do differently and might do better.	Having staff with greater capacity and ability to manage with professional autonomy.	Finding that professional standards are observed.	Knowledge that staff are working to a clear direction, standards etc.
Help in managing caseload, workload and the emotional impact of their work.			Reassurance that staff are identifying and managing risk.
			Professional staff acting with autonomy but subject to appropriate scrutiny from peers, line manager, patients and service users.
			A source of potential challenge regarding organisational policy and practice.

with reasonable frequency and worthy of comparison. Coaching has been defined by Holroyd and Field (2012: 2) as being 'a focused discussion whereby one individual assists another to achieve their desired outcomes'.

Table 5.2 summarises the differences between supervision generally and coaching.

Probably the most significant difference between supervision and coaching concerns whether the conversation is directive or not. Coaches are expected to be non-directive in their work, helping their coachees discover options for action, to decide which one to take and to plan for it to happen. Supervisors, however, frequently direct or guide supervisees to a solution and therefore normally share the same professional background. Coaches however often have entirely different backgrounds from their coachee; relying on process skills rather than technical skills or knowledge to be effective.

Whilst coaches are generally expected to be non-directive, supervisors need to be more flexible being directive much of the time, yet able to adopt a coaching style if they believe this to be the best way of supervising in that moment. For some supervisors, adopting a coaching strategy is natural, yet if this was to be the basis for all their conversations they would be highly unlikely to meet their supervisory responsibilities.

So as well as being a helping discipline in its own right, coaching is also one of a number of supervisory strategies that Howe and Gray (2013: 35) suggest also include

Table 5.2 Comparison of supervision and coaching

Comparison of Supervision and Coaching

Supervision	Coaching
Process orientated, systematic review.	Goal orientated.
Often an ongoing process.	Usually a defined number of sessions.
Often part of quality assurance process.	Not an essential quality assurance process.
Connected with organisational governance requirements and professional obligations.	Not linked to organisational governance requirements and professional obligations.
Focused on ensuring supervisee follows best standards and safe practice.	Not necessarily focused on standards and safe practice.
May involve a blend of teaching, supporting, facilitating and conceptualising about professional issues and practice.	More of an inquiry led process.
The supervisor may tell the supervisee what to do.	The coach works to help the coachee identify solutions for themselves.
Exchange of advice with an experienced practitioner.	The coach may have less, little or no experience in the coachee's field of practice.

directing, supporting and delegating. These four strategies are based on Hersey and Blanchard's theory of situational leadership (1993) that recognises different levels of support and direction needed by different staff. Howe and Gray (2013: 36) link these strategies to different levels of professional maturity as summarised in Table 5.3, as adapted from earlier work by Morrison (2005) and Hawkins and Shohet (2006).

It is essential that supervisors understand and are able to use all four strategies effectively, all of which require good relationships, mutual commitment, the ability to craft good questions, to listen actively and catalytically, summarise, reframe, etc.

Mentoring, another popular helping discipline has been defined by Clutterbuck (2004: 12) as being:

> *off-line help from one person to another in making significant transitions in knowledge, work or thinking.*

Mentoring is similar to supervision in that the relationship between the mentor and mentee often has a directive quality, this may also last a significant period of time and typically the supervisor will be more experienced than the supervisee and in the same sector or profession. However, mentoring differs in that it is not normally a professional requirement or part of formal governance and usually the mentor is 'offline' and not, therefore, managing or supervising the supervisee.

Counselling and therapy are other interventions that staff may benefit from but which should only be practised by appropriately qualified staff. It is important to note that, as with coaching and mentoring there is an ever-present risk that supervision conversations develop a counselling quality. This is risky if the supervisor is untrained

Table 5.3 Supervisees professional maturity and supervisors approach

Supervisee's level of professional maturity	Supervisor's approach
Novice	**Directing**
Staff member has little experience of task and is governed by rules and tasks.	Provision of structure, teaching in formal and informal supervision.
Is dependent on supervision for guidance and advice and can be anxious about completing role/task.	Offer regular and constructive feedback.
Likely to over-focus on detail and content and sees tasks simplistically.	Needs encouragement to reflect and learn new skills.
Draws conclusions from discrete pieces of information, does not have a holistic approach.	Regular monitoring and observation.
Developing competence	**Coaching**
Staff member fluctuates between independence and dependence, and can sometimes be over-confident and other times overwhelmed.	Will still need some structure and direction, but less than novice level.
May sometimes blame supervisors for mistakes.	Supervision should allow time to reflect on own practice.
Starting to engage with complexity.	Support and develop own style of working and independence.
Starting to own the role and matching interventions to service user.	Allowance to make mistakes and learn from them.
	Focus on realities and wider context.
Competent practitioners	**Supporting**
Developing increased professional confidence and consistently able to perform tasks.	Supervision is more collaborative and discursive.
Able to generalise about learning needs and skill development and sees wider context of service and user needs.	Provision of new challenge and further development needed.
Danger of boredom and habitual practice.	Promote independence/responsibility to maintain interest in role.
Mature/expert	**Delegating**
Staff member has a significant level of professional maturity, integrated skills, knowledge and awareness into deep professional understanding of role within organisation.	Recognition of expertise.
	Give wider responsibility.
	Ensure experiences is used in agency.
Developed areas of expertise and able to help others learn skills.	Supervision is collaborative and can look at wider issues.
Awareness of own strengths and gaps.	

and inappropriate if this is not the basis of the contract with the supervisee. If a supervisor believes that a supervisee might benefit from counselling this should be suggested during supervision for later actioning rather than allow the conversation to drift into this area.

Supervisory conversations – dimensions and forms

Howe and Gray (2013: 6) suggest that supervisory conversations can involve a wide range of topics that fall into four broad categories as shown in Figure 5.1 and outlined below.

- Work/case discussion is normally a major focus for supervision, particular for staff who carry a caseload. The aim here is for a skilful exploration of work completed taking account of professional standards and operating protocols.

- Aspects of management and leadership including for example caseload and workload, targets and performance. There is some concern that with the current challenges facing health and social care that too much time is being devoted to discussing stress, worrying about the future and morale, at the expense of other domains.

- The quality of relationships with team members and people working in other parts of the wider system is a third area for conversation. Health and social care is not practised in isolation and supervisees potentially have a wide range of relationships that need to work well irrespective of the different, shifting and potentially conflicting demands placed on those involved.

- Discussion about professional development often flows from conversations about cases, management and relationships but can also be prompted by ongoing assessments of future changes in the service, patient or service user groups and shifts in professional practice.

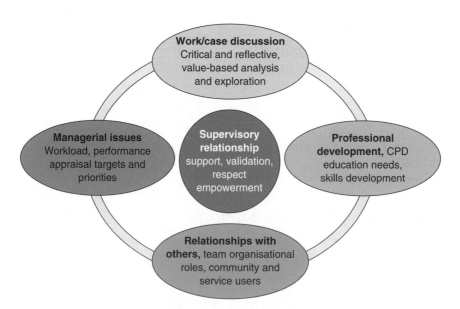

Figure 5.1 Dimensions of supervision

Source: Effective Supervision in Social Work Howe and Gray, 2013

These four dimensions are inter-related, all of which should be considered within each supervisory conversation, balanced according to the context. It is important that the supervisor is alert to the risk of a dimension being neglected, particularly if this is habitually the last one to be considered in supervisory conversations.

Supervisory models

A number of supervisory models exist, some developed by academics and trainers and the rest by practitioners. In the case of the later such models may simply be lists of areas to be covered in supervision based on what has historically worked for an individual supervisor. Individual supervisors may or may not acknowledge that their practice is based on a model and similarly, may or may not understand why what they do, and the way they do it works. If supervision is to be practised with conscious competence with the supervisor effective with a wide range of supervisees, topics and contexts, it is important to know which model if any is shaping the process, its features and how the use of it might need to be tweaked to meet specific contexts. Conscious competence should also mean that a supervisor can explain their expertise to others, in the process helping them to become consciously competent.

Used with skill, supervisory models increase the chance of conversations being appropriately challenging and supportive, therefore ultimately productive. Such models vary considerably in terms of complexity and it is important to be able to select one that fits the context and preferences of the supervisor and supervisee, and to be able to use this flexibly. Two of the easier to use models are detailed below.

The 4×4×4 model advanced by Wonnacott (2012: 54) is driven by a four-stage process based on Kolb's (1984) learning cycle (Figure 5.2). The process typically starts

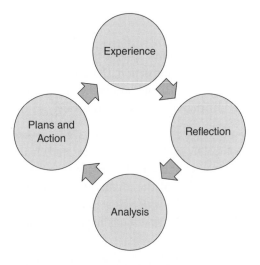

Figure 5.2 Experience, reflection, analysis, plans and action

with the supervisee recounting an experience which might be related to a particular case, an incident or more generally to work. At this point, the supervisor is working with the practitioner to develop a rich understanding of their experience. Recounting moves into reflecting on experience which allows for the emotional responses of the practitioner to be explored along with any intuitive response or gut feeling. This experience plus reflection are then analysed in the light of desired outcomes, relevant theory, research, policy, formal knowledge, previous experience and wisdom of the supervisee and supervisor. From this analysis, options for possible required action are identified, assessed and a preferred one chosen.

The focus of the process are four different stakeholders; service users, staff, the organisation and partners to be considered in terms of the interest they might have, the impact of what has happened and how they might be affected by planned action.

The model recognises four functions of supervision; helping with staff management, development, support and mediating between the needs and priorities of different stakeholders, parts of the system, etc.

A second model devised by Peter Hawkins (2012: 66) is CLEAR which has the following five stages:

- **Contract Stage** during which the desired outcomes from this supervision session are established and the scope of this session confirmed, along with the ground rules that apply including for example confidentiality. Questions could include for example 'what would you like to focus on today' and 'how might I be of most help?'.

- **Listen Stage:** where the supervisor listens in a way that helps the supervisee articulate the situation they face using active listening and catalytic questioning, making connections, paraphrasing and offering reframes.

- **Explore Stage:** where the aim is to generate new insights about, and options for handling the issue being discussed through questioning and guided reflection. Questions could include 'Who else is affected by this situation and in what ways?', 'Could you tell me a little more about...?'.

- **Action Stage:** having identified some options the next stage involves choosing a way forward, testing feasibility and taking action. Questions could include 'What would you like the outcome to be?', 'What would you really like to happen?', 'How might you tackle this issue?' 'How else might you tackle this issue?'.

- **Review Stage:** where the supervision session ends with a review of the planned actions and the process by which these have been generated, leading to insights regarding what has worked and why and how this process could be even better next time. Questions could include 'Which of the identified options do you think is the most attractive and why?', 'What will be your first step in taking this action?', 'What are the risks associated with this option?' 'What if anything do you need from me?'.

With all models there are risks. Firstly, that a structure and sequence is followed even when it does not seem to be working, Secondly, two or more stages may become blurred and the full potential value lost. A third risk is that one more stages is skimmed or omitted for example in Wonnacots (2012: 54) 4*4*4 model, by short-circuiting the process by missing out reflection and analysis resulting in a conversation that goes straight from experience to action. Familiarity with these models and how they are thought to work will improve the chances of success.

There are other models in the literature that can be useful when supervising, some of which are labelled supervisory models, such as the seven-eyed model developed by Peter Hawkins (2012: 86), whilst others such as Whitmore's (2010: 55) GROW (Goal, Reality, Options and When) or Caplan's (2003: 20) SNIP (Situation, Needs, Ideas and Plan) that come from the coaching literature are useful when a coaching style of supervision is appropriate.

Contracting

The foundation of effective supervision is a contract between supervisor and supervisee that recognises both parties have rights and responsibilities. The contract which may be written or verbal, covered once at the outset of supervision or revisited at each session, typically focuses on:

- Administrative matters concerning, for example, the frequency and length of supervision sessions, location, how agendas are set, proceedings recorded and responsibilities regarding cancellations and/or interruptions.

- Professional aspects including being clear about the purpose and benefits of supervision, underpinning principles, values and behaviours and how difficulties will be dealt with.

For supervisors that are external to the organisation, there is also a commercial aspect to the contract regarding fee levels, cancellation charges, etc.

The supervisory relationship

Successful supervision cannot be guaranteed solely by the use of a recognised model, however appropriate, sophisticated and well executed. Also required is proficiency in skills associated with building and sustaining productive relationships where messages are given and heard, questions asked and answered, points of confusion clarified, areas of disagreement worked through, learning takes place and development occurs. Wonnacott (2012: 73) suggests that supervisors should aim to be authoritative where they combine clear expectations regarding performance, standards and behaviours coupled with responsiveness to the perspectives, needs and emotions of the supervisee. This style should result in supervisees that are confident, clear and secure in their practice. Being clear about expectations whilst being unresponsive to a supervisee, is likely to result in a style that is authoritarian in nature and may cause supervisees to be anxious and defensive. Failing to be clear about expectations whilst responsive leads to a permissive style that might result in an unfocused and/or overly autonomous supervisee. Arguably, the worst case scenario is a supervisor who is both unclear about what is required from the supervisee and unresponsive, a neglectful style that can leave supervisees being unclear about what is required of them, feeling isolated, unsupported and unlikely to develop.

In terms of knowledge, experience, abilities and skills that supervisors need, the following are of particular importance:

- knowledge and understanding of:
  - o what constitutes good professional practice, organisational policies and requirements;
  - o supervisory models, frameworks and approaches;
- experience of professional practice coupled with an ability to offer this sensitively;
- a good level of conscious competence, understanding why they do what they do, how they tailor their approach to fit different contexts, etc;
- an ability to:
  - o link theory and practice;
  - o critically reflect;
  - o stimulate and support reflection in others;
  - o create and maintain a safe and productive environment;
  - o be non-judgemental and respectful of different perspectives;
  - o be interested, keep focused, maintain an appropriate structure and observe boundaries;
  - o give feedback, challenge performance and tackle unhelpful behaviour and other issues;
  - o sense how supervision is progressing real-time and to adjust behaviour accordingly.
- relational skills such as rapport building and attending to feelings and emotions, giving space and feedback, asking good questions, listening, paraphrasing, etc.

Central to effective supervision and excellent professional practice is a capacity for critical reflection, without which supervision is likely to lack depth, competence is likely to remain unconscious, theory and practice remain detached, etc.

Critical reflection

An important element of supervision in the caring professions is critical reflection. The aim of critical reflection is to create at least some doubt and critique of ongoing actions. The whole process can, therefore, cause anxiety but this is an essential element in unsettling preconceived notions and taken for granted assumptions and bias in decision making. It should involve both a cognitive and emotional element. It is important for practitioners to engage in critical reflection about their own world of practice, synthesising and evaluating this experience as they exercise professional judgement. Critical reflection involves challenging notions of 'certainty' and unsettles taken for granted assumptions and ideas. This is not just a process of re-evaluating our practice world, but also ourselves as practitioners, and as a result, self-realisation should be a key component of reflection (Barnett, 1997). A critically reflective stance, therefore, helps the individual to examine personally held assumptions (that can be 'hidden' and socially dominant) about the individual in the social world. This process can bring about a change in awareness and actions, and ultimately transform professional practice (Fook and Gardner, 2007).

A critically reflective stance is underpinned by critical reflection, and this helps the individual to develop an awareness of cognitive biases and assumptions. This includes:

- Not 'jumping to conclusions' or accepting the first thoughts;
- Recognising the importance of context;
- Exploring alternative explanations and options;
- Using systematic processes;
- Being open and flexible.

(Adapted from Brookfield 1987 in Rutter and Brown, 2012)

At the heart of supervision is learning and this is facilitated and supported through the medium of critical reflection in which the supervisor is the facilitator (Carroll, 2014). The emotionally charged nature of health and social care practice can prove stressful and challenging, and reflective supervision can create a safe space in which in which the supervisee can be supported to think more critically about their practice (Carpenter et al, 2012). Indeed, it has been suggested that regular professional supervision can increase the retention of social work employees, who often face burnout due to high-stress work environments (Chiller and Crisp, 2012).

In addition to management, development, support and mediation previously identified by Wonnacott as being the four functions of supervision (2012: 54), (McPherson et al, 2016) added safety, referring to these as elements rather than functions. Safety is vital to creating a culture in which critical reflection is supported and nurtured. As McPherson et al (2016: 76) suggest 'a foundational requirement for effective supervision is safety within the supervisory relationship for the supervisee, given what can be experienced as an unsafe practice context'.

REFLECTION POINT **5.1**

Thinking about critical reflection in your practice …

- *What is its purpose?*
- *What are your experiences of using critical reflection?*
- *As a supervisor – what models do you use – why?*
- *As a supervisee – what models do you use – why?*

Using reflective supervision is crucial to help underpin sound decision making and well-evidenced professional judgement. The need for good reflective supervision is highlighted by a recent serious case review which found that practitioners too often believed what adults involved in the case told them and concentrated on their needs rather than those of the three children (Donovan, 2016). This report highlighted a lack of good reflective supervision as a factor in services' willingness to believe the adults despite the buildup of evidence contradicting their claims. Reflective supervision is crucial when addressing erroneous thinking and decision making, and supervision can provide a safe space to honestly explore practice and challenge thinking. This is important to when challenging intuitive bias. For example:

* Confirmation bias – clinging to our beliefs.

* Availability heuristic – paying most attention to the evidence that is available: first impressions, emotion-laden evidence, recent. Rather than evidence which is abstract, emotion-free or dull.

* Optimism bias – wanting to see situations positively.

* Repetition bias – the more often it's heard, the more likely it is believed.

Another serious case review (Carmi and Walker-Hall, 2015) highlights some of the professional dilemmas faced by practitioners who are supporting a family where there are safeguarding concerns for children who have complex health needs. One of the recommendations of this review suggests that it is important 'to establish if the designated professionals receive professional supervision, and if not, what arrangements should be in place to ensure that this is available' (Carmi and Walker-Hall, 2015: 11). This would support practitioners to think critically about their assumptions underpinning the case.

As discussed earlier in this chapter, the 4x4x4 model proposed by Wonnacott (2012: 54) is driven by a four-stage process based on Kolb's (1984) learning cycle, and can be used to facilitate critical reflection within supervision. This model includes the following stages:

* EXPERIENCE

* REFLECTION

* ANALYSIS

* PLANS/ACTION

By supporting the supervisee to critically reflect upon their practice, the supervisor can facilitate change in thinking and action.

A practitioner stuck at the EXPERIENCE stage may experience anxiety, lack of confidence and paralysis. A supervisor has a duty of care but can also support critical reflection on specific tasks. By supporting a critically reflective stance at this stage

Table 5.4 Levels of reflection

Technical	Comparison of performance to standards and procedures. Focus on compliance and 'getting it right'.
Practical	Using practitioner's experience as a source of evaluation, insight and learning. Reflecting in and on action. Looks at solving problems and finding ways forward.
Process	Looking at the impact of unconscious processes and the interaction of thoughts and feelings; how these have shaped the worker's judgements and decisions. Aims to increase worker's awareness of unconscious intra- and inter-personal forces.
Critical/in-depth	Encourages the practitioner to question and challenge how knowledge about practice is created; to consider existing power relations and the interests served.

the supervisor can slowly build confidence. However, they should not assume that practitioners stuck in this phase can hear positive feedback.

A practitioner stuck in REFLECTION can often become self-absorbed whilst drowning in feelings. By supporting a critically reflective stance at this stage the supervisor can help to clarify expectations and help the supervisee to focus away from feelings whilst planning time-limited tasks.

A practitioner stuck in the ANALYSIS stage tends to intellectualise, avoid feelings and make over-generalisations. The supervisor can encourage critical reflection by focusing on feelings and on specific issues and tasks.

Finally, practitioners stuck in the DOING stage are often fire-fighting, undertaking reactive practice with short-term aims. They rarely reflect on what they are doing and 'just know' what to do. It is important for the supervisor to use reflective questions to support the supervisee to develop analysis and longer-term plans.

Ruch (2007) has described the above four levels of reflection which are useful to develop critical thinking within supervision (see Table 5.4).

The levels of reflection described by Ruch (2007) highlight the importance of developing effective questioning which encourages learning and supports the supervisee to reach their own conclusions. The following are examples of open questions that encourage critical reflection.

- What appeared to be most important to the client?
- What other facts or issues do you feel are/were relevant to the situation?
- What other courses of action were open to you?

REFLECTION POINT 5.2

Create at least ten open questions that you can use in supervision which will encourage critical reflection.

Reflect upon a recent supervision and consider how you encouraged critical reflection.

Tips for successful supervision

Opportunities to learn from supervisory experiences are unlimited, some of which are general and transferable to a range of contexts, the rest are more specific and individual. Generally applicable tips for success include:

Planning and preparing supervision

- Attend to domestic details such as securing an appropriate, comfortable meeting place that allows for confidential conversations without interruption.

- Read the supervision file, think about the person and their current context noticing any known changes since the last session.

- Remind yourself of the purpose and value of supervision, the four domains of conversation and your selected supervision model and strategy for this specific conversation.

- Think about how you create a safe space within supervision to enable to supervisee to explore difficult issues.

- Remind yourself of the need to enter and remain in an 'authoritative' state prepared to be demanding and responsive.

- Think about what questions you will use to support critical reflection during supervision.

- Remind yourself of any changes to your supervision practice that you plan to implement.

Starting a supervision session

- Reconnect with the supervisee in a way that helps you both shift into a productive supervision conversation.

- Agree on an agenda that looks feasible for the time available.

- If need be, remind the supervisee of the 'supervision contract'.

During supervision

- Monitor how the supervisee appears to be responding to this supervision modifying your approach if appropriate.

- Maintain focus, observe boundaries, monitor the support/challenge and domain balances.

- Check whether you are being 'authoritative' and successfully deploying your selected strategy (directing, supporting, delegating or coaching).

- Review whether the model or framework you're using to structure your conversation is working.

- Review how your approach facilitates critical reflection and learning for the supervisee.

- Review actions agreed at the end of the session and ensure recording is complete and appropriate.

Key learning points

- Effective supervision offers significant potential benefits to the supervisee, supervisor, the organisation, clients patients and carers.

- An effective supervisor is able to select and use different strategies such as directing, supporting, delegating and coaching according to context.

- A number of supervision models are available which when used with skill can help structure supervision conversations.

- Maintaining an authoritative style of supervision requires knowledge, abilities and a set of relational skills.

- Critical reflection is essential to learning which in turn is at the heart of effective supervision.

Chapter 6

Leading successful teams in health and social care

Sue Ross

CHAPTER OUTCOMES

As a result of completing this chapter you will:

- Appreciate that the skill base for leading successful teams in health and social care comprises professional knowledge and expertise, managerial competency and skill together with leadership skills.

- Appreciate the importance of investing in the psychological contract that you and your organisation have with staff.

- Understand the importance of dealing with 'road-blocks'.

- Be able to develop strong professional resilience.

Introduction

Most people's stereotype of a social worker reflected in the literature of the profession is…a profoundly uncreative being, a passive, reasonable, dull, smiling sponge which soothes troubled surfaces with abundant soft soap: a Uriah Heep figure without the redeeming evil intentions.

(Jordan, B., 1979, p8)

I became a social worker in the 1970s when the fledgeling social work profession was just beginning to learn its first bitter lessons. The critical Maria Colwell Inquiry and the subsequent, minority report, written by the inspirational Olive Stevenson, set out the stark daily challenges of the reality of trying to protect a child in under-resourced, ill-conceived organisations, with largely inexperienced managers, who had little or no knowledge of the scope and complexity of their responsibilities. In 2016 I am still proud to be a social worker, with the same cynical wonderment that I had back then, about the resourcefulness and endurance of my colleagues and the seemingly endless disregard given to improving the quality and skills of managers, amid the ever harsh criticisms of their failings. It appears endemic that the leadership and management of social care and health services are routinely criticised to the point of demonisation, particularly for their failure to protect children from abuse, but the government response is to name and shame the managers and to look for others to fix the failing systems, not to seek to develop the quality and skills of the management and leadership within our services and to support their endeavours on behalf of society's victims.

Over the decades I have managed and led many teams and, as a Director and a Chief Executive in the NHS have also led many organisations with all their infinite variety and challenges. I remain convinced that successful leadership and management lies at the very core of high performance for individuals and their organisations. This chapter is written from my experience (sometimes bitter in nature) of trying to provide that management and leadership effectively. I am writing this from my desk, in a local authority, where I have the responsibility for the day-to-day delivery of children's social care. It is genuinely based on that daily experience of the real world of children's social care.

It is not intended to be 'recipes' for success, because there is no science which can be applied to guarantee success in highly complex social systems. However, I offer some 'menu cards' for working successfully, which will describe some of the key components I find helpful to focus on, some tips for achieving progress and some short case studies, all drawn from my daily experience, which attempts to show how key components may be applied, particularly in the rapidly changing context of public sector organisations.

Underpinning this chapter is a view that for any leader or manager in the health and social care field, there are three vital categories of knowledge and skills which all must be evidenced, if they are to succeed and for the teams and services they run to be successful. Firstly, these are that they must have sufficient specialist skills in their subject area of their team or service. That means they must understand the business of the team(s) for which they are they are responsible. In the chapter that follows, I will refer to this as 'specialist expertise'. Whilst it is not implied they must be expert on everything within their responsibilities, they must know enough about the deliverables, constraints, costs, legal requirements and so on, of the business to be a credible manager, who can command the respect of their staff and the wider workforce, their service users and the agencies with whom they work. Secondly, they must have skills, competency and knowledge of a general management nature – what I refer to as 'managerial skills'. These involve areas such as budgetary control and finance, for example, how to read a balance sheet and a budgetary forecast, human relations – such as how to deal with managing sickness and absence in the workplace, grievance and disciplinary and capability matters, the selection and recruitment of staff and how to review and audit work and undertake project planning and management. The final area of successful leadership and management are 'leadership skills'. This refers to the softer skill set of knowledge and behaviours around how the manager inspires, motivates and energises their teams and importantly how they deal with conflict in and amongst teams and develop consensus in decision-making. The daily successful interface between managerial and leadership skills is the place where great careers are forged and sadly, where reputations are lost and mistakes are made, some of which have devastating consequences.

In my experience, most managers in the health and social care sector do have the necessary specialist skills. There is usually significant attention paid during recruitment and selection for managers' posts as to their degree of knowledge of the 'business' they will be required to manage. Far less attention is paid to managerial skills and particularly for front-line posts, where managers are still too often recruited for their expertise as a worker, but where their knowledge of managerial skills is extremely limited and may stem only from their personal experience (good and bad) of their managers' behaviour towards them. Once in post, there are a variety of professional development opportunities available which address the leadership skills – motivating teams, creating shared objectives, managing conflict and achieving consensus and so on. These are relatively frequently offered to managers but the critical area of deficit often remains the manager's lack of knowledge and skills about how to behave as a manager, their understanding of the tasks they are required to perform and their capacity to undertake those demands. Without those managerial skills, the capacity to be an effective leader is severely curtailed.

As Matt Bee recently wrote in *Professional Social Work* (May 2016) that: 'Broadly speaking this is how you end up a social work manager. Some plan for it, others fall into it and yet more – I suspect – have it thrust upon them'. He goes on to say: 'We don't actually train our managers to be managers and once we've appointed them into a position they're not trained for, we do everything they tell us. That is a bit like mid-flight, asking one of the passengers to fly the plane'.

Such deficits are often exposed in the routine issues in which most managers will be engaged, in health and social care settings. Complaints investigations, data breaches, dealing with grievance of disciplinary matters, case reviews, audits, investigations, inquiries and so on, all tend to highlight failures of managerial practice and where the manager's decision-making is not clear and defensible, the manager becomes exposed – often personally as well as professionally – and this can be a bitter experience, with confidence-sapping, career limiting results.

When it comes to the area of leadership skills, health and social care organisations often invest resources into creating 'high performing' leaders. Job advertisements very often describe our desire to produce 'exceptional' or 'inspirational' leaders. When the leadership of services is judged to have 'failed', we blame individuals for their personal shortcomings – what has been dubbed 'football manager syndrome'. There is a clear narrative that leaders can solve systemic problems by the application of strong leadership skills and when this fails, they are blamed and replaced. As one leadership course for social care managers states, 'an outstanding leader... consciously manages power dynamics to empower social workers to influence their system'. The reality in health and social care teams is that successful leaders manage their resources within their budgetary constraints, control their costs, recruit and retain the best staff, set high professional standards based on best practice and deal fairly with their staff. The over-blown hyperbole of leadership training struggles to address the daily demands of how to be a good leader and a decent manager in our complex, ever-changing and high-pressured organisational world.

REFLECTION POINT **6.1**

To what extent do you feel that you have been encouraged and supported to develop managerial competency and leadership skills?

As a manager to what extent have you encouraged and supported your staff to develop managerial competency and leadership skills?

What might you do in response to your reflections?

Three key areas for skills development

This rest of this chapter attempts to address some of the key skills and behaviours in all three areas of leadership – specialist skills, managerial skills and leadership skills, but it will give particular significance to some of the core managerial and leadership areas which front-line managers need to become proficient in to run successful teams in health and social care. It will tackle three key areas in particular:

- How the manager can build the psychological contract with their staff.

- How the manager can deal with 'road-blocks' which undermine achievements.

- How the manager can stay positive and focused and develop their own resilience and skill.

Developing the 'psychological contract'

> *Many people remain members of teams for large parts of their life, whether it is a quiz team at the local pub, bowls in the park or team games on a family evening. And many people enjoy the sense of belonging, the sharing of effort and the working things out that is restricted to playing the game (more usually winning the game) that creates such a concentrated experience of working together and being together. Some team experiences provide people with intense experiences of 'belonging' that they may not have in other parts of their lives.*

> (Taylor, B. 2014)

Leadership and management of teams in social and health care require artistry, resilience, perseverance and strenuous effort. Success is based on developing with your staff and in the wider organisation and its partners, respect, trust and a mutual appreciation of the goals and challenges. Successful leaders in our field are not so because of who they are, or how much power they can wield, but comes by virtue of how they engage their staff in delivering their aspirations and ambitions. A very helpful concept to describe one of the key elements of that success is the idea of the 'psychological contract'. This term has been widely used since the late 80s and was best described by Denise Rousseau (1989) as a term to describe the belief systems, perceptions and informal obligations between the employer and the employee. It is particularly relevant for staff in the public sector at the current time because as Maslach, Schaufeli and Leiter pointed out in 2001:

> *Now employees are expected to give more in terms of time, effort, skills and flexibility, whereas they receive less in terms of career opportunities, lifetime employment, job security and so on. Violation of the social contract is likely to produce burnout because it erodes the notion of reciprocity, which is crucial in maintaining well-being.*

In health and social care settings, a manager needs to spend considerable time building the psychological contract with their staff individually through supervision, appraisals, meetings and all their operational contacts and with their wider organisation as a whole. This contract is not only the formal elements such as job descriptions, procedures, instructions, job profiles and so on, but also the day-to-day interpersonal interactions and relationships within the workplace where managers and staff negotiate what they must do to satisfy their side of the bargain and what they can expect in return. A satisfying psychological contract between managers and their employees does not come about by accident. The negotiations are sometimes explicit (e.g. supervision, appraisals, peer reviews, etc.) and sometimes, and more often, through the interactional behaviour of each and the reactions to each other where parties explore and draw the boundaries of what each expects of the other.

Where the expectations and the mutual lived experience of staff and managers in the workplace match, the performance of teams and organisations will be high. Where it does not, there will be a significant mismatch in expectations leading to poor performance, disenchantment and resentment which can become increasingly toxic for managers and their staff alike. Examples of such environments are commonplace and characterised by tell-tale signs such as the leaving party which no one wants to attend, closely followed by the embittered rant from the disaffected staff member as they are given their leaving gift. The untidy and unloved office whose walls are littered with the organisational graffiti of unfunny sarcasm, disguised as humour 'You don't have to be mad to work here but it helps', and the team meetings in which the only real communication is non-verbal and more is discussed outside the meeting than inside it.

In organisational environments such as these, managers and leaders often respond to the negativity by becoming more authoritarian in their approach, or more rule-bound in terms of issuing more instructions or procedures. The section below suggests ways of dealing with such 'road-blocks' and avoiding these 'more of the same' traps. The positive development of a healthy psychological contract between managers and their staff is relatively straightforward to create if the managers are focused on the importance of it at all times. It involves a number of key steps:

The manager must firstly fully understand that the feelings and attitudes of their staff and their expectations in the workplace are strongly influenced by their treatment at work, how they see themselves and their relationship with their manager and how they see their colleagues are being treated. Simply put, making your staff are confident in expressing their honest views, and enjoying their work challenges is fundamental to operational and organisational performance. Securing the commitment of staff through the careful negotiation of a strong psychological contract is vital for success. Yet, with the dramatic acceleration of the pace of change in public sector organisations over the last 20 years, there are signs that ever decreasing time is given to its development. Some writers have attributed this to workers becoming more mobile, because of the globalisation of employment markets and to the increasing use of new technology. Within the health and social care fields, huge changes in the organisational structures underpinning education, hospitals, community care services and the provision of welfare, have led to some leaders and managers cutting corners to achieve results, and being more preoccupied by survival than attending to the wishes and feelings of their staff. The pressure to deliver targets at any price can lead to ignorance about the fundamental requirement to explain what is required of staff. In such an environment there will be failures to hear and act on the views of employees. Undoubtedly, the increasing complexity of the psychological contract between managers and their staff, where employees can move jobs easily and have complicated work–life arrangements which can fragment and distort that relationship. It is key that the manager knows and understands what the employee wants from their work (what a former colleague of mine used to describe as 'knowing what makes bunny run') and is able to match those expectations within the work environment. Where there is a poor match, or worse, no match, the working environment will be negatively affected.

The manager must create regular and frequent opportunities for their staff to talk about how they feel about their work, their colleagues and their manager(s). There are many very easy ways to do this formally through such mechanisms as supervision, appraisals, 360-degree feedbacks, staff surveys, team building exercises and so on, but also through the daily organisational contact of taking the time to ask team members about their feelings and experiences in the workplace. The manager in social care organisations has to be observant and vigilant, taking notice of the way their team behave towards each other and towards them. They must keep the channels of communication continually open and they must act on the feedback they receive from their staff.

Secondly, the manager needs to work at deepening the benefits, within the psychological contract, for the employee in order to encourage and develop loyalty, dedication, commitment and investment in organisational success. There are lots of ways (even when greater financial rewards are not possible) to deepen the level of commitment from staff. Sometimes these can be part of a formal retention strategy or workforce development strategy, but formal or not, there needs to be real, genuine positive benefits for staff to increase their loyalty through, for example, training opportunities, paid sabbaticals, research opportunities, travel and opportunities to see different approaches, good quality supervision and appraisal and a fundamental respect for the contribution individuals make to success. All these things (and many more) breed respect and investment in the workplace. If the staff are ashamed of where they work, they will not stay and they will not give their best in the highly pressurised and world of public sector service delivery. It is the manager or leader's responsibility to ensure their staff want to come to work and want to do the best work of which they are capable.

Again, there are lots of formal ways to build loyalty and commitment, such as long service awards, retention bonuses, sabbaticals, education and training opportunities, personal development opportunities such as coaching, mentoring, work shadowing, secondments, employee recognition schemes and other such approaches. There are also lots more informal ways to build loyalty such as team events, away-days, compliment letters, etc. When a manager notices that their team member has 'gone the extra mile' and gives them genuine, positive feedback and praise, the 'social capital', for the employee and their team, rises. Conversely however, when managers routinely fail to notice and acknowledge good performance, the psychological contract will be severely curtailed.

Thirdly, having developed feedback mechanisms and worked at building loyalty and trust, the manager then has a responsibility in building the psychological contact to promote the work their team is doing. This needs to be done with care because the manager must be authentic, fair and honest in the way they promote achievements. Crucially, they must be very careful not to seem to be claiming the achievements of their staff for themselves but they must always take care to attribute them to the work of their team and to be very clear why the achievements are significant. An example of this is taken from a recent communication I sent to my staff where it is possible to see my attempts to build positive commitment to core activity for the team on recruiting and retaining good staff:

> *A big thank you from me to all of you who have assisted with the recruitment process – particularly <name withheld> and her team who have given so much of their time and energies to this and to <name withheld>, our HR business partner who is advising and supporting me in our recruitment and retention strategy work. For 2016/17 our allocated budget for agency staff is half what we spent last year so we have a real challenge, which I know you can meet, to reduce our dependency on agency staff and make sure we grow and keep our own talent.*

Newsletters, blogs, team talks, staff forums, etc. are all formal ways to promote and celebrate success. However just as importantly, informal mechanisms are also effective. Notes to staff when they achieve an objective or resolve a problem, inexpensive tokens such as cakes or sweets to mark achievements, taking teams for a meal, etc., can all be appreciated and serve to strengthen the sense of group belonging and well-being. Frequently, the manager saying 'thanks' is valued more than anything else, when it is sincere and appropriate.

Bond building

A brief case study to illustrate how to help build the bond between team members and the organisation is described:

A new team of senior managers was coming together. Some of the individuals in the team knew each other from previous roles in other organisations and had some 'history'. Some were newly appointed and had little awareness of each other and the senior manager for whom they would be working. The manager met them and explained her expecta-tion that they would work closely and effectively together and be able to represent each other, support each other, co-work projects and show and loyal team approach to the wider organisation by being loyal to each other and the team in public and honest and open and challenging where necessary, in private. She explained that to help this process there would be an 'away day' where she would spend the day with them outside the normal working environment, with no other distractions so they could get to know each other better, talk to each other and to her in confidence about their individual hopes, dreams and aspirations in their roles and what they wanted from their colleagues and from her.

She developed a programme for the day combining fun 'games' where she and team mem-bers could get to know each other better, some work planning where each team member could talk about their immediate and medium term priorities and how they could support each other in achieving them and the final element was designed to encourage them to take more risks with their relationships in the team by being more direct in giving feed-back about their likes and dislikes about the team. For this she used a 'game' drawn from social group work which was adapted from the work of Donna Brandes (1981), described in her 'Gamesters Handbook'. Here the team sit in a circle and each person in turn goes around the group finishing the sentence 'I resent...' then adding one thing that they do not like about that person from their interaction with them. The sort of examples that come out are, 'I resent the way you interrupted me when I was speaking', 'I resent the way you didn't give me a proper induction when I started working for you', etc. Whilst each person is speaking no one reacts or interrupts, in order that each team member can really concentrate on saying what it is they really want to say. The leader's role is to encourage team members to give genuine clear feedback and to help them look at each other when they are giving their 'resents' and to speak personally and openly. Key to that is modelling that in the way the leader gives feedback to each member and listens and respects the feedback they get. Most importantly the leader must give their feedback to each person clearly and honestly, not missing anyone out. Then the same process is followed but each person does a round of 'I appreciate...'. Examples might be, 'I appreciate John the way you always seem to notice when I'm having a difficult day and ask what you can do to help', 'I appreciate Liz the way you encouraged me with that project I was struggling with', etc.

(Continued)

CASE STUDY **6.1** *(CONT.)*

Then when everyone has finished both rounds of 'resents' and 'appreciates', the leader should allow a little time for team members to talk about their feedback and what they will take from it in terms of how they work together more effectively in future. At the heart of this exercise (there are many other similar 'games' that can be used in this way) is the belief that teams which are effective develop strong bonds which are forged by their ability to give and receive feedback. These strong bonds are unlikely to occur naturally unless they are actively encouraged by putting team managers in 'safe' situations where they are encouraged and supported to take risks to improve the strength of their interactions within the team.

Dealing with road-blocks

I believe that the students were right in the sixties: there was something very wrong in their education and indeed in their whole culture. But I believe they were wrong in their diagnosis of where the trouble lay. They fought for 'representation' and 'power'. On the whole they won their battles and now we have student representation. But it becomes increasingly clear that the winning of these battles for 'power' has made no difference to the educational process. The obsolescence to which I referred is unchanged and, no doubt, in a few years we shall see the same battles, fought over the same phoney issues, all over again.

(Gregory Bateson, 'Mind and Nature', 1978)

Managers, especially when they are inexperienced, are often concerned when they discover that improvements and changes they want to make in their teams are more difficult to achieve than they assumed. Sometimes this is due to resistance by their staff to make changes to their working practices, but more often it is because the organisation they are working for, seems to have a built-in inertia which makes some changes unnecessarily complex or protracted, or sometimes seemingly impossible for less than clear reasons. It is tempting, in these sort of circumstances, to feel disheartened or a personal failure, or to assume it is just impossible to make progress, particularly where the problems you are trying to solve are long-standing or complex. Sometimes the lack of ability to make positive changes is put down to the behaviour or personalities of particular individuals. My experience tells me that all effective managers and leaders in the health and social care field, will meet head-on this inertia – what I term 'road-blocks', and these are to do with the systemic nature of organisational life, not the individual characters or personalities of the actors within the organisational system in which they work. Managers and leaders have to develop skills in working in complex systems and overcoming the resistance of road-blocks in order to be effective.

Margaret Power (in Walker and Beaumont (1985)) talking about the probation officer's role in the juvenile court, summed up that helpless feeling that managers and social care workers can experience in working in, organisations: 'There are dangers for those on the margins of powerful institutions. They tend to draw you in, take you over, incorporate you, write you off as an irrelevance'.

There are numerous examples of how social work and health managers attempt to bring about changes but the new policies, procedures, or working practices are absorbed or incorporated in a way which leads to little alteration in the operation of the system. In our book 'Social Work Management and Practice', Bilson and I (1999) describe these systems challenges in some detail and outline some systems principles and practice for overcoming them. Of particular significance for managers in health and social care is the characteristic of social systems to draw the 'eyes' of managers to those parts of the system most resistant to change or to those parts where change will have little or no effect. Forrester (1972) writing about social systems sums this up as follows:

> *Social systems are inherently insensitive to most policy changes that people select in an effort to alter the behaviour of the system. In fact, a social system tends to draw your attention to the very points at which an attempt to intervene will fail.*

When making changes aimed at improving the functioning of their teams, managers need to plan carefully what changes are to be made, how best to introduce them to gain ownership and how to work to reduce the potential for significant resistance. The paradox for new managers is that early on in their management of their teams they have the optimum capacity to introduce new ideas and ways of working, but seldom the wisdom and knowledge about how the teams are likely to respond to changes. The wise system's manager will go with the 'ecology' of the system, taking care to emphasise their team's capacity to successfully make changes and to be reassuring about concerns and reservations by helping their teams to 'own changes' rather than impose them. Attempts to force through new policies, procedures and ways of working on the basis of power and status are most likely to be ignored, disqualified and undermined. Whereas if changes are well explained and team members are given space and opportunity to work out the implications for their work, they are far less likely to be met with resistance.

Significant road-blocks to change are an everyday part of a manager's challenge but so often they are seen, not as a characteristic of organisational life to be managed, but 'caused by' the behaviour of individuals in the workplace who are seen as 'difficult' or 'dysfunctional'. Whilst it is undoubtedly true that every manager will encounter difficult people in their teams from time to time, and will be required to respond effectively to their behaviour if it is damaging progress or performance in the workplace, nevertheless personalising difficulties in bringing about changes ('this problem exists because of X') is unhelpful thinking, and often contributes to significant cultural and wider systemic problems not being addressed and becoming chronic. A classic example of this is the knee-jerk reactions which have been so much part of the social care environment over the last 10 years where OFSTED inspections have judged a children's service to be 'inadequate' and the Council concerned has then 'blamed' the managers of that service for the inadequacies, and got rid of them one way or another, only to find that, even with new managers, the service continues to fail repeat inspections and standards drop even further. So the 'more of the same' systems problems are not addressed, but increasing resources are ploughed into dysfunctional attempts to fix parts of the system which show little or no progress.

Health and social care services are part of complex organisational systems which require systems leadership in order to achieve significant, lasting, positive changes. These can only be achieved by changing the nature of way we define problems and the way we intervene to resolve them.

CASE STUDY *6.2*

Dealing with systems road-blocks

The following case study illustrates the systemic nature of a manager's dealing with systems 'road-blocks'.

A manager took over responsibility for a service that exhibited very clear signs of poor morale. Evidence of this was an organisation-wide staff survey where her staff had the poorest rate of response to the survey within the organisation and those staff who did complete the survey were very negative in their views. They indicated they had little trust in their managers, felt that changes were imposed on them, rather than consulted on, and that their managers had little or no ability to understand their concerns and little confidence that if they expressed them, they would be heard and acted upon. The service, whilst having some areas of good performance and some talented staff, generally under-performed, failed to meet financial targets and lacked a wider credibility alongside similar services in other areas. The lack of effective communication mechanisms between managers and the staff was a constant theme and the culture of 'them' and 'us' between managers and their teams was evident in much of the dialogue.

The manager worked with her team managers to develop some clear priorities for change which then were discussed with all the managers in large and small group sessions and in individual meetings. At the heart of this work was the articulation of a clear message about the direction of travel for the whole service and in which all the managers would play a part. Managers were encouraged to voice their fears, concerns and challenges and asked their opinions, especially if they had criticisms. Team meetings for all the staff were established and a manager went to all of the team meetings, to hear their views and drop in slots were set up so staff could talk about any concerns they had, without having to go to their manager, if they felt they could not discuss them directly, for whatever reason. A plan of support for front-line staff was developed which included individual and peer supervision, a workforce development plan, which was accessible and shared with all staff and other elements, and constituted a more supportive offer for front-line staff and their managers. Over time, and after a great deal of discussion, a reconfiguration of team structures was undertaken that enabled work flows to be more fairly distributed and staff resources more fairly allocated. Improving performance in key areas of activity (such as budgets, performance data, recruitment and retention of staff and sickness and absence management) were always

CASE STUDY *6.2* *(CONT)*

noted and praised and a brief bi-monthly newsletter from the senior team re-iterated those achievements. Within six months the budget pressures were eased and performance in all the key areas of activity improved. New staff were recruited across the service and the pressures, which had been perceived by staff as being ignored by their managers, were now seen as something which the whole service was addressing and making progress on.

Staying positive, focused and resilient

What would happen if deliberately I disobeyed? I knew what would happen: nothing. Nothing would happen and that knowledge depresses me. I suppose it is just impossible for someone like me to rebel anymore and produce any kind of lasting effect. I have lost the power to upset things. I can no longer change my environment, or even disturb it seriously. They would simply fire and forget me as soon as I tried.

(Heller, J., *Something Happened,* 1974)

Many thousands of books have been written about what makes a successful manager/ leader. For decades the debate was whether great leaders had innate personal characteristics rather than acquired skills or learnt behaviour. Whilst the 'great man' theory occasionally resurfaces, most writers now accept that leadership, and to a great extent management too, is about functional behaviours which are inextricably linked to the context in which they occur. For example, in a crisis where time is critical, a leader or manager who is able to weigh up information quickly and make clear decisions based on his/her judgement, will be seen as successful. Whereas a leader with a more reflective approach, who needs to consider all the available facts and options and being really certain in their own mind about how to proceed prior to making decisions, will be far more appropriate in high-risk activities, where getting it wrong is more dangerous than making progress.

In the social care and health arena, most decisions managers/ leaders have to make will be based on somewhat limited 'facts' – the 'grey areas', which so often involve deciding between potentially bad options. In the introductory chapter of our book 'Social Work Management and Practice – Systems Principles' Andy Bilson and I (1999) described the cartoon in a social work journal which showed one caption of a social worker being hung by an angry mob which read, 'Social worker who takes a child from family' and the second caption which shows the same scene with 'social worker who leaves abused child with family'. We go on to describe the ultimate irony of our personal experience of being involved with two inquiries whose reports were published in Scotland on the same day – one which criticised Fife Council for not taking enough children into care, and the other which criticised Orkney Council for removing too many children who were believed to be the subject of sexual abuse (Kierney Report, 1992; Clyde Report, 1992). The themes of these inquiries mirrored those south of the border, where within two years of each other the inquiry into the death of Jasmine Beckford (Blom-Cooper, L., 1985) criticised 'under-reaction' to abuse whilst the Cleveland Inquiry (Butler Sloss, E., 1987) criticised over-reaction to child sexual abuse. One only has to look at the huge rise in numbers of looked after children throughout the UK in the months and years following the Baby P murder and the 3 million signature petition orchestrated by the 'Sun' newspaper which called for the sacking of all social workers involved in the case, to see the volatility and reactivity of managerial decision-making in some critical areas of social care. Despite the reassurances in the Laming Report which followed Peter Connelly's death (2009) the support to child care practitioners in their 'demanding task' has been slow to materialise.

In this climate where the verdict of the court of public opinion has a default setting of guilty, the social work manager has to have a focus and a resilience which allows them to follow their professional judgements in the best interests of their service users and which will not be swayed by pressure to be risk-averse or to attempt to court popularity. It might be assumed that social workers are innately resilient people based on the very nature of their profession – and therefore their management style reflects this when they become a manager. I would suggest that the personal exposure that many social work managers and leaders get in the course of their work, produces a much more significant requirement to develop strategies for developing and sustaining their personal and professional resilience and the organisational resilience in those whom they lead. This is well summed up by Loehr and Schwartz (2003):

> *Leaders are the stewards of organisational energy (resilience) they inspire or demoralise others, first by how effectively they manage their own energy and next by how well they manage, focus, invest and renew the collective energy (resilience) of those they lead.*

The challenge for managers is to build their professional resilience. These are some ways which I have found to help with this to develop the resilience of those they lead in their teams and organisations. I describe below three key areas – building a network system, using coaching/ mentoring to develop your professional range and expertise and finally to build collective resilience.

The essence of all three of these areas is summed up by Johnson-Lenz (2009):

> *People with trustworthy relationships and personal support systems at work and with friends and family are more able to cope with stress and organisations more likely to hold up in a crisis.*

Definitions of resilience are varied but all refer to the capacity of individuals and groups, teams and communities to successfully adapt to life tasks even in the face of highly adverse or stressful conditions and to 'bounce back' despite adversity. Successful managers and leaders in health and social care organisations need to strengthen and develop their personal resilience and to build collective resilience in their teams.

Building a network

Some of the American writers on resilience talk about 'developing resilience buffers' (Armendariz et al, 2009). In simple language what most writers are actually suggesting are ways which help managers develop resilience by building positive professional and personal networks which allow them to talk through, with people they trust, the demands of their work, the challenges and the positives. As Liz Bingham writing in the Guardian in 2014 says, 'at its most basic level, networking is about forming and maintaining relationships... it should be about inspiring ideas, sharing information and collaborating'. These networks are far more than professional friendships or building effective relationships with colleagues. They are links which the manager needs to develop to ensure they have access to people who can help them focus on doing their best work, solve problems and look for new ideas. There are lots of ways to develop effective networks but they will take an investment of time and energy and some degree of determination. In my experience, they will not just develop by accident.

The best professional networks to develop your resilience as a manager and a leader will be formed of people in your field who have acknowledged expertise, and people who are 'connectors' – able to help you find resources, ideas and people who can help you achieve in your work environment. They are different from friendships and social connections in that they are aimed at helping you to be better at your job and they will need to take different forms depending on your professional context at any one time. Sometimes networks develop which are aimed at supporting people who are tackling similar projects, or developing new approaches. Sometimes they are specific to particular groups or shared interests or concerns, such as 'women manager networks' or LGBT networks. Sometimes they work best when they are just professionals getting together to help each other progress with problems and share common interests.

Using coaching and mentoring

For social work managers there is sometimes confusion about the difference between coaching and mentoring and the relationship both have with counselling. Mentoring is a developing a formal professional link with someone who has expertise in a role you are performing or in aspects of that role, or in a related discipline. The mentoring activity is outside of any supervisory of accountability relationship and is aimed at helping you gain skills and ability in those areas of the role in which they have expertise. Mentoring is often helpful when you are faced with a very new challenge or a significant increase in the scope and complexity of you job. It usually takes the form of planned face to face or virtual meetings in a conducive environment outside of work pressures where you can talk through some of the challenges and share thoughts about how to proceed based on the mentor's 'take' on the best advice they can offer, given their experiences. Good mentoring will help the manager to develop their plans, take stock of what they need to accomplish and avoid making mistakes through lack of experience. Mentoring can take the form of a relationship, often reasonably informal, with a senior professional, sometimes lasting a significant period of time, where the mentor focuses on the career and personal development of the manager.

Coaching, however, is not about advice giving. It is using techniques which help the coachee to focus on areas of their work and or life to explore ideas and develop ways to move forward successfully in problem-solving. The coach may be from a social care or related background but often will not. It is usually short term (4–6 sessions) and will be structured and time-limited. I recommend that managers in health and social care consider working with a coach in circumstances such as where they are facing new challenges which are likely to be very personally/ professionally demanding or if they are facing significant organisational or professional change which they are uncertain about or if they are experiencing tension between their job demands and their personal aspirations and wishes (what is often referred to as the 'work–life balance'). A skilled coach can help you focus on the things that are important to you and will challenge you to have the confidence to pursue options and to think through wider possibilities.

Coaches will use a range of techniques sometimes drawn from neuro-linguistic programming techniques, some from social psychology, narrative therapy, group work, gestalt therapy, psychodrama, cognitive behaviour therapy, etc. but whatever techniques are used, they will are merely mechanisms to help you focus on the things which you identify as areas you want to progress

Building collective resilience

Building collective resilience is about helping members of teams you lead and teams you are part of, to trust each other and to have the confidence to believe they can achieve more together than individually and apart. Resilient teams are confident that they can cope well with changing circumstances and support each other through competing, or increasing demands. Research (Bandura, 2000) into team effectiveness suggests that where team members can openly express their views, talk about their feelings and their needs, they are more likely to feel able to show strong collective resilience and they will usually, therefore, perform better. Resilience in teams will only develop once members develop an awareness that they work better together than as individuals. This means that they have to know each other's strengths and weaknesses, practice achieving things together and understand how they can overcome problems and resolve conflicts. All these skills have to be worked on by the manager so that the team develops a confident identity.

CASE STUDY **6.3**

Developing professional and collective resistance

A case study to describe a way in which a manager was able to develop her professional and collective resilience is described below:

A female manager was internally promoted to a senior role managing a team which she had previously been part of. Several members of the team had unsuccessfully applied for the post and were resentful that she had been successful. There were significant improvements which were required in the functioning of the team and her service and efficiencies which were required which she needed team members to commit to and work on. She quickly lost confidence in her ability to manage the team and motivate them to make the service improvements. She described to her boss how she was feeling somewhat overwhelmed by the size and scope of the challenges and was worried about her inability to manage the difficult dynamics in the team she had taken on.

She agreed that some sessions of coaching with a suitably trained and experienced coach would be helpful to her. The coach met with her for six sessions at monthly intervals in a confidential environment away from the workplace. They worked on helping her to define her work and life goals, particularly her priorities. Using coaching exercises like the 'Life story Wheel', described in Jenny Rogers book 'Coaching Skills' (Rogers, J., 2004) she described how she and her husband had a plan that they had wanted to establish a business together running training events but, after the birth of their children, they felt reluctant to pursue their dream and were reliant on the security of her income. She felt her husband was a little resentful of the demands her new role was placing upon her time and her marriage and her relationship with her children were somewhat threatened by her concentration on the requirements of her work role. Through the coaching conversations, she was able to sort out what she wanted to achieve for herself in the short and medium term. She was able as 'homework' to have a frank and open conversation with her husband about her wishes and feelings and her need for his total support in meeting the demands of her post on a practical and emotional way. He explained to her that he was proud of her achievements but was worried she would be very undermined if she could not achieve the success she wanted in her new role. They talked about how sorry they both felt that they had not pursued their hopes to set up a company themselves but agreed that whilst their children were young, the financial risks were too great.

She was then able, with the coach's support, to work out a plan for having some difficult individual and team conversations with her team members and to role play some of the 'games' she feared they might attempt to play with her which could derail her from getting some clear messages across to them. She also planned what support she would ask for from her manager and worked out a more realistic time-frame in which she felt she could reasonably make the changes to the team which she needed.

Coaching provided a vehicle for her to think through the demands on her – not just in work but in her marriage, her family life and in her relationships with her peers, her staff and her manager. It helped her recommit to the role she had accepted and to develop the confidence to achieve the goals she set herself and which her role demanded.

To what extent have you personally developed and maintained a strong professional network?

Is coaching or mentoring something which you could access for yourself or offer your staff?

To what extent do you think that your team trust each other and believe that they can achieve more together than individually and apart?

What will you do in response to considering these questions?

Key learning points

- The skill base for leading successful teams in health and social care is based on three elements:

  o Professional knowledge and expertise.

  o Managerial competency and skill.

  o Leadership skills.

- Three skills are required in combination in order to produce highly performing teams:

  o Building the psychological contract with staff.

  o Dealing with 'road-blocks'.

  o Staying positive and developing resilience and skills.

- There is a need to address the challenges of strengthening the psychological contract through formal and informal mechanisms which promote and encourage loyalty within and to the role which the team member fulfils.

- Successful managers seek ways to ensure that positive changes gain traction within the system to enable positive changes to occur. Managers should not allow themselves to become distracted or diverted into thinking that problems of a systemic nature are the responsibility of individuals or the result of dysfunctional behaviour by those individuals.

- Ways to develop strong professional resilience are key to being a successful manager and leader in social and health care organisations. Three ways by which managers can develop their professional resilience are:

  o Building strong networks.

  o Using coaching and mentoring.

  o Building collective resilience.

Chapter 7

Strategic thinking, commissioning and planning

Richard Field

CHAPTER OUTCOMES

As a result of completing this chapter you will:

- Be aware of the importance of strategic thinking and planning.

- Appreciate commissioning as a strategic process and understand how this is likely to develop over the next few years.

- Be able to develop and implement an effective planning process leading to the preparation of a successful service or business plan.

- Be able to participate in strategic thinking, commissioning and planning through contributing to environmental scanning, undertaking strengths and weaknesses analysis and exploring opportunities and threats.

Introduction

This chapter looks at three aspects of organisational life; strategic thinking, commissioning and planning. What it means to be strategic is explored as well as strategic analysis and strategic thinking. Commissioning, which for many people is the latest approach to strategic public service management, is outlined; we then consider service and business planning in detail. The final section outlines three popular tools that can be used to support strategic thinking, commissioning and planning. Although covered in a separate chapter it is important to stress that budgeting – which is the process by which the resources required to support planned activity are secured and managed – should be fully integrated with strategic thinking, commissioning and planning. A failure to integrate budgets nearly always leads to pressure to deliver a quantity and quality of service for which there are inadequate funds or to make budget cuts while maintaining planned activity. Failing to maintain a clear and strong relationship between activity and finance is a major cause of the problems facing public services.

Strategy

The terms strategy, strategic planning and strategic management feature a lot in management literature and development programmes. At its simplest, strategy is defined as being 'the long term direction of an organisation' (Johnson et al, 2014: 4). Byars (1992) extends this a little by defining strategy as 'the determination and evaluation of alternatives available to an organisation in achieving its objectives and mission, and the selection of the alternatives to be pursued'.

Johnson et al (2014: 7) recognise that in larger, more diverse organisations strategy may be set for different levels and, or parts, of an organisation. A local authority, for example, may have an overall corporate level strategy for the whole authority as well as service levels strategies for adult social care, highways, trading standards, etc. Below this may be service or business unit strategies and perhaps individual team strategies. In practice, therefore, strategy is the longer-term direction of a whole organisation or relatively discrete part. Planning documents are a major means by which leaders express direction for their organisation. These plans are of varying length and style and are called by many names including short, medium and long-term plans, strategic plans, operational plans, corporate plans, commissioning plans, service and business plans. The variety of names, practices and a general confusion of terms reflects development in the public sector, different thinking about strategic management, fads, organisational history, culture, political and personal preferences. The shift to a more commercial way of working in the early 1980s and more recently commissioning have both prompted new terminology and approaches to planning.

In practice, those leading whole organisations, departments, services and units need to work with three or more different time-frames that are linked, compete for attention and occasionally conflict.

- The first time-frame, which for many leaders consumes most time and energy, is the short-term. What constitutes short term varies but normally covers the current or next financial year for which a plan and budget will be agreed. This period is usually broken down into quarters or months, for each of which there is a target against which actual performance can be measured, variances calculated, investigated and action is taken to rectify. Planning and action in this timeframe is short-term, detailed and operational in nature, usually taking place in a context where there is relative certainty, at least compared to longer time-frames.

- The second, medium-term time frame concerns a longer period, often of two to five years, in respect of which there is usually a degree of certainty regarding some aspects of the wider environment, service provision and delivery. Many service and business plans are set on a three-year rolling basis, with the first year considered in detail and years two and three in outline. These plans contain a mix of strategic and operational analysis, synthesis and action.

- The third time-frame addresses a still longer time perspective, typically between five and 10 years, but may be longer. Planning for this time-frame has a very high level of associated uncertainty and is almost entirely strategic in nature.

Planning for medium- and longer-term periods can be difficult because of the time-frame involved and a high level of inherent uncertainty. However, the long-term survival and success of the organisation depend on being able to anticipate and respond to early signs of shifts in the far and near operating environment. Working with these three time-frames is not easy but essential for continued success; delivering today while preparing for the future. Inevitably a number of tensions arise, including, for example, decisions to divert money that could be spent on today's services to investing in tomorrow. It takes confidence as a leader to sacrifice performance today in order to prepare for a better tomorrow.

While much strategic thinking focuses on the whole business of teams, services, and organisations, this is also needed to tackle specific issues, particularly ones that exhibit characteristics such as:

- Being novel, complex and multi-faceted.

- Affecting a number of stakeholders who may well be interested in conflicting outcomes.

- Requiring collaboration within and between agencies and beyond this to other parts of the whole system.

- Being of significant interest to the media.

- Carrying a range of risks, the full extent of which may be unknown but are a challenge to managers and politicians.

Being strategic

Taking a wide view of strategy suggests that our involvement should be widespread and it is, for we are being strategic whenever we:

- Try to make sense of the current and future likely operating environment.

- Identify and respond to opportunities and threats.

- Critically reflect on current operation and the fit with the environment.

- Ensure a 'golden thread' exists between vision, longer-term objectives and short-term goals.

- Invest energy in understanding 'how things work round here'.

- Improve operations over time and against competitors or similar organisations.

- Discuss with staff the wider picture, the response of the organisation and their part in it.

The benefits of being strategic are many. The strategic process should result in a clear sense of what the organisation is trying to achieve, which is important to service users and citizens as well as to staff who benefit from understanding how what they do matters. Strategic plans and similar documents support applications for funding, inform business cases and enhance accountability through ongoing performance monitoring against strategic objectives. It is all too easy to focus only on day-to-day operations and lose sight of what you are trying to achieve or to fail to spot or anticipate changes in the environment. The twin dangers of 'drifting' away from purpose or being 'beached' as the environmental tide goes out are greatly reduced through constant thinking about 'what next', 'what probably after that' and 'what possibly after that'. Strategic plans and particularly strategic engagement enable more junior staff to make informed decisions about priorities and to better plan for their own work areas.

Being a manager requires the ability to manage a number of balances, of which the following relate to being strategic, these include:

- Deciding how much time should be devoted to being strategic rather than managing operations.
- Determining how much time should be spent identifying and exploring issues as opposed to taking action.
- Deciding what level of performance sacrifice should be made today to enable better performance tomorrow, particularly where performance management focuses on the short-term.
- Managing to be grounded while also viewing the future or an issue from a great height, often referred to as adopting the helicopter view.
- Managing to focus on effectiveness when external pressure is towards ever greater economy and efficiency.

For a variety of reasons being strategic is difficult for many managers. These include:

- There being limited opportunities for, or poor experience of, 'being strategic' within the organisation.
- Organisational approaches to strategy that focus on the production of documents, rather than strategic thinking and dialogue.
- The pull of the operational, which is usually more urgent, familiar and tends to yield quicker results.
- High levels of uncertainty regarding the future.
- A lack of time for strategic thinking.
- Personal preferences for problem-solving and acting rather than talking or thinking.

It is not just corporate leaders that need to be strategic, so too do leaders of departments, services or business units. While the context, restraints to be worked within and freedom enjoyed differ with level, role and culture there is still a need to be strategic and to avoid the risk of over-focusing on the operational.

- *How much of your time do you spend on 'being strategic' and is this sufficient?*

- *What if anything do you find stops you being strategic?*

- *What could you do to be even better at 'being strategic'*

Strategic analysis, thinking and planning

In order for an effective strategy to be developed, there is a need for analysis and exploration or thinking. Strategic analysis is the deliberate gathering and processing of data in order to inform strategy development, while thinking involves:

- Looking at this data from different perspectives.

- Sense checking.

- Being creative by challenging assumptions, reverse thinking, use of metaphor, etc.

- Playing with 'what if ?'.

- Valuing intuition, etc.

Good quality data is required to stimulate and inform thinking. While the specific data sets required will vary with the entity being planned for, these will typically include the current and future operating context, how the service is performing, strengths and weaknesses, the market, competitors, etc.

Too little analysis and you run potential risks of being ill-informed and making poor decisions whereas too much data gathering and analysis is burdensome, confusing and can lead to procrastination and paralysis.

Because planning tends to be undertaken regularly at a predictable point in the year, there is a risk it becomes a largely incremental process whereby the current plan is simply updated to form the one for next year. There is a risk that data is gathered in a mechanical and predictable fashion using one or two established tools. As the saying goes 'familiarity breeds contempt', perhaps a bit harsh but if you always gather the same data in the same way, you are likely to view the strategic context, performance and responses as now. It is, therefore, essential to vary the models used to underpin analysis, to spend time being creative and to allow intuition to be voiced and valued. Thinking is far more important than planning.

The whole process of analysis and thinking or exploration constitutes strategic planning, defined by Johnson et al as being:

systematic analysis and exploration to develop an organisation's strategy.

(2014: 405)

For larger organisations, particularly in the public sector there tends to be a pre-occupation with producing strategy or planning documents to feed established governance processes. While planning documents may serve a purpose, they are often out of date by the time the 'ink is dry' and organisations run the risk that document writing is viewed as more important than the thinking process. If there is a tight planning timetable, thinking may not happen at all with next year's plan being no more than an incrementally modified version of the current plan.

The future operating context for public service leadership is such that economy, efficiency and effectiveness will remain vital, with planning and budgeting critical to ongoing success. Traditional approaches to strategy development, in particular, writing documents that are little more than an incrementally updated version of earlier ones and failing to integrate plans and budgets, have tended to result in over-focusing on economy and efficiency, often at the expense of effectiveness. This needs to stop and be replaced with more sophisticated and sensitive analysis, feeding into quality thinking.

REFLECTION POINT **7.2**

- *To what extent is there evidence of strategic analysis and thinking within your organisation?*
- *How much opportunity is there for you to be strategic?*
- *What might you do to improve your strategic capability?*

Commissioning

Commissioning is a relatively new, widespread and rapidly developing process adopted by much of the public sector. Commissioning practice differs significantly as reflects the variety of policy contexts, operational environments and cultures along with preferences of senior leaders. Accordingly, there is no single definition of commissioning although the one issued in 2009 by the Department for Communities and Local Government is reasonably typical, where commissioning is seen to be:

> *The means to secure best value and deliver the positive outcomes that meet the needs of citizens, communities and service users.*

Three key points flow from this statement; best value, positive outcomes and the needs of citizens, communities and service users. Each of these is explored below.

- Best value – a concept that emerged during the Tony Blair administration, elected 2nd May, 1997 still applies in a commissioning context, at the heart of which is the pursuit of economy, efficiency and effectiveness. This goes back to the idea of value for money – introduced by the first administration of Margaret Thatcher in 1979. Whether framed as value for money or best value, public service performance has traditionally focused on economy and efficiency which entails measuring inputs and outputs. However, this is only part of the performance story – if a service is not effective in meeting the need for which it was designed it will represent a poor use of public money, irrespective of how economic or efficient it may be. While often difficult to understand and measure, it is essential that the needs a service intend to address are identified and the extent to which these are met, understood.

- Positive outcomes. Understanding and embedding outcomes in public service management may not be unique to commissioning but is essential for this approach to work. Outcomes are changes, benefits, learning or other effects that happen as a result of action taken. If a manager fails to place outcomes at the centre of their thinking they are highly unlikely to realise the full benefits of commissioning. The risk is that they and others will continue with a mindset that causes them to want to respond to each and every 'need' with a service, for which they then become responsible for designing, funding and delivering. This builds unhealthy citizen expectations of the state, which the public purse can no longer fund and ignores the possibility that there might be non-service ways of achieving outcomes, some of which may need little or no funding. If a manager thinks only in terms of commissioning services, they are likely to continue buying what they have always bought albeit with a focus on reducing cost to the taxpayer – a process that is much closer to traditional procurement than to commissioning. A manager who commissions outcomes is much more likely to consider a wide range of ways of achieving these, including for example via:

  o Shifting citizen behaviour to eliminate, delay or reduce the need for traditional public services (e.g. prompting people to dispose of their own litter reduces the need for paid 'litter pickers').

  o Collaborating with other agencies to provide integrated effective and efficient responses to outcomes.

  o Influencing businesses, voluntary and community groups to work in ways that help achieve social outcomes (e.g. encouraging shops, cafes, places of worship, etc. to provide toilet facilities reduces the need for public conveniences).

  o Helping communities to identify and use the assets they control, the priorities they seek and actions they might wish to consider.

Of course, it may be the case that the best way of meeting an outcome is actually via state funded services but this is often the most expensive option to the state and should be considered last.

The cost to the state of meeting or helping to meet outcomes varies significantly with the means adopted and effective commissioning involves considering each option. Continuing, however, with the mindset of commissioning services rather than outcomes is likely to limit thinking to internal provision or external purchase of services.

- Needs of citizens, communities and service users. The focus of commissioning goes well beyond current service users to include communities and citizens. This raises the prospect if not certainty of disagreement between stakeholders, for while they may share some common needs, others will be unique. Some of these outcomes may conflict,

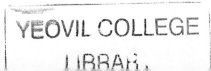

a relatively common situation which needs to be worked through. Traditional service provision focuses on current service users whereas there is a pressing need to delay service take-up which means working with 'could be' service users earlier, either via prevention or more widely and earlier through focusing more generally on well-being outcomes.

While commissioning shares a number of characteristics with processes such as strategic management, business planning, procurement and outsourcing it is fundamentally different. As our understanding of commissioning develops it is increasingly clear that:

- Commissioning is a strategic process that involves a greater number of stakeholder groups than conventional strategic management and frequently necessitates collaboration with other public service organisations. In addition, commissioning organisations increasingly work towards two visions, one for the community expressed in terms of social, economic and environmental outcomes and the other concerning the role of the commissioning organisation(s) aiming to bring or help bring this about.

- Many of the tools used when generating business plans are applicable to commissioning, however, business planning is more commonly adopted by organisations offering goods and services. Commissioning is a broader process with greater emphasis on understanding and meeting citizen needs and outcomes and featuring greater citizen involvement to the extent that the citizen and state practitioners are approaching, if not in, an equal relationship.

- Recognising that while ultimately it might be necessary to procure a service, commissioning seeks to achieve outcomes by the best appropriate means not just through service provision. It is, therefore, a broader process than procurement.

- Outsourcing can be an appropriate means of acquiring goods and services but this is not always the case. Arguably, 'right-sourcing' should be adopted, the concern being to identify the best way of securing supply, irrespective of internal or external status, political ideology, etc.

The commissioning process

The common presentation of commissioning is as a four-stage, analyse, plan, do and review process as shown in Figure 7.1. Table 7.1 outlines the tasks involved in each of the activities.

The typical sequential representation of commissioning is an over-simplification, implying a nice, orderly process whereas in practice there is iteration and significant interaction between activities. There is also a risk that the stages are linked to a calendar, therefore implying that analysis only occurs in May or June perhaps, planning in July and August and so on. We see commissioning stages as more like cogs in an integrated process as shown in Figure 7.2.

How commissioning has evolved

Current public sector commissioning practice has come a long way. Previously public service organisations tended to operate largely independent of each other with

Figure 7.1 Commissioning as a four-stage process

professionals and elected members determining services to be offered largely through in-house providers supplemented by some external provision. Outputs tended to be the focus of performance measurement and there was an emphasis on procurement and supplier management rather than market management. Prior to the emergence of commissioning, there had been years of financial constraint and a strong emphasis on cost reduction. Early experimentation with commissioning saw growing interest in and use of outcomes as a basis for decision making and management although these were often unsophisticated, partial in coverage, confused with outputs and determined by professionals. Over time, there has been a realisation that commissioning is not the same as procurement and market management is needed to ensure that the services required are available to buy at the right price and quality, with the user having some choice. Although early practice tended to be service-centric there has been growing interest in other ways of meeting outcomes, including nudging citizen behaviour, pursuing social value, digitisation, etc. While there is growing collaboration between state agencies, much resource is however still locked in silos. Many organisations are now moving on to embed commissioning in all their practices including for example performance management and contract management, more actively engaging citizens in identifying desired outcomes and designing ways of bringing these about, drawing

Table 7.1 Commissioning tasks and activities

Commissioning Activities	
Activities	**Tasks include**
Analyse	Gathering and interpreting data relating to anticipated changes in the environment, desired outcomes, assets, actual and potential demand, performance, suppliers and market, etc.
Plan	Deciding priorities, identifying different ways of addressing need, designing services and other responses, determining desired market shape, aligning and allocating resources, etc.
Do	Managing demand, launching and decommissioning services, influencing other agencies and people, procuring supply, shaping the market, managing contracts, etc.
Review	Evaluating impact, measuring performance, sense making, reporting performance, sharing learning, etc.

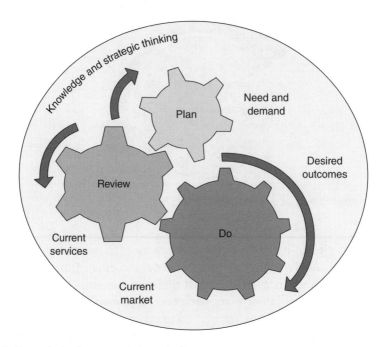

Figure 7.2 Commissioning as an integrated process

on personal and community assets, pursuing greater integration and responding to individual personal needs. In future, there are likely to be further movements towards more effective community engagement, greater use made of community assets, deeper integration of health and social care, wider collaboration and whole systems leadership.

How different is commissioning from conventional approaches to public service management?

The answer to this question has to be 'it depends on what is meant by commissioning' and 'it varies with organisation and sector' both in terms of the practice of conventional public service management which it replaced and the extent to which commissioning has been adopted. Field and Miller (2016 in press), suggest that the practice of commissioning ranges from the embryonic to collaborative and co-designed to asset aware and asset based, brief descriptions of which are included in Table 7.2 along with conventional public service management, which this is generally replacing.

Asset-aware and asset-based commissioning are actually two emerging versions of latest commissioning practice similar in certain respects yet with significant differences that fall outside of the scope of this text.

Few organisations fit neatly within one column, most exhibit characteristics associated with two or more columns – due sometimes to operating in a complex environment and other times a lack of conscious thinking about the adopted approach to commissioning.

Table 7.2 Practice of commissioning

Conventional Service Management	Embryonic Commissioning	Collaborative and Co-designed Commissioning	Asset Aware and Asset Based Commissioning
Service design and management is driven by politicians and professionals within organisations who also determine who should receive services, how and when. Little use is made of outcomes and contract management tends to be tight, based on detailed technical specifications rich in input and output measures. There is a strong emphasis on cost reduction through 'salami slicing' and managing suppliers rather than markets. The voice of the client and citizen is seldom heard.	Early moves away from conventional approaches to public service management with limited service user/ citizen involvement in decision making, early use of outcomes that tend to be binary in nature and partial in coverage. Single organisation commissioning rather than collaborative is practised. Relationship with suppliers is generally formal but becoming less adversarial. Early attempts to 'manage markets as well as suppliers', appears.	Commissioning basics are in place and evolving to become more sophisticated. There is greater involvement of users and citizens and more nuanced and embedded use of a broader range of outcomes. There is limited collaboration between state agencies and an appreciation that outcomes may be achieved through a wide range of strategies including demand management, citizen behaviour change and influencing state, private, voluntary organisations to work in different ways. Market management is more sophisticated involving pre-tender, tender and contract management stages.	Far greater involvement of citizens, including them leading the commissioning process. Joint decision making by professionals and service users as equals. A wide range of community assets contributing to outcome achievement. Collaboration between state agencies becoming more sophisticated and extending to include commercial providers and community groups. Options for achieving outcomes extend to include unsupported and supported self-help together with co-production.

Some people liken the evolution of commissioning to a journey which sees organisations moving from left to right, from embryonic, through collaborative and co-designed to asset aware and ultimately asset based. For some organisations, this may be true but for others, their operating environment and culture restrict such movement or render it inappropriate. Public organisations vary in the freedom they enjoy about what they do and how they conduct business so if it is a journey then different organisations have different destinations which they approach in different ways and to timescales that work for them.

REFLECTION POINT 7.3

- *Does your organisation practice commissioning?*

- *If so which column or combination of columns included in Table 7.2 best describe this practice?*

More detail regarding commissioning in health and social care can be found in *Effective Commissioning in Health and Social Care*, another text in this series.

Planning

The third section of this chapter concerns planning, with a focus on service or business planning, a form that many managers contribute to, and or, lead. Much of the content, however, is relevant to the preparation of other plans.

Typically, service and business planning are medium-term forms of planning experienced early in managerial careers.

Planning can be defined as:

> *The process by which a desired future state is conceived and an effective way of delivering this developed and resourced.*

> (Field, 2012: 2)

The definition of planning makes three important points; that planning is a conception or design process, is future based and seeks to ensure the desired future state is delivered.

While all people plan in respect of their personal lives we differ in the extent to which we plan, the detail we engage in and our overall approach. Organisational planning differs from personal planning in that it normally involves preparation of a planning document, the use of planning techniques and approval by a more senior person or body. Organisational planning should be an integral part of performance management and flow from strategic thinking.

Plan and budget integration is illustrated in Figure 7.3, where an annual planning process leads to the preparation of a three-year rolling plan with the first year expressed as a detailed budget and years two and three as broader financial forecasts.

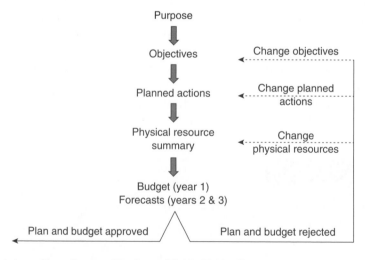

Figure 7.3 Integrating plans and budgets (Field, 2012: 6)

There is a logical flow in this diagram. All units or parts of an organisation have a purpose and are expected to achieve certain things that may be expressed as objectives, goals, targets, etc. In turn, we plan to achieve these by acting in particular ways, often referred to as actions or perhaps strategies, for which a certain quantity and quality of resources are required. It follows, then that the cost of accessing these resources determines the budget required. Plans and budgets, therefore, should be integrated, from which it follows that:

- Planned activity cannot be changed without this affecting the budget.

- Any changes in budget will impact on the quantity and/or quality of planned activity.

- Managers will start the project or year with sufficient money to resource plans.

- Approval or rejection decisions apply to both the plan and the budget.

As public sector resources are limited there will inevitably be occasions when a perfectly good plan will be rejected. If an attempt is made to approve a plan but with a reduced budget a dangerous mismatch can occur, the manager should stay true to the principle of integration, making changes in planned quantity and/or quality of activity, or deploying different physical resources such that the cost of required resources reduces to the point that the plan and budget once again match.

Planning and budgeting processes should go far beyond the simple preparation of action points and the calculation of the budget required to purchase physical resources. Effective planning involves strategic thinking and significant challenge regarding the level and quality of resources required, where and how these are purchased – all with a view to ensuring value for money.

However, this integrated approach, despite its associated logic and attractiveness has historically been rare. Continuous pressure to increase service quantity and quality while reducing or at least constraining budgets have led to years of budgets based on figures for previous years rather than what is needed. This crude incremental approach, particularly when accompanied by inadequate provision for inflation or cuts, often results in poor service prioritisation, gains in economy and efficiency at the expense of effectiveness, game playing, poor value for money and undue managerial stress.

Incremental approaches to budget preparation completely fail when the size of the required budget reduction is significant, as has been the case since the last recession started. There is more interest now in linking or integrating plans and budgets, at least temporarily as part of fundamental reviews.

Why plan?

Undertaken with enthusiasm and care, the planning process should ensure that services and activities continue to be relevant to the community, that service development is stimulated, value for money achieved and management control facilitated, all of which contributes to sustainable performance improvement.

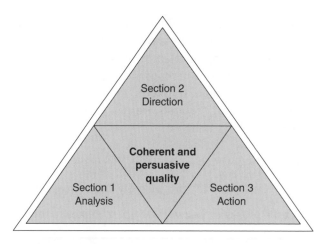

Figure 7.4 Planning to plan (Field, 2012: 9)

Types of planning and plan documents

Approaches to organisational planning and the preparation of plan documents differ between organisations, vary over time and change to reflect managerial fashion. Such variations include the organisational scope, plan format, the extent to which planning is strategic or operational, and the time period addressed.

The format of a plan is often determined by another agency or by managers operating at a more strategic level within the organisation. Where there is freedom regarding plan format the broad structure outlined in Figure 7.4 should be considered. It features three main sections (analysis, direction and action), which combine to result in planning proposals that are coherent and persuasive.

The analysis section should include relevant historic, current and forecast information regarding various aspects of the service which helps the reader understand the current and likely future context for the plan.

The direction section explains why the service exists, identifies key objectives for the planning period and explains in broad terms how these will be achieved.

The action section should convince the reader that proposed actions will deliver the objectives, are realistic and will happen if the plan is approved.

What constitutes a good quality plan?

The quality of a plan can be assessed using a number of criteria presented as questions in Table 7.3.

What constitutes a good planning process?

Good quality plans arise from effective planning processes, which typically involve six steps as shown in Figure 7.5.

Table 7.3 Criteria – quality plans

Plan evaluation questions

1   Is the plan written in a way that can be understood by the intended reader(s)?
2   Does the plan have a persuasive quality?
3   Are short and long-term outcomes recognised and balanced?
4   Do the planned objectives and actions fit the current situation?
5   Is the plan document of appropriate length?
6   Does there appear to be sufficient analysis?
7   Does the plan content flow?
8   Does the plan contain sufficient detail regarding the internal and external context?
9   Does the plan appear to be the product of a sound planning process?
10 Does the plan show how this links to other plans?
11 Is the plan self-critical?
12 Does the plan take account of the views of key stakeholders, balancing the different desired outcomes?
13 Is there evidence that planned performance is being stretched, yet targets are realistic?
14 Does the plan include a clear statement of direction and SMART objectives?
15 Does the plan indicate the level of resources required to support activity?
16 Does the plan reassure the reader that planned actions will happen?
17 Have risks been considered?

The first stage concerns planning to plan and involves addressing 10 questions (see Table 7.4).

The second stage, analysis and strategic thinking, is at the heart of the planning process and is covered in more detail later in this chapter. With the content of the plan generated, attention turns to the third stage, which involves writing the document in preparation for the fourth stage; approval and feedback. Once approved, the plan is implemented leading to the final stage, involving periodic performance review.

Figure 7.5 The planning process

Table 7.4 Planning questions (Field, 2012: 14)

Planning to plan

1   Who will receive the plan and for what purpose?
2   What plan format will be used?
3   Who should be involved in planning, and how?
4   What guidance and support will be given to those involved?
5   What will be communicated to those not directly involved in planning?
6   What timetable will be adopted for planning?
7   What criteria will be used to evaluate the plan?
8   How does the plan link with other systems?
9   Who will write the plan?
10 Who will present the plan?

Thirteen key questions – analysis, direction and action

The 13 key questions in Table 7.5 offer a framework for analysis, direction and action planning.

Analysis

Questions 1–7 in Table 7.5 provide a framework for completing the analysis section of a plan, the quality of which can be greatly enhanced by using planning tools such as strengths, weaknesses, opportunities and threats analysis (SWOT) or environmental scanning (SPELT). These two tools, which are in widespread use, are explained in the final section of this chapter.

Table 7.5 Thirteen key planning questions

Question	Purpose and approach
Analysis	
1. What do we know about our performance?	Plan readers need to understand how successful a service is, whether performance is improving or reducing and how this compares with similar services or organisations.
2. What do we know about how we operate?	Most services have strengths that contribute to successful operation which, depending on the future environment and direction, will be important to maintain in the immediate term. Similarly, most services have one or more weaknesses that if sufficiently serious should be addressed within the plan.
3. What do we know about the environment?	The plan should reflect the environment within which the service will operate, how this might change in the future and the implications this poses for the service.

Question	Purpose and approach
4. What do we know about those that use our services and the services we provide or commission?	The plan should identify current service users and their level of satisfaction together with targeted future users and the needs that should be addressed. The resource implications of running these services together with the associated unit costs should also be included.
5. What do we know about others that provide similar services?	Understanding how this service compares to similar ones is important either because of operating in a competitive situation or because there is potential to learn from other organisations.
6. What do we know about opportunities and threats?	Arising from the earlier analysis will be opportunities and threats, which should be drawn together and the implications explored.
7. What restraints affect our planning?	Most plans are prepared within frameworks that in effect limit the actions planners can propose.
Direction	
8. Why do we exist or act as we do?	The plan should include a succinct statement that captures the purpose of the organisation.
9. What do we want to achieve?	The plan should include a small number of key objectives some of which are likely to relate to ongoing service delivery, others to one-off initiatives or specific required actions. These should flow from the earlier analysis, be consistent with the purpose statement and expressed in SMART terms (Specific, Measurable, Achievable, Realistic and Timed).
10. How will we achieve what we want?	This section outlines the broad approach to achieving each key objective expressed as headline actions with more detail appearing later in the action section.
Action	
11. How will we ensure that the plan will happen?	This section identifies the detailed actions required to make the plan happen, the person responsible for taking action and how progress will be monitored.
12. What resources are needed to support the plan?	It is important that the level and cost of resources needed for planned activity are clearly stated.
13. What risks are plan activities exposed to and how will these be managed?	The plan should identify the risks to which the service is exposed, the potential impact, likelihood of occurrence and the approach proposed for managing this risk.

Direction

Having addressed the seven key questions relating to analysis, attention turns to stating the purpose, key objectives and the high-level actions associated with direction.

All plans benefit from the inclusion of a high-level statement of purpose, which helps the reader understand why the service, unit, organisation, etc. exists and provides a focus for objectives and planned actions. The following is an example of such a statement for a home care service.

We aim to provide a range of tailored services to users in a way that promotes their independence, secures an improved quality of life and helps them remain in their own homes.

Statements of purpose, mission or vision are usually expressed in relatively general terms and are a high-level expression of direction. More specific information about direction is normally provided in the form of key objectives such as:

To undertake a rolling programme of service reviews resulting in savings of:

* £0.5 million in 2017/18

* £1.5 million in 2018/19

* £2.5 million in 2019/20

While there are potentially numerous objectives relating to a service, only those that are key to success should be included in this part of the plan. When stating objectives care should be taken to ensure that they are stated in SMART terms (Specific, Measurable, Achievable, Realistic and Timed).

The direction stage of planning concludes with the identification of high-level actions needed to achieve the key objectives. Both the objectives and high-level actions can be captured in a grid as shown in Table 7.6, (Columns 1 and 2) the detailed preparation of which is completed during the action planning stage. Identifying the purpose, defining the objectives and stating high-level actions answers key questions 8, 9 and 10 in Table 7.5, which concern the direction phase of planning.

Action planning

The action plan element should reassure the reader that thought has been given to how the plan is to be achieved, that risks have been considered and contingency measures are in place. The first stage of action planning is to identify the detailed actions that will lead to the achievement of each high-level action, thereby ensuring that each key objective is met. The action grid included as Table 7.6 and started during the direction phase can be used to record detailed actions together with information regarding responsibility and monitoring. The grid is completed by:

* Breaking high-level actions down into detailed actions and inserting these in Column 3.

* Entering key dates in Column 4.

* Stating in Column 5 the person responsible for ensuring each detailed action occurs.

* Specifying monitoring arrangements in Column 6.

Completing this action plan addresses key question 11 in Table 7.5.

Question 12 in Table 7.5 requires the resources needed and associated budget to be identified, the process for which is outlined in Chapter 8, Effective Budget Management.

Table 7.6 Action grid

Objectives	High-level actions	Detailed actions	Detailed action – key dates	Responsible person	Monitoring arrangements
(1)	(2)	(3)	(4)	(5)	(6)
Undertake a rolling programme of service reviews resulting in savings of; • £0.5m in 2017/18 • £1.5m in 2018/19 • £2.5m in 2019/20	Develop a three-year review programme by 30th April 2017	Identify and prioritise a full list of reviews. Submit priorities list for approval by Senior Management Team	By 14th March 2017 By 30th April 2017	Director of Operations	Monthly line management monitoring and consideration by Senior Management Team

When approving a plan those involved need to be assured that potential risks have been identified, assessed and will be managed. This information can be conveyed via the grid provided as Table 7.7, completion of which involves:

• Describing risks in Column 1 indicating the source.

• Describing the likely impact in Column 2.

• Indicating in Column 3 the potential severity of this impact, using a score of 1–10 where 1 is low.

Table 7.7 Risk grid

Description of risk and source	Description of likely impact	Impact (Score 1–10, where 1 is low and 10 is high)	Likelihood (Score 1–10, where 1 is low risk and 10 is high)	Risk score (Column 3 x Column 4)	Risk management
1	2	3	4	5	6
Level of cuts imposed is greater than planned budget reductions, arising from planned service reviews.	Likely to be even tougher financial targets imposed by senior managers, probably on a pro-rata basis Possible failure to achieve cuts with subsequent overspend	8	6	48	Priority will be given to services expected to yield more significant resource savings Second optional schedule will be prepared with a much faster pace of review

- Indicating in Column 4 the likelihood that this risk will occur, using a score of 1–10 where 1 is low.

- Multiplying the impact and likelihood scores to give a total risk score and entering this in Column 5.

- Indicating in Column 6 the management arrangements in respect of risks where scores are considered high.

Useful tools

There are many tools that can be used to help structure data gathering, analysis and interpretation when thinking strategically, commissioning or planning. Some tools are very well established such as SWOT and Environmental Scanning, others less so. Some of these tools have uses that are much wider, such as for decision making, change management and innovation. The quality of commissioning and planning depend on quality thinking which is more likely when data has been gathered and interpreted from different perspectives. Using a good range of appropriate tools and varying these over time brings new insights, disrupts existing thinking and helps keep processes fresh.

The following section introduces three tools commonly associated with strategic management, commissioning and planning. It should be stressed that there are many others and to continually rely on a small number of tools is ill-advised.

SWOT

A SWOT analysis is used to capture the internal strengths and weaknesses of a service together with the external opportunities and threats, typically presented as four cell matrix as shown in Figure 7.6.

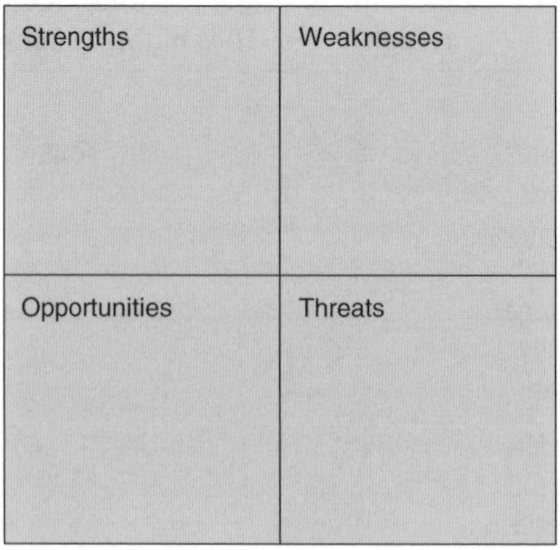

Strengths	Weaknesses
Opportunities	Threats

Figure 7.6 SWOT analysis

A variation on the traditional approach to SWOT is to split this analysis into two tools; a strengths and weaknesses analysis undertaken at the start of the analysis phase of planning and an opportunities and threats analysis, completed towards the end. This split is adopted in the following material.

Strengths and weaknesses analysis

Any service is likely to have a number of strengths and weaknesses, some of which are key to ongoing success and others of relatively minor importance. As a general rule, a strength or weakness should only be included in a plan document if it is relevant to the service, significant in size and its impact is differential when compared to other services. When stating strengths and weaknesses it is important to avoid the common practice of simply producing a list of bullet points (e.g. our staff are a strength) as this leaves readers unaware of why a factor is a strength or weakness, the nature and significance of the impact this has on service performance and so on. The analysis can be improved by using the grid included as Table 7.8, which contains five questions intended to help determine which strengths and weaknesses feature in the text of a plan.

Where a strengths and weaknesses analysis is undertaken prior to completing an environmental scan and determining future service direction there is a risk of focusing on factors that will be less important in future or failing to identify ones that will be important given anticipated changes in the future environment and direction. The initial strengths and weaknesses analysis should, therefore, be reviewed once the proposed direction is known.

Table 7.8 Strengths and weaknesses analysis

Strength/ weakness	How does this impact on the service	How significant is this factor? (high, medium or low)	How do similar organisations compare?	Is the significance increasing/ decreasing/ or static?	What evidence is there to support this view?
E.g. Well equipped staff – all have high specification laptops, PDAs, etc.	Staff are in constant touch with the office, information is entered once only and efficiency is high. Responses to client enquiries can be immediate. Staff feel that they are well equipped for the work they undertake.	Medium	A number of similar organisations appear to have failed to make this investment.	Decreasing as technology costs fall and other organisations invest.	Customer response times and qualitative feedback. Staff feedback from annual Attitude Survey.

Environmental analysis

Understanding the environment and how it might change provides the context for planning. Environmental scanning is a process which helps develop this understanding, one version of which (SPELT) provides a framework for identifying five major sources of environmental influence; sociological, political, economic, legal and technological, and three time-frames; influences that are impacting now, those expected to impact over the next three years and those that might impact in the longer term as shown in Figure 7.7.

When using SPELT the first stage is to identify environmental influences that might impact on the service under consideration. This might affect all organisations, all public services or only those offering, receiving or employed within, a particular service. The five sources are used to prompt rather than constrain thinking across the environment and an influence will often relate to two or more categories. It has to be accepted that despite best endeavours there is always the chance that a significant and unexpected shift in the environment occurs, such as factors linked to war, acts of nature and politics, etc.

The second step is to identify the likely impact of each influence on the service concerned using low, medium and high descriptors to indicate the extent of the impact and the probability of it occurring. Table 7.9 illustrates how one significant economic influence can impact on a service.

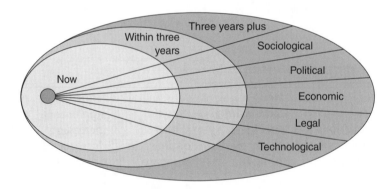

Figure 7.7 SPELT analysis (Field, 2012: 22)

Table 7.9 SPELT influences – economic example

SPELT Category and influence	Impact	Possible implications	Impact and probability
Slow economic recovery coupled with a political commitment to balance the books and eradicate the national deficit within five years.	Cuts in grant funding to public bodies and new limits on local tax raising powers.	Reduced funding Increased emphasis on efficiency.	High impact and high probability.

The final step is to use the impact/probability assessment to determine whether to:

- Respond to the influence in this plan.
- Investigate and possibly act in response to this influence during the period covered by the plan.
- Monitor this influence during the life of the plan.
- Ignore the influence.

Opportunities and threats analysis

Opportunities and threats face all organisations, the implications of which range from minor to very significant. Considering opportunities and threats at the end of the analysis stage allows thinking to be influenced by factors that have emerged while considering key questions 1–6 (see Table 7.5). However, it is also worth allowing time and space for more opportunities and threats to be identified – perhaps via the use of creativity techniques, such as brainstorming.

As it is likely that there will be a significant number of opportunities and threats it is helpful to filter these to isolate those that are both potentially significant and likely to materialise. This process of filtering can be assisted by the use of a grid such as the one included in Table 7.10, where the first column identifies opportunities and threats and the second, potential impact. Columns 3 and 4 record the significance and likelihood scores using a scale of 1–10 where 10 is high. Where those planning decide that an opportunity or threat looks significant, Column 5 should be completed, describing one or more possible responses.

Table 7.10 Opportunities and threats analysis

Opportunity/ threat	Potential impact	Potential significance (Score 1–10 where 10 is high)	Likelihood of occurrence (Score 1–10 where 10 is high)	Possible responses
(1)	(2)	(3)	(4)	(5)
Imposed efficiency target	Need to increase efficiency year on year	8	9	Establish a rolling efficiency review programme

---

REFLECTION POINT 7.4

Planning is a significant management process, competence in which is important to future organisational survival and leadership success. The following five questions comprise a framework for reflecting on current practice in the workplace, the application of learning and planning further personal and organisational development.

(Continued)

REFLECTION POINT **7.4** *(CONT.)*

1 To what extent do the plans you prepare, contribute to or work with:

    a) meet the evaluation criteria identified in Table 7.3?

    b) address the 13 key questions detailed in Table 7.5?

2 If you undertake strengths and weaknesses analysis is the output meaningful to the user (Table 7.8)?

3 If you undertake environmental scanning is the potential impact of each factor clear and the likelihood that it will occur stated (Table 7.9)?

4 If you undertake an opportunities and threats analysis is this:

    a) informed by the answers to key questions 1–6 (Table 7.5)?

    b) presented in a way that clearly identifies the potential impact and likelihood (Table 7.10)?

5 What is your experience of using other planning tools and how could you improve the value this yields?

More detail regarding planning, particularly the use of tools can be found in *Planning and Budgeting Skills for Health and Social Work Managers*, another text in this series.

Key learning points

- Being strategic is important to the long-term success of organisations and proposed resolution of significant issues.

- Being strategic is something that can and should occur at different levels in organisations. The capacity of, and need for, individuals to be strategic is widespread and requires individuals to balance how they spend their time, the extent to which they focus on now and the future, etc.

- Commissioning is a relatively new way of managing public services, the practice of which varies across the public sector.

- Commissioning takes different forms, needing to be tailored to context, culture and leadership preferences. Practice is constantly evolving, generally becoming more asset aware or asset based.

- Plans and budgets must be integrated with a recognition by all stakeholders that a change in one will lead to a change in the other.

- Effective service and business planning ensure products, services and activities are relevant to individuals and communities.

- Good plans arise from effective planning processes and an appropriate investment of time.

- Good use of planning tools improves strategic thinking and analysis that underpin an effective plan.

Chapter 8

Effective budget management

Richard Field

CHAPTER OUTCOMES

As a result of completing this chapter you will:

- Understand why and how planning and budgeting processes should be integrated.

- Understand types of budget responsibility.

- Be able to prepare, monitor and manage a budget.

Introduction

The future operating context for public service leadership is such that economy, efficiency and effectiveness will remain vital and budget management will play a key part in ongoing success. The most recent recession has impacted on budget management in a number of ways including:

- Forcing public sector agencies to recognise that the old incremental approach to budget preparation and in particular budget reduction, are no longer workable. The size of the cuts demanded of the sector rule out the 'salami-slicing' approach much favoured by politicians and managers over the years.

- Prompting senior managers to reverse what had been a widespread trend towards devolving budgets to lower managerial levels. While the arguments for devolution remain valid the twin imperatives of ensuring very tight financial control and budget reduction have prompted financial re-centralisation. This is a logical response to financial stress that is also seen in private and third sector organisations.

One implication of leading in a period of relative centralisation is that many managerial levels that would have exercised budget responsibility years ago do not now, and some managers have lost this aspect of their role. This position is likely to change once the economy recovers and public sector borrowing comes under control for in the longer term, high level, central financial control will be seen to be increasingly disempowering, inflexible, stifling, stressful and ineffective.

Developing financial competence now, in particular with regard to budget management, will help those currently holding such responsibilities to discharge these effectively. For other people, this development is slightly ahead of the time when either re-devolution will occur or promotion success bring financial responsibility.

This chapter explores budget management which Field (2012: 58) suggests is the 'total process by which budgets are prepared, negotiated, monitored and acted upon', offering ideas intended to help the reader develop competence and confidence. For many people, the prospect of studying a subject involving numbers is unappealing often due to a mistaken belief that budget management is a technical process detached from day-to-day service delivery and involving high-level mathematical skills. The reverse is actually true; good budget preparation and control requires detailed knowledge of the service, a tolerance of uncertainty and quite limited mathematical ability. In fact, budget management is more of a political/behavioural process with a potential for different people to legitimately take different views about the volume and the cost of physical resources needed to fulfil a plan.

Integrated planning and budgeting

In the Strategic Thinking, Commissioning and Planning chapter the importance of integrating planning and budgeting was introduced using the following diagram, where the annual planning process leads to the preparation of a three-year rolling plan with the first year expressed as a detailed budget and years two and three as broader financial forecasts.

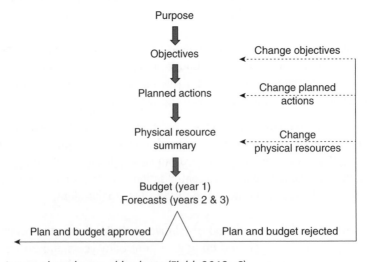

Figure 8.1 Integrating plans and budgets (Field, 2012: 6)

The service, project or activity to which the budget relates will typically be accompanied by a very high-level explanation of why this is thought necessary. This purpose, which can take many forms including as a mission statement, will be accompanied by a set of objectives that articulate what the service, project or activity is to achieve leading to a strategy which sets out actions intended to deliver the objectives. These actions require physical resources, for example, staff, buildings, telephone calls to be made, miles to be travelled. Usually, physical resources need to be purchased, rented or leased, the cost of which will determine the budget required. There should be a golden thread that links purpose, objectives and planned actions to the required physical resources and associated budget.

Accepting the idea of plan and budget integration it follows that:

- Planned activity cannot be changed without this affecting the budget.

- A change in the level of budget available will impact on the quantity and/or quality of planned activity.

- Managers will start the project or year with sufficient money to resource approved plans.

- Approval or rejection decisions apply to both the plan and the budget.

As public sector resources are limited there will inevitably be occasions when a perfectly good plan will be rejected. If an attempt is made to approve the plan but with a reduced budget, the manager should stay true to the principle of integration and propose measures such as:

- Reducing planned quantity.

- Reducing intended quality of activity.

- Deploying different physical resources or changing the resource mix.

- Responding with other cost-cutting proposals.

Planning and budgeting processes should go far beyond the simple listing of action points and calculating the budget required to purchase physical resources. Effective planning involves strategic thinking regarding the prioritised needs of service users, target quantity and quality of services or activities and how resources are purchased – all with a view to ensuring value for money.

This integrated approach, despite its logic and attractiveness, is historically rare in public service management. Continuous pressure to increase service quantity and quality while reducing or at least constraining budgets have led to years of budgets based on figures for previous years rather than what is needed. This rather crude approach often results in poor service prioritisation, gains in economy and efficiency at the expense of effectiveness, game playing, poor value for money and undue managerial stress.

Budget management

Budget management is a key responsibility for most managers and one which with career progression, tends to become more significant. The exact responsibilities, organisational rules that apply and the processes by which budgets are managed vary significantly between and even within some organisations. The experience that an individual budget manager will have of budget management depends on a number of factors including the:

- Number of budgets they are responsible for and the extent to which they can exercise control – at its simplest this responsibility will be limited to a small number of budgets over which reasonable control can be exercised. At its most onerous budget responsibility includes budgets that relate to all the resources used by the manager, irrespective of controllability.

- Extent to which the financial regulations or rules of the organisation allow managerial control – for example the degree to which the manager is free to make purchases from wherever they wish, whether they can switch money between budgets, have permission to carry forward under/overspends, etc.

- Nature of budget responsibility, this generally being devolved or delegated.

It is essential that budget managers are clear about which budgets they are responsible for, the rules they are required to operate within and whether they have devolved or delegated responsibility.

Devolved and delegated responsibilities

Devolved budget management is defined by Bean and Hussey (1996) as being:

> the process whereby budgets are devolved to an individual who becomes the budget holder and who will be totally responsible and accountable for that budget. Ideally management and financial responsibilities are aligned such that the budget holder is accountable for the financial implications of his/her management decisions.

(Bean and Hussey, 1996: 5)

By contrast, the delegated approach is defined as being:

> where budgets are delegated to nominated budget holders who are responsible for monitoring the budget, but are not accountable for the budget as they will have little or no control over its construction and its usage.

(Bean and Hussey, 1996: 6)

Devolved budget managers have total responsibility and are expected to exploit opportunities or remedy problems as they arise during the year. However, the word 'total' is somewhat misleading as there are circumstances where the only responsible action a manager can take is to escalate the budget situation to a more senior budget manager. For managers of a delegated budget, responsibility is limited to ensuring they spend appropriately, monitor levels of income and expenditure regularly, investigate apparent problems and report these to the person who holds devolved responsibility.

Devolution, which prior to the recession was quite popular, requires:

- Organisational leaders to relinquish a degree of power, which some find quite difficult.
- Managers to engage appropriately in budget setting.
- All those involved to understand their role, responsibilities and rights.
- Managers to have reasonable managerial and financial freedom.

Where these conditions are not met there is a serious risk that budget managers will end up feeling responsible for a budget they do not understand or believe to be sufficient and in respect of which they have little freedom to act.

While managers tend to have some understanding of their role and responsibilities with regard to budget management relatively few are aware of their rights. The following questions provide a framework for addressing rights.

1. What rights do I believe I have with regard to budget management? Table 8.1 includes some rights typically identified by budget managers.

2. Are these rights being met?

3. What can I do to help my organisation meet these rights?

Regarding competence, budget managers with delegated responsibility should be able to monitor a budget, identify causes of variance between budgeted and actual figures, correct errors and propose possible actions. Those managers with devolved responsibility should also be able to prepare and negotiate a budget, complete a year-end forecast, interpret financial performance in the wider context, take thoughtful action and escalate issues promptly when necessary. All managers should understand the responsibilities and rights associated with their post, the financial regulations and procedures relevant to their responsibilities, the budget reporting process and budget reports.

In practice, budget management comprises two important interlinking processes; preparation and control. Budget preparation involves calculating how much resource is needed and negotiating this in the light of planned activity and available budget. Budgetary

Table 8.1 Devolved budget manager rights

Include the right to
- Proper involvement in preparing, negotiating and agreeing a budget
- Know the amount of the agreed budget before the financial year starts
- Know the financial regulations and procedures within which they are required to work
- Budget management training before assuming such responsibility
- Good quality and timely information

---

control involves periodically checking the reported financial position, investigating any worrying variances, projecting a year-end position and taking action.

Effective budget preparation leads to a greater understanding of service operation and costs, which can greatly assist in budgetary control. Similarly, good budgetary control involves analysis of actual spending and service operation, which in turn can improve the next cycle of plan and budget preparation.

For planning and budgeting to be effective these processes need to begin well before the start of the period covered by the plan. Early preparation means starting the process before the total available resource is known, so early drafts of the plan and budget may need to be revised several times in the lead up to the start of the new financial year. Final plan and budget approval tends to occur just before the start of a financial year after which attention turns to monthly performance monitoring, including budgetary control. Towards the end of the financial year and continuing into the early part of the following year attention turns to preparing final performance statements and annual accounts.

Budget preparation

Effective budget preparation results in budgets that are challenging yet sufficient to resource planned activity. A robust process and the active involvement of budget managers is essential to effective budget practice and should result in budgets that match planned activity and managers who understand how the budget has been calculated and are committed to staying within the agreed sum while achieving the plan. Where the preparation process is poor, agreed budgets may be too generous or insufficient, managers are unlikely to know how their budget is calculated and will probably suspect it is insufficient. Stress, delayed spending, game playing and low morale can be expected.

Ineffective budget preparation is caused by a number of factors including:

• Budget managers who not are involved in preparation.

• Little or no opportunity for budget managers to negotiate the plan and budget.

• Budgets being calculated by reference to historic spending levels rather than what is required.

• Percentage budget cuts or 'salami-slicing' as it tends to be known.

In practice, budget managers are often presented with a budget that has been calculated by someone else; in which case they have three options.

Option 1: Accept the budget figures given to them, which will probably have been calculated on a historic basis and possibly 'salami-sliced'.

Option 2: Check that the budget looks broadly reasonable given plan and budget performance so far this year and what they know about the service to be delivered next year.

Option 3: Calculate the budget they believe necessary to resource the plan, compare this with the budget provided and negotiate accordingly.

The first option is risky as provided budget figures may bear little relation to planned activity, and the third one can be time-consuming. In practice, a mix of options two and three should be adopted. For budgets that are unlikely to be affected by planned changes in the service or where changes are expected to be minor and well-understood option 2 is fine. Option 3 which involves building the budget from the plan should be used for more significant and complex changes or where a fundamental review is needed. Combining options 2 and 3 will work well providing that: the budget manager has reasonable knowledge of the existing service together with likely and planned changes, is willing to assert their right to have resources and planned activity that match, and is prepared to argue for greater resource, a reduction in the quantity and quality of planned activity or to change the way in which a service is resourced.

Budgets can either be prepared with regard to planned activity (rational) or by reference to budgets set, or actual income and expenditure, for previous years (historic or incremental).

Rational approaches

Rational approaches to budget preparation involve identifying the cost of resources needed to act in a planned way to achieve the set objectives and ultimately the purpose of the service. Policy-based budgeting, thematic, plan-led, needs-led and zero-based are all forms of rational budgeting, each of which should result in a budget that is sufficient to resource planned activity.

The financial calculations involved in rational budget preparation are typically straightforward, however estimating the volume of required physical resources can be challenging. Clarity about the purpose of the service, the objectives and actions required is essential and once these are identified the following five questions need to be addressed.

1. What types of physical resource are needed to act in the way we plan?

2. What minimum quantity of physical resources is required?

3. What is the minimum quality of physical resource needed?

4. What is the cheapest way of securing the required volume and quality of physical resources?

5. How much will these physical resources cost based on the answers to questions 1–4 above?

The quality of rational budgeting depends on the rigour of the whole process, in particular, the extent to which assumptions have been challenged and radical delivery options explored. As a consequence, rational approaches to budget preparation tend to be time consuming and expensive.

Incremental approach

Incremental or historic budgeting is a simple approach to budget preparation whereby the budget for next year is based on the budget relating to the current year.

In its more sophisticated form, the current budget is adjusted up or down to reflect the financial implications of anything which is likely to be different next year e.g. changes in planned service volume and quality, organisational structure, processes, inflation, etc.

In practice, many organisations, particularly in times of budget pressure, use a poor variant of incremental budgeting where appropriate downward adjustments to budgets are made but necessary upward adjustments are ignored or understated, resulting in a mismatch of plan and budgets. Where the mismatch is relatively minor, managers usually try to cope by improving economy and efficiency. However, if minor mismatches occur over a number of years, or there is a large mismatch in any one year, the scope for making sufficient improvement in economy and efficiency is very limited. The consequence of this is that the budget may become overspent, the quantity and quality of services fall and/or physical resources deteriorate through under-investment. With incremental budgeting, there is usually a lack of challenge with budgets evolving slowly over time and often lagging behind service development.

Up until the current recession, widespread use was made of incremental budgeting in public service organisations accompanied by the occasional use of rational approaches. Several years of financial restraint and significant resource cuts, together with a relatively bleak short-term outlook for government funding has changed this, forcing politicians and public service leaders to engage in more rational budgeting. Although uncomfortable in the decisions rational budgeting often brings this is an inherently transparent and honest approach.

Inflation

All budgets reflect two factors; the volume of physical resource to be purchased or sold and the cost or price per unit. An expenditure budget for gas, therefore, comprises a number of kWh to be purchased at a particular tariff or rate. At the point at which budgets are prepared the actual future price that will be paid per unit is difficult to estimate due to the effect of future inflation, something which can be accommodated by either:

- Setting budgets at prices that apply when the budget is prepared and updating the value of these as and when actual prices change; or

- Including within budgets an allowance for the anticipated impact of inflation between the date the budget is calculated and the end of the year to which it relates. This rate is normally provided by accountants to ensure consistency across budget managers.

In practice, the second approach is widespread with budget managers given an estimated allowance for inflation together with responsibility for handling the impact of any difference between estimated and actual inflation. The ability to predict inflation and honestly incorporate this in budgets is crucial as there is an attendant risk of under-inflating budgets which, unless the manager reduces the volume and or cost of purchases, will lead to overspending.

Example 1 – Gas budget on a rational basis and allowing for three per cent inflation

It is estimated that next year 215,000 KWh of gas will be needed to deliver a planned service, the price of which is 5p at the point the budget is prepared. The budget has to include an allowance for future inflation and the best estimate of this is three per cent for the period.

	£
Estimated consumption * current rate (215000*5p)	10,750
Inflation adjustment * £10,750 * 3%	322
	11,072

Whether in practice this budget proves to be sufficient will depend on whether the estimated volume of required gas proves accurate and whether future inflation is actually 3.0 per cent.

Example 2 – Postage budget on an incremental basis and allowing for 2.5 per cent inflation

Using the incremental basis, the budget for next year is based on the current year rather than on an estimate of how much postage is likely to be required. Assuming future inflation is likely an adjustment is required to re-price the current budget. The rate in this example is assumed to be 2.5 per cent. If the current postage budget is £800 re-pricing this for 2.5 per cent will result in a budget of:

	£
Current budget	800
Add effect of inflation 2.5%	20
	820

Whether in practice this budget proves to be sufficient depends on the current budget being adequate to meet the cost of current consumption, the volume of post-age remaining constant and actual inflation proving to be 2.5 per cent. As a budget manager, it is essential to know how inflation is treated and where budgets include an inflation allowance, the rate used. If the rate and/or the overall budget appear incorrect this should be challenged at the earliest opportunity.

Budgetary control

Budgetary control is the process by which managers check and respond to the evolv-ing position on actual income and expenditure budgets during the year. Effective budgetary control is an integral part of performance management, provides early warning of emerging underspends or overspends and helps budget managers spot opportunities as they arise and act if needed. Figure 8.2 shows budgetary control as a five-stage process.

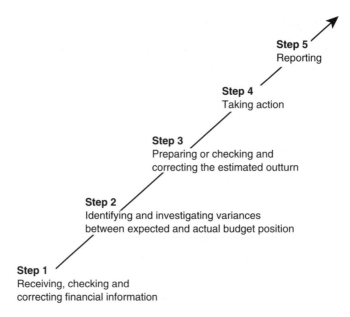

Figure 8.2 Five-stage budgetary control process

Knowledge of the budget profile or the rate at which income is expected to be earned or expenditure incurred over the budget period is crucial. While the amount spent might be constant over time it often varies according to one or more factors such as service demand, contract terms and conditions or weather, etc. Up-to-date information regarding actual income and expenditure is also vital. Where the accounting system only records expenditure at the point payments are made it will be necessary to manually take into account the value of orders placed in respect of which invoices have yet to be processed.

Once financial information has been received the manager should check and correct this for errors before identifying and investigating any variances they consider significant. The next step involves either preparing a projected year-end/project end budget position or checking and correcting year-end figures that have been generated elsewhere. This figure, which may be referred to as a year-end forecast, budget forecast or estimated outturn, relates to the key performance measure of keeping within the approved budget for the whole year or project. Many organisations require estimates of the likely year-end position for each budget at the end of each month, producing these either by:

- Scaling up actual income or expenditure at a particular point in the year or life of the project. If for example, postage spending three months into the year is reported at £1,000 the estimated outturn will be £4,000 (based on (1,000/3*12)). This approach however can be risky as it assumes that the rate of income and expenditure is the same each month, which is not the case for many budgets; or

- Combining current actual income or expenditure figures with estimates of how much is expected to be earned or spent over the rest of the project or financial year. So for the postage budget example it would be £1,000 actual spend for months one to three plus estimated postage spend for months four to twelve.

Irrespective of approach it is essential that the budget manager is involved in preparing or checking an estimated outturn.

The final steps in the budgetary control process are to take action and report performance as required. While budget responsibility normally rests with the manager it is likely that an accountant will be involved in providing financial information and offering technical advice. It is important that accountants do not become too involved; otherwise there is a blurring of accountability with a risk that managers disengage from the process. It should be noted that there are very few financial actions that can be taken to bring a budget under control – they are almost all managerial in nature.

Understanding budget reports

Budget information is central to the budgetary control process and tends to take the form of regular screen or hard copy statements that show the latest financial position based on transactions recorded by the main accounting system. While the exact layout of these reports varies (Case Study 8.1) they tend to include as a minimum:

- The budget for the project or year in question.

- The expected budget position at this point in the project or year (profile).

- Actual income and expenditure to date, the latter based on payments made or payments made plus outstanding orders for goods and services.

- The variance or difference between the expected budget position and actual income or expenditure.

- Estimated year-end position – either based on scaled up figures or a year/project end estimate.

EXAMPLE 8.1

Below is an example budget report prepared in respect of the period 1 April to 30 June. The budget relates to telephone expenditure and is profiled according to the predicted pattern of spend, which for the first three months is £300. The projected year-end figure is £1,300 based on the actual to date which has been scaled up for the full year.

Central services budget report 1 April to 30 June

Budget Detail	Annual Budget (£)	Budget to Date (£)	Actual to Date (£)	Variance (£)	Estimated Year-End (£)
Telephone	1200	300	325	25	1300

(Continued)

EXAMPLE *8.1* (CONT.)

This report shows that after three months the telephone budget is overspent by £25. By the end of the year, it is estimated that this overspend will have grown to £100 (£325*4). Investigation reveals that service activity is higher than planned and inflation is slightly higher than allowed for when the budget was set. There is nothing that can be done about inflation but perhaps call volume (numbers and/or length of calls) could be reduced and other actions considered such as transferring money in from another budget. It should be noted that the reported variance figure will only be true if the rate of spend should be constant throughout the year.

When interpreting financial information, it is essential the budget manager under-stands how:

- Each budget has been prepared, the volume of activity it relates to and how inflation is being treated.

- The profile has been calculated and whether this appears realistic.

- Actual income and expenditure are recorded – whether it is up to date or it is necessary to adjust for transactions that relate to the period covered by the report but which are not yet included in the figures.

- Favourable/unfavourable variances are shown which might include the use of minus signs, brackets or colour. There is no standard approach to how variances are shown so it is good practice to check understanding before interpreting.

- If an estimated outturn is included, this has been provided and calculated, and to have a view as to its accuracy.

REFLECTION POINT *8.1*

Budgeting is a significant management process, competence in which will be important to future organisational survival and leadership success. We end this chapter by asking you to answer nine key questions:

1. If you are a budget manager is your responsibility devolved or delegated?

2. With regard to budget management:

    a) What rights do you consider you have?

    b) To what extent are these met?

    c) What might you do to help your organisation meet these rights?

3. On what basis are your budgets prepared – rational or historic?

REFLECTION POINT **8.1** *(CONT.)*

4. Do you engage in budget preparation and negotiation either by:

   a) Checking provided figures to see if they are broadly reasonable given current budget performance, recalculating these where this is not the case? or

   b) Independently calculating the budget you need to resource planned activity?

5. Do you integrate your plan and budget?

6. Do you seek to negotiate your plan and budget at the same time?

7. Do you know how inflation is treated with regard to your budgets and do you consider this to be adequate?

8. Does your budgetary control practice appropriately match estimated and actual figures for the same period?

9. Do you either:

   a) prepare estimated outturns, or

   b) check and correct estimated outturns prepared by others?

Key learning points

- Plans and budgets must be integrated with a recognition by all stakeholders that a change in one will lead to a change in the other.

- Appropriate engagement by managers in budget management is essential and this starts with the planning process.

- In order to be effective, budget managers may need to assert their rights in order to discharge their responsibilities.

- Budgetary control is essential to performance management.

The next few years are likely to see significant development in public service organisations with knock-on implications for leadership and management. More sophisticated commissioning practices, significantly reduced agency resources, pooled budgets and greater use made of 'free' community assets can be expected. However, many of the principles and practices involved in effective planning and budgeting are likely to remain largely unchanged despite the very different context within which these will be practised. There is a need for continual review of what competence looks like, periodic self-assessment and planned development to ensure that leaders are equipped to meet this challenge and confident of their ability.

Chapter 9

Integration through effective change leadership

Catherine Driscoll

CHAPTER OUTCOMES

As a result of completing this chapter you will:

- Understand the value of leadership to successful integration and outcome delivery.

- Appreciate the growing importance of system leadership and how to apply these principles to health and social care integration.

- Understand the ingredients that are essential to leading change when pursuing integration in the context of whole systems leadership.

This chapter sets out the policy context for integration and whole systems leadership, outlines different types of integration and why effective change leadership is vital. Included is a case study illustrating how integration was approached in Bournemouth, Dorset and Poole from which key learning points are identified and tips for success offered.

Introduction

The current public sector context is challenging. Customer expectations are increasing whilst there are significantly reducing resources. In addition, the health and social care system is fragmented and complicated to navigate, which can lead to delay, duplication and people being lost within the system. Delivering integrated care has the potential to achieve person centred outcomes and promote people's interests by making sure that services are coordinated to meet their needs. It can also achieve more personal involvement of people using services, recognising their experience as crucial to achieving positive outcomes from their care and support. This is a significant leadership challenge particularly as the health and care landscape is complex and undergoing major change. This chapter explores this leadership challenge from a policy context and through the lens of a specific integration programme in Bournemouth, Dorset and Poole.

Health and care integration: the policy context

A consistent policy theme over the past 40 years has been a concern that welfare services could be improved if statutory agencies worked together more efficiently. In adult health and social care, a variety of strategies have been introduced to encourage or direct agencies to work together. The 1970s saw policymakers focus on developing mechanisms through which health and Local Authorities jointly planned services. In the 1990s attention focused on efforts to overcome the fragmented responsibilities for adult social care as well as initiatives, such as intermediate care services, conceived to improve the coordination of services to support people making the transition between acute, primary and social care services. The Health Act 1999 attempted to remove some of the obstacles to joint working, for example allowing statutory agencies to pool budgets and jointly commission services. This was followed by an agenda supporting greater structural integration of Local Authorities and primary care services, which included establishment of care trusts.

The Health and Social Care Act 2012 radically reformed the NHS, with the establishment of Clinical Commissioning Groups designed to ensure that commissioning was clinically led. The legislation also established health and wellbeing boards, hosted by Local Authorities, to bring together the NHS, public health, adult social care and children's services, including elected representatives and Local Healthwatch to act as system leaders to plan how best to meet the needs of their local population and tackle local inequalities in health. Public health responsibilities were transferred from the NHS to local government.

The NHS Five Year Forward View (5YFV), published in 2014, set out the challenges facing the health and care system over the next five years, characterised by three gaps which must be closed if the health and care system is to continue to meet the expectations of patients and the public in a sustainable way:

The health and wellbeing gap

If the nation fails to get serious about prevention and wellbeing then recent progress in healthy life expectancies will stall, health inequalities will widen, and our ability to fund beneficial new treatments will be crowded-out by the need to spend billions of pounds on wholly avoidable illness.

The care and quality gap

Unless we reshape care delivery, harness technology and drive down variations in quality and safety of care, then patients' changing needs will go unmet, people will be harmed who should have been cured and unacceptable variations in outcomes will persist.

The funding and efficiency gap

If we fail to match reasonable funding levels with wide-ranging and sometimes controversial system efficiencies, the result will be some combination of worse services, fewer staff, deficits and restrictions on new treatments.

But the Five Year Forward View also sets out a vision for how the health and care systems can rise to this challenge, through working differently with patients and the public; through a greater focus on health and prevention; working to clear national quality standards; and changing the way in which services are commissioned and delivered to patients. The scale of this challenge should not be underestimated, and in order to succeed, large parts of the health and care system will have to change the way in which they work.

What does integration mean in practice?

The increasing rhetoric around integration often fails to clarify the type or level of integration that is sought. This lack of clarity over definitions, and consequently the benefits expected to accrue, can create confusion and inertia. Table 9.1 provides definitions of the different types of integration.

This demonstrates how important it is to be crystal clear about the vision for future ways of achieving integration at the outset of discussions about making it real. Proposals stall if there is a misunderstanding of expectations. The leadership challenge is to create an environment where shaping the vision for integration is present and that sufficient attention is paid to this task.

Table 9.1 Types of integration

Horizontal	Bringing together organisations providing services at the same level e.g. merger of two acute hospitals
Vertical	Bringing together organisations providing services at different levels e.g. merger of primary and secondary care organisations
Virtual	Partnerships and networks between organisations
Real	Structural merger of organisations
Organisational	Organisations working together or joining e.g. mergers or networks
Clinical	Integrating care through coherent processes e.g. shared guidelines and protocols
Service	Integration of different services provided within one organisation e.g. multidisciplinary teams
Commissioner	Groups of commissioners coming together
Macro-level	Delivering integrated care to populations
Meso-level	Delivering integrated care to a particular population sub-group e.g. for a certain condition
Micro-level	Delivering integrated care to individuals

Leadership and management

Integration of health and social care is a key context for leadership and management within Local Authorities. The policy drive is clear at a strategic level as expressed by the Department of Health, however there is no clear blueprint for how to make integration work in practice. This then is the leadership challenge and is distinct from the management responsibility for implementing the vision which is just one aspect of how management and leadership is seen to differ. Bennis (2009), Ellis and Bach (2015) and many others offer distinctions between management and leadership which suggest that managers are typically seen as operational, attending to detail with a focus on short-term performance compared to leaders who are seen as more strategic, taking a longer term view with a focus on the horizon. Whereas managers tend to be concerned with planning and control – investing time and energy in structures, systems and frameworks, leaders, it is argued, rely on relationships and trust to co-ordinate and align staff. There is a view that managers essentially work within the culture, maintain the status quo and administer the business, whereas by contrast leaders create culture, challenge the status quo and think differently.

CEB: SHL Talent Management (2013), offer a leadership report based on the competencies incorporated in the well established Occupational Personality Questionnaire (OPQ 32). This leadership report sorts the competencies into those that are managerial or transactional in nature (analysing and interpreting, adapting and coping, supporting and cooperating, organising and executing) and those that are leading or transformational (creating and conceptualising, interacting and presenting, leading and deciding, enterprising and performing). As might be expected, individuals vary as to their individual mix and strength of competencies associated with leadership and management, with some people having more of a management focus, some more of a leadership focus and others a balanced mix of both.

Local Authority cultures are often focused on successful project management. This means being clear about aims and objectives, governance and reporting back to a board, all important management skills. However, this approach can be counter cultural to the type of messy and complex work involved in system leadership. In the context of making system changes across organisational boundaries and professional practice, leadership is required in order to imagine and shape a new way of working, inspire trust around the vision and build relationships to affect positive change, whilst ensuring that current services stay on track. To be effective, leadership will be a practice rather than limited to a specific position. In this context leadership is required to:

- **Develop a vision** – of the future, establishing direction and strategies for producing the changes to achieve the vision.

- **Align people** – communicating the direction through words and deeds to all those whose co-operation may be needed so as to influence the creation of teams and coalitions that understand the vision and strategies to achieve it.

- **Motivate and inspire** – energising people to overcome major political, bureaucratic and resource barriers to change by being both inspired and inspiring.

133

- **Produce change** – often to a dramatic degree and having the potential to produce transformational change.

- **Be resilient** – leaders need to find creative ways of managing the emotional impact of constant change.

Importance and key characteristics of effective system leadership for integrated care

This section highlights a number of the factors that contribute to a complex and challenging environment, within which a model of integration needs to be shaped. The planning guidance and associated requirements present three major challenges for leaders in the NHS and Local Authorities. The first is the sheer size and complexity of the agenda they are faced with in achieving sustainability and delivering transformation within the timescales set out. Every organisation will need to be clear on the priorities it is pursuing, and national bodies must lend their support by recognising that not everything can be delivered. Now more than ever, honesty and realism are needed at all levels about what really matters when the health and care system increasingly appears to be on a war footing.

The second challenge is for organisational leaders to engage and support staff to lead work on sustainability and transformation with a focus on improving value for residents and not crude cost-cutting. There are many opportunities to deliver better outcomes at lower cost with a particular focus on changes in practice. Framing the sustainability challenge in this way is critically important if staff are to engage in the work that now needs to be done with the support of experienced managers. A vision that focuses on cost-cutting will not be inspiring, whereas one that is about delivering better outcomes for people can be.

The third challenge is for organisational leaders to work together in place-based systems of care. This is essential in the preparation and implementation of sustainability and transformation plans and in ensuring the resources are used to deliver improvements in health and care for the populations covered by these plans. Work under way in the new care models programme is showing what system leadership means and is also illustrating the challenges facing experienced organisational leaders in collaborating with their peers. National bodies need to support system leadership at a local level by themselves acting collaboratively in their interactions with providers, partners and commissioners.

System leadership will be absolutely crucial in delivering required changes. This means:

- Taking a wider role in the local health and care system and accepting shared responsibility for the sustainability of the local health and care economy.

- Promoting collective leadership within and between organisations, creating a culture of collaborative working across the partnership.

- Shifting from a hierarchical focus ('looking upwards') to a place-based one ('looking outwards').

- Agreeing shared metrics of success with local partners, against which leaders can hold each other mutually accountable.

- Taking a role in public health, prevention and wellbeing.

- Fostering relationships with local partners that are capable of sustaining collaboration alongside competition.

The 2014 BBC Reith lecturer, Atul Gawande argued that we are living in the 'century of the system' (Gawande, 2014). By this he means that individuals and organisations cannot solve the problems facing today's society on their own. Instead, we must design new ways in which individuals can work together in teams and across systems to make the best use of collective skills and knowledge. Although this adds complexity it is crucial for a chance of success.

Systems leadership: local vision – Bournemouth, Dorset and Poole

Systems Leadership: Local Vision was developed by the Systems Leadership Steering Group, a consortium of local and national government, NHS, social care, public health, voluntary sector and private sector members who support the development of systems leadership in UK public services. It was designed to promote and facilitate radically different ways of leading transformation in public service to address complex social issues. Its core aim was to develop shared leadership capability to generate solutions to 'wicked' issues that cannot be solved by one organisation or sector alone.

The Better Together partnership in Bournemouth, Dorset and Poole was selected as one of the first cohort of 25 localities in 2013. This partnership consisted of eight organisations (one Clinical Commissioning Group (CCG), three Acute Hospital Trusts, one Community Services Trust and three Local Authorities) which had successfully bid for Department for Communities and Local Government (DCLG) transformation challenge funding to develop and implement integrated health and social care across the patch. The CCG and three Local Authorities also committed resources to fund the programme. It was a complex, high level strategic initiative that involved bringing a diverse group of organisational leaders together, many of whom were competitors in other areas of funding and provision.

Part of being a Local Vision programme involved facilitation by a skilled and experienced enabler. This person worked with local senior leaders to scope the vision for the programme and create a space where relationships could develop. This was particularly helpful in facilitating an agreed vision and strategic approach which would need to hold strong in the face of other elements of competition and challenge. From this work four principles were developed that all eight organisations were happy to commit to as the foundation on which to build the detailed programme:

- People first, agency second.

- Focus on quality.

- Built to last.

- Best use of the public pound.

The evaluation of the Local Vision programme included a case vignette of the Bournemouth, Dorset and Poole partnership and this is included here:

CASE STUDY 9.1

Bournemouth, Dorset and Poole

In Bournemouth, Dorset and Poole, Local Vision was used to support a number of large strategic projects around the integration of health and social care across three local authorities, including the Transformation Challenge Fund and Better Care Fund. Local Vision offered an alternative platform for engaging partners and, in particular, developing a sense of shared purpose and leadership.

Local Vision funding of £27k was agreed in November 2013 through to spring of 2014 to address group leadership development and to support tackling of the challenges the newly formed partnership was facing. Local Vision, despite representing a very small proportion of the total funding available to the partnership, occurred at a timely moment, just as eight CEOs had arrived together in the room with a highly challenging agenda and the appointment of a skilled systems leader as Programme Director.

The memorandum of understanding (MOU) agreed for Local Vision stipulated that systems leadership would be demonstrated through the ability of the Sponsor Board to 'make high level decisions with respect to the vision, the guiding principles, ensuring operational activity and with demonstrable behaviours to support the core values or openness, honesty, ability to listen, empathise and ability to think and express differently, build authentic relationships and form guiding coalitions'.

The MOU further articulated that the sponsor group will make change happen through strategic decision-making, removing barriers to change and focusing on key outcomes including ownership of agreed principles and ways of working, together with political engagement and ownership of the transformation work, shared resources and greater coordination.

The package of support from Local Vision included one-to-one coaching for partner members, as well as cross partnership activity to develop new styles and ways of working in business meetings. The linkage with the King's Fund was also recognised as useful in coordinating a shared policy direction with the involvement of Acute Hospital leaders.

'We've done more in the last six months than in six years! All of the changes going on are about bringing systems together. We've succeeded in bringing in cash. Locality teams are moving into place and we are pulling together IT through Dorset Digital. It's a glass

half full. How many of us could have named each other round the table and have a discussion rather than a row in picking up the phone?! You're either in for the long haul or the short wins. It has built some pretty good foundations in moving forward.'

"The partnership was successful with the highest allocation of £750k and then levered in matched funding of £1m for commissioners to oversee the Better Together Programme. The Better Care Fund came along and in one way it was a help, but in other ways it constrained. In total though, the partnership achieved a pooled budget of £60m. There were 4 areas that got pooled budgets including Manchester. We came in the next tranche. From a leadership point of view, the question is what do we want to achieve together? Our partner principles are agreed: its customer before agency! It's easy to say and difficult to do. As a Chief Operating Officer with accountabilities that's a real tension. But it has allowed us to move forward and do some difficult things. The Leadership aspect (Local Vision) has been one of the most important strands."

Source: Bolden, R., Gulati, A., Ahmad, Y., Burgoyne, J., Chapman, N., Edwards, G., Green, E., Owen, D., Smith, I. and Spirit, M. (2015) The Difference that Makes the Difference – Final evaluation of the first place-based programmes for Systems Leadership: Local Vision. Project Report. University of the West of England, Bristol. Available from: http://eprints.uwe.ac.uk/27932

Reproduced with permission from the Leadership Centre and Systems Leadership Alliance

The Better Together programme consisted of eight agreed workstreams which flowed from the agreed principles:

- **Early help** – focusing on preventing, reducing and delaying the need for intensive support from both health and social care services, harnessing the vital role that the voluntary and community sector has in this.

- **Integrated locality teams** – bringing health and social care staff together around 13 GP localities to integrate care for individuals. Including a skills development programme and key features for the way the teams would operate.

- **Joint commissioning** – agreeing joint investment plans for services to deliver better outcomes for residents, increasing the use of evidence to inform these decisions.

- **Carers** – integrating support for carers to enable them to continue in their caring role.

- **Tricuro** – establishing the first tri-Council Local Authority Trading Company for adult social care provider services.

- **Dorset Care Record** – common system to enable shared access to patient data.

- **Information sharing** – integrated approach to allow data sharing across organisations to improve timely access to patient information.

- **Workforce** – joint approach to workforce planning, training and development support to work in integrated settings.

During the operation of the programme the system conditions changed within which the partnership was operating. The CCG launched a Clinical Services Review of the hospital and community system; the Department of Health launched the Better Care Fund nationally; the financial context worsened and rates of emergency hospital admissions increased significantly with a consequent impact on delayed transfers of care. These factors individually and collectively had the potential to undermine the Better Together programme and there was certainly some evidence of attention being focused into these competing priorities. However, the health and care integration landscape is complex and ambiguous, so it would be naïve to assume that the programme would follow a linear process towards integration. With competing priorities, changing national expectations, shortage of resource and very different organisational cultures, there will inevitably be challenges. The strength of the Better Together programme was evidenced by the very fact that the relationships between partners held up through this difficult environment:

We've reflected on how important the relationships are and this makes a difference at every level and are the key to success.

(quote from a Better Together programme partner)

The Better Together programme came to its planned end on 31st March 2016. The system leaders discussed the outcomes from the programme locally and identified significant achievements in the specific workstreams, for example:

Our integrated locality teams are an outcome of (the programme). There are now 13 localities engaged in new discussions and good work around health and social care. Ground work, shared vision and relationships are key. Now we have coordinators to deal with admissions and readmissions and if proven, they will continue. It's all a build, a layering thing.

(quote from a Better Together programme partner)

Part of the local evaluation was to ensure that the workstreams were either appropriately closed down as they moved from development to business as usual, as well as identifying the outcomes that had been delivered, and areas where progress had not been as much as had been anticipated at the start of the programme. This discussion highlighted the value that senior leaders placed on the Better Together sponsor board as a unique place where they came together across the system, including both commissioners and providers, to set the direction for the future of integrated services. Consequently, the partners agreed to continue to meet as a Systems Leadership Group to fulfil this role on an ongoing basis, building on the shared vision, agreed principles and relationships in order to navigate a way through the continued complexity of the health and care environment. This group will provide leadership for overseeing integration, changing acute and community service structures and development of the sustainability and transformation plan required by the Department of Health as the blueprint for future service design. In this respect Bournemouth, Dorset and Poole are in a stronger position than many other health and care systems nationally because the commitment to joint working has already been established through the Better Together programme, and relationships have withstood the pressure of external events and challenges. However, the leadership challenge continues and requires sustained time, attention and commitment in order for its potential to be realised.

Leading change

This chapter has identified the policy context for health and social care integration, has talked about leadership characteristics and the challenges for system leadership. It has then described the Better Together case study as a real example of approaching change in a complex environment and the factors that had an impact on outcomes from the programme. One of the leadership approaches that the programme used was public narrative as a technique to support change and create social movement. A social movement emerges when individuals assert new public values, form relationships rooted in those values and mobilise to translate values into action. This approach which was developed by Marshall Ganz of Harvard University (Ganz, 2008), describes leadership as accepting responsibility to enable others to achieve a shared purpose in the face of uncertainty, accepting responsibility for the whole system not just for their individual part of it. Leadership in social movements is required at all levels and not confined to the stereotypical heroic leader at the top of an organisation. Public narrative is described as a leadership art that draws on the power of storytelling to motivate others to join in taking action. Leadership requires both strategic and motivational skills. Strategy is focused on how to turn resources into the power needed to achieve goals. Motivation focuses on asking why the goals matter enough to find the courage to act despite uncertainty and to inspire others to act as well. Effective leadership engages the head – the strategy – and the heart – the narrative – to engage the hands – the action (as captured in Figure 9.1). Public narrative is the why – the art of translating values into action through stories.

Public narrative is a leadership skill and provides a way of motivating people to join in action. It can be used by presenting the case for change to engage the head as well as engaging heart and hands by weaving a story of self to reveal why we are motivated to take action, a story of us to hold up the values that are jointly shared and a story of now calling on people to join in taking action. The narrative structure is to describe the challenge, to set out the outcome hoped for and to be clear about the choice to make the change.

These techniques can be very powerful in sharing a clear vision that has a value base, motivating others to feel inspired by and share in the vision and calling people to translate the vision into reality. This disperses the leadership effort to all those working to achieve change and helps to build strong relationships grounded in shared values.

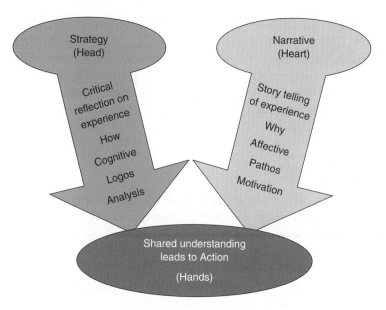

Figure 9.1 Mobilisation of others (Ganz, 2008)

As part of the Better Together programme, public narrative was employed as one of the techniques to engage people at all levels throughout the partnership. It allowed leaders to share their value base and experience of where a lack of integration had failed people who needed high quality care and support, to highlight the current challenges faced by people on a daily basis and using this motivation to engage staff to make a difference. It was helpful in building commitment to change, even when that change was challenging for individual services or organisations.

Public narrative enabled leaders to inspire people to commit to the principles of integration through engaging at a values level. However, the direct experience of service users, patients and carers was pivotal in making the case for change. This started with the first of the four principles – people before agency – that grounded the programme in what was right for people needing health and care services, rather than what was best for individual organisations. This work drew upon a national programme that had worked intensively with people to identify what was important to them in receiving services. This was National Voices (2013) a Department of Health piece of work that had developed a number of 'I statements' that mattered to patients and service users.

These statements were tested out with local patients, service users and Voluntary and Community Sector (VCS) organisations and garnered general support and approval. They were so reasonable that these became the heart of the vision for the integration programme and were consistently referenced during the work, particularly when progress became challenging. Video clips of people sharing their local experience were consistently used to keep the vision clear.

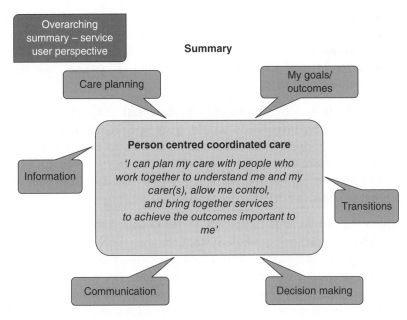

Figure 9.2 'I' statements summary

Learning points from the Better Together Programme

There were a number of factors that contributed to the programme having a chance of success. These included practical factors such as allocating appropriate resource, recruiting an experienced and skilful programme director and establishing robust programme governance structures. These are important managerial tasks that ensured action could be scoped, implemented and problems escalated for resolution.

Leadership commitment was crucial, spending time understanding individual motivation, working through the principles and vision for the programme and building trust and relationships. This started with the most senior leaders across the system in order to provide legitimacy and mandate for the work. The time that this relationship and vision work took, should not be underestimated, even though there will inevitably be temptation to shortcut this work and move to delivery instead. Without sufficient personal connection, delivery would stall once complex challenges arose. Relationships need to be sufficiently secure to enable them to survive challenge, conflict and changing context. They also need to be continually nurtured and developed to maintain them.

Managerial and leadership focus will only deliver better outcomes if the vision is sufficiently compelling and rooted in what matters to people who use services. When established systems like health and care are challenged to change, there is inevitably a defence reaction in order to maintain the status quo. This is grounded in organisational and professional power and control systems, so there must be a very strong motivation in order to overcome this resistance. Approaches to change are based on either commitment or compliance. Successful change happens through commitment to a powerful and compelling vision and then compliance follows.

It was also helpful to focus on engaging frontline staff and community representatives in exploring how integration would work in practice. Meaningful change in practice can only happen from the ground and time to carry out this work was important. It is important that the development work with staff is congruent with the vision agreed by system leaders and that there is time to engage with staff values and beliefs in order to improve outcomes for residents.

Complexity in the system adds complexity to the change and this is exacerbated by multiple partners. In delivering whole system change, there is a tendency to move at the pace of the slowest partner or to allow one partner to have a veto on change if they are not prepared to move. There is a judgement call to be made about when partial progress is preferable to no progress at all, or when consensus can be reached with sufficient time to work through the issues and interests at play. This leads into a focus on making sure that the principles agreed by all partners at the outset are being demonstrated in reality, and that individuals are prepared to hold each other to account when these principles are not being lived. This will only work effectively when there are developed relationships and trust that all partners are signed up to the vision.

It can be challenging to ensure there is a clear and robust connection between the change principles and vision and the work programmes that are designed to make the vision a reality. Making the whole system work in a person centred, outcome focused way can mean different things to different partners. Using data and shared metrics to inform the progress being made will be crucial to maintain commitment. This is a continued challenge in order to understand the levers for change and where it is important to focus most effort.

Top tips for leading change for integration

- Agree and explore shared values – without these there is no chance of success.

- Vision – shape and share a clear and compelling vision and keep on sharing it to ground the change.

- Build relationships and trust – this will take time and will require each partner to relinquish power on occasions. Make sure it is not always the same partner who has to compromise as this will erode trust over time.

- Motivate service users, patients, community to push for integration – create a social movement that engages leaders throughout the system.

- Work with a coalition of the willing – some partners will be more open to change than others so start with these.

- Focus on front line workers, as well as senior leaders.

- Remove the organisational barriers to integration at frontline – trust staff to do the right things for people.

- Financial incentives/disincentives inhibit progress, so pay attention to these issues.

- Invest in workforce, training, what works to shape the culture.

- Keep going back to the reason for doing the work – be clear about the case for change and why the status quo is not serving people well.

- Start and keep on going!

Key learning points

- Systems leadership and integration are crucial to meeting the challenges facing health and social care.

- The scale and nature of the change involved in moving to a whole system integrated approach to public service requires effective leadership.

- Agreed principles and a compelling vision are essential to change leadership.

- Effective personal relationships and trust are key – they have to be developed and nurtured over time.

Chapter 10

Impact evaluation of leadership programmes

Emily Rosenorn-Lanng and Keith Brown

CHAPTER OUTCOMES

As a result of completing this chapter you will:

- Understand why and how impact should be measured.
- Understand the different types of measures that can be used to assess impact.
- Be able to develop an evaluation framework including a logic model methodology.
- Be able to interpret and assess the impact of programmes within leadership and management.

Introduction

This chapter is intended to help leaders and managers develop awareness of the importance of impact evaluation, the key processes and considerations to be thought about before starting to evaluate. As with other aspects of management, such as budgeting, employment law and contracting there is a limit as to how much specialist expertise a general manager can be expected to possess. Therefore, it is likely that at some point the manager will need to talk to colleagues who possess expertise in data gathering, analysis, question phrasing, etc.

This chapter explores impact evaluation of leadership and management development programmes, exploring varying methodological approaches to support the development of a robust framework within which impact can be accurately assessed. Evaluation can be defined as:

> *The assessment of ... effectiveness and efficiency during and after implementation. It seeks to measure outcomes and impacts in order to assess whether the anticipated benefits have been realised.*

> (HM Treasury, 2011: 14)

Although a considerable number of organisations do evaluate leadership programmes, the approach tends to be limited to what participants thought of the event and possibly what they learnt against predetermined learning outcomes. Often incidental, short-term impacts will be discovered, all of which whilst helpful, fall short of an impact evaluation.

Impact evaluations can be defined as being:

> *Evaluations that assess the contribution of an intervention towards some outcome or goal. The contribution may be intended or unintended, positive or negative, long term or short term. Impact evaluations attempt to identify a clear link between causes and effects, and explain how the intervention worked, and for whom.*

> (CDI, Centre for Development Impact, 2016)

Consistent with this definition we see impact evaluation as being much wider than traditional evaluation with the focus on desired outcomes for a range of stakeholders, in particular patients, service users, carers, etc. With this approach, assessing whether learning outcomes have been met is only part of the story, at best a step towards the wider outcomes – the ones that really matter.

A key area of evaluation, therefore, is to ensure that a measure of impact is captured and not solely the individual's experience of the intervention. Although often over-looked, evaluating the impact and effectiveness of any professional development or intervention is essential to support the development of robust programmes and frameworks, ensuring that both individual and organisational objectives can be met (Carpenter, 2011).

An evaluation must, therefore, consider two key aspects:

- Assessing whether the development has supported effective change, which is key to improving professional practice.

- Within a sector of limited and finite resources, assessing if there is an effective return, both in respect to time and financial input.

Why evaluate?

When considering the time and resources invested in leadership and management programmes the reasons to evaluate are numerous, including:

- Establishing whether the intended benefits have materialised and if so to what extent.

- Identifying and assessing unintended impact.

- Learning about what worked, why and what you would do next time.

- Identifying as appropriate the return on investment.

There is, of course, a cost implication of undertaking programme evaluation and this cost is frequently cited as the primary motivation for not accessing impact; however, this logic has an obvious flaw. Yes, it is possible that by not undertaking an evaluation, the programme may be available to a marginally larger population, but the question remains as to whether there has been an adequate return on investment. This can only be established if we understand whether the programme is having the required impact on those who undertake it, and beyond.

To be able to say a programme provides a good return on investment, the following questions need to be answered:

• Has the learning become embedded and is it relevant?

• Has the programme had a long-term impact on an individuals practice?

• What is the nature of the impact and does it effectively align with the strategic aims and organisational culture?

• What is the impact of the programme on others (service users/clients/team)?

Research shows that whilst significant investments are made in continuing professional development (CPD), evaluations of the impact of these programmes are rare (Brown et al, 2008, Draper and Clark, 2007), and therefore it is rare that the above questions are addressed. Evaluating impact is about more than considering an individual programme, it is a cultural shift. Evaluation is an important component of organisational learning (Hafford-Letchfield, 2007), providing an evidence base for future programmes and ensuring that programmes continue to be improved to meet expectations and organisational requirements.

Evaluation provides real evidence that a programme has or has not achieved the intended learning. Further to this, the information collected can be useful for internal and external audit, and inspections from regulatory bodies such as Ofsted and the CQC. Tight budgets and limited organisational resources mean that CPD programmes must 'prove' their value. Those unable to do so will be increasingly vulnerable (CIPD, 2010).

A well-designed impact evaluation may capture additional and unanticipated benefits such as the transferability of the learning to an alternative professional context or the dissemination of the learning to a wider team or organisational culture. The key to a well-designed evaluation is to ensure it is truly embedded in the programme design, this means it runs concurrently with the programme, having full engagement from participants and developed to align with course and strategic aims. This can also mean using outputs from the learning to assess the level to which it has become embedded. Assessment tasks become essential for this purpose and a well-designed assessment task will not only help learning become embedded but will also provide an opportunity for the learning to be applied directly to practice, supporting the long-term integration of learning into the wider organisational context.

What is impact?

As defined earlier, impact is a wider concept than the evaluation of professional development and occurs when the learning is applied and contributes to enhancing

Table 10.1 Five levels of impact evaluation (Holroyd and Brown, 2014)

Levels	Focus	Questions
Level 1	Learners' reaction to development	What did the student think about the training?
Level 2	Learning attained	Did the student learn what was intended? Did they demonstrate newly acquired skills?
Level 3	Behavioural change at work	Did the learning transfer to the job?
Level 4	Impact on team, departmental, organisational level	Has the training helped organisational performance?
Level 5	Impact on users and careers	Has the development improved services, and is there any evidence?

performance to make a beneficial difference to practice. Therefore, impact should be assessed not only in relation to programmes of professional development but also where, for example, new models of working, organisation change or restructuring have been employed, to ensure the desired outcomes are effectively being met.

Examples of impact include:

- Improvement in performance (individual, team or organisational).

- Identifiable outcome benefits for others (service users/clients/patients/colleagues/ team).

- Quantifiable return on investment.

- Key performance indicators that have been met or improved.

- Long-term behavioural change.

Holroyd and Brown (2014) argue that Kirkpatrick's (1959) model, which is frequently utilised to assess programmes, may not provide an adequate strategic framework to truly assess the impact of a programme, and that a five-level model may offer a more robust and comprehensive understanding of impact.

Evaluations frequently address levels 1 and 2 of the above model, but this is arguably not an assessment of the impact of the programme but rather the participant experience of the programme. For the impact of a programme to be assessed; levels 3, 4 and 5 must be considered, as it is in these areas where it is possible to explore the true impact of the learning in practice.

How to evaluate impact?

It is clear that all programmes should be evaluated for impact; and therefore, this leads to the question as to how programmes can be evaluated to provide a robust, balanced reflection of impact most effectively. Generally, when evaluating there is a choice to be made as to whether to adopt a data-driven analytical approach or to use an evaluation framework. This chapter focuses on impact evaluation of leadership programmes that is designed not just to understand what has changed but why, how and who has been affected. In this context, an evaluation framework would normally be the best way forward and forms the basis of the rest of the chapter.

An evaluation framework, as the name suggests, is an overarching approach to undertaking an impact evaluation. Included within this framework is a model that drives the approach, an evaluability assessment, research design and a methodological approach.

The evaluation of impact is a development process, which starts with understanding the research question in more detail. The broad question asked in reference to programme impact evaluations would be, 'has the programme positively impacted on practice?' This initially seems like a relatively simple question to answer, although answering this leads naturally to further questions as to how it has been impacted, to what extent and how does this align with strategic priorities.

As public sector resources are limited, programmes are often delivered to meet or address a specific service need or requirement. It therefore follows that, to ensure these limited resources are providing an effective return on investment; any evaluation should assess the programme with particular reference to the particular need or requirement.

Evaluation framework and evaluability assessment

In order to identify how to evaluate a specific programme; it is first necessary to create or identify a framework by which the programme can be assessed and its impacts captured.

The framework is dependent on a variety of factors including the following:

- Strategic outcomes and priorities.
- The intended learning outcomes.
- Course design/activities.

An evaluation cannot successfully occur in isolation and requires engagement with a variety of stakeholders to ensure all factors are adequately addressed. This includes understanding that the specific strategic outcomes and priorities can occur at multiple service levels and ensure all stakeholders are engaged in identifying the priorities specific to the evaluation. This is essential to ensure that the impact measured is consistent with the intended outcomes. In addition, a detailed understanding of the programme/intervention is required and consideration given as to how the intended learning outcomes align with the aforementioned strategic priorities. If the two do not align, questions are raised as to whether there would be a reasonable expectation that the programme or intervention would impact on that stated outcome or priority.

Having a comprehensive understanding of programme design and activities will influence the operational methodology of an impact evaluation and significantly aid the analysis and interpretation of the data. The level and detail of understanding, however, is a complex issue, as it is necessary to understand the context of a programme, whilst retaining an unbiased view, in order to provide a balanced overview of the programme or intervention.

Impact evaluations should normally be undertaken by someone external to the programme design team. Internal evaluations should be undertaken cautiously, if at all. Typically, these consist of 'happy sheets' relating to the course facilitation, resources provided and individual experience of the intervention. Essentially these gather data that can, using Kirkpatrick's model as adapted by Holroyd and Brown (2014), be used to assess the learners' reaction to development. Very little else can be drawn from these sheets and as they are often handled and processed by the programme or project leads, this raises questions about the independent nature of the conclusions drawn from the data obtained.

When adequate information is gained in each of these areas, a logic model can be created to underpin the research and create a theoretical framework in which the programme can be assessed. Frameworks allow a greater sense of balance than a data-driven analysis, allowing a greater sense of parity between all measures. Logic-driven impact evaluation is a developmental tool in and of itself; in addition to highlighting areas in which the desired impact has been achieved this approach may yield constructive information as to how a programme can be developed and improved to meet the desired outcomes.

Developing an evaluation framework

Central to an effective evaluation framework is a model. One which is popular and relatively easy to use is the logic model, which the following section explores in some detail.

Prior to developing a framework, however, it is necessary to consider the context of the evaluation, considering whether it relates to a new development programme, an existing programme or a pilot programme. This will influence the questions underpinning the model as shown in Table 10.2.

Logic models

When considering which approach to undertake, it must first be decided whether the evaluation is going to be driven by inputs, for example, the intended learning outcomes of the programme or long terms outcomes, such as the strategic priorities identified. This section will consider three approaches to building a logic model; a theory approach, activities approach and an outcome approach.

It will also consider how an Evaluability Assessment can be employed throughout the evaluation period to ensure the process is both practical and remains consistent with the overarching aims of the programme.

Table 10.2 Focusing an impact evaluation

New Programmes	• What characteristics of the programme implementation process facilitated or hindered programme goals?
	• Which initial strategies or activities of the programme are being implemented?
	• How can those strategies or activities not successfully implemented be modified or adapted to the realities of the programme?
	• Is the programme reaching its intended audience?
	• What lessons have been learnt about the initial planned programme design? How should these lessons be utilised in continually revising the original programme plan? Do any changes in programme design reflect these lessons or other unrelated factors (e.g., personalities, organisational dynamics, etc.)?
	• How can we better connect programme design changes to documented implementation lessons?
Established Programmes	• Which programme operations work? Which aren't working? Why or why not?
	• What programme settings (facilities, scheduling of events, location, group size, transportation arrangements, etc.) appear to be most appropriate and useful for meeting the needs of clients?
	• What strategies have been successful in encouraging client participation and involvement? Which have been unsuccessful?
	• How do the different programme components interact and fit together to form a coherent whole? Which components are the most important to programme success?
	• How effective is the organisational structure in supporting programme implementation? What changes need to be made?
Piloting Future Programmes	• What is unique about this programme?
	• What programme strengths can we build upon to meet unmet needs?
	• Where are the gaps in programme activities? How can the programme be modified or expanded to meet still unmet needs?
	• Can the programme be effectively replicated? What are the critical implementation elements? How might contextual factors impact replication?

Adapted from W.K. Kellogg Foundation (2004)[1]

Creating a logic model

A logical model is a systematic, visual representation of the theory, assumptions and evidence underlying the rationale. This model communicates the interactions and intended relationships between a programme design and its intended outcomes. There are a number of suggested formats for logic models including the Kellogg Foundation model (2004) and the Local Government Association model (2015).

Two differences across such models are the extent to which the impact is looked at in terms of breadth and time period covered.

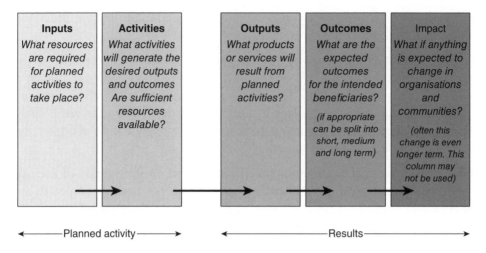

Figure 10.1 Example logic model

Some models have a narrow focus, aiming to assess impact on the intended direct beneficiaries, for example, staff attending learning programmes. Others look beyond this to other stakeholders which for learning programmes might be service users, organisations, partner agencies, the wider community, etc.

Some models focus on impact at a single point (often short term) while others help assess the nature, extent and permanence of impact over time.

Depending on context, preference and the need to be proportionate the approach used might, therefore, be limited to only reporting impact on direct intended beneficiaries at one point in time. A more sophisticated approach could include measurement of short, medium and long-term outcomes together with wider impact. Figure 10.1 illustrates a mid-complexity approach.

Table 10.3 illustrates a logic model for a learning programme with three timeframes for outcomes, but no impact column. However, in this case this is not needed as the

Table 10.3 Key components of a logic model for a learning programme

Key Components		
Resources/ Inputs	The resources required or available for implementing the programme, this could include any training, financial implications or staff time.	
Activities	The programme design, resources, and processes which are intended to create the impact on practice.	
Outputs	The direct products of a programme, this may include the completion of assessment related tasks and/or KPI and audits.	
Outcomes:	**Short term**	Changes in knowledge, skills or attributes
	Medium term	Changes in professional behaviour
	Long term	Changes in direct practice/ culture / service improvement

151

long term outcome measure is also wider in breadth and fulfils the purpose of what some researchers would classify as impact.

The Kellogg foundation suggests three possible approaches to developing a logic model; theory approach, activities approach and outcomes approach, which are explored in more depth in Table 10.4. There is no one right approach to developing a logic model and the way in which it is undertaken depends on the wider contextual issues relating to the programme. Logic models are rarely static and often require redefining as strategic needs change and develop.

Choosing the most appropriate approach will depend on the context of each specific impact evaluation. If a programme or intervention has been developed to meet the criteria of a specific framework, such as the National Competency Framework for Safeguarding Adults, using this to underpin a theoretical approach would be appropriate if your priority is to verify that this framework has been addressed. However, if there is a pre-existing programme or intervention and this theoretical underpinning is not forthcoming, an activities approach may be more appropriate. Similarly, if the scope of the research is to assess how the current provision of programmes aligns with strategic priorities then an outcomes approach may be more appropriate.

Table 10.4 Approaches to developing a logic model

Theory Approach	This approach starts with the thinking that underpinned the original design of an existing programme or is informing the design of a new programme.
	In practical terms, this means it is underpinned by a theory of change which may be based on pre-existing national frameworks or national guidance.
	Sadly, it may be the case that there is no articulated theory of change which makes this approach inappropriate unless through carefully guided conversations the theory can be teased out from the programme designers. If not, an activities approach should be considered.
Activities Approach	This approach uses 'forward logic', taking input and activities involved in the process and mapping them to outcomes. Users are encouraged to focus on the implications of each stage of the process and its impact on the next.
	In practical terms, this is perhaps most helpful when there is a pre-existing programme in place as it involves mapping from the programme specification and design to the possible impacts. In effect, the theory of change is built as a result of the mapping.
Outcomes Approach	This is a 'reverse logic' model, focusing on outcomes first and working backwards.
	In practical terms, this would involve mapping the greater strategic priorities, over the long, medium and short term, against the inputs, activities and outputs. Seeking to answer the question as to how the outcomes can be achieved in relation to the inputs.
	This is particularly helpful when designing a new programme having been tasked with achieving outcomes.

Evaluability assessment

An evaluability assessment examines the extent to which a programme can be evaluated in a reliable and credible fashion. The assessment calls for the early review of a proposed programme in order to ascertain whether its objectives are adequately defined and its results verifiable.

The overall aim of an evaluability assessment is to decide whether an evaluation is worthwhile in terms of its likely benefits, consequences and costs. Also, the purpose is to decide whether a programme needs to be modified, whether it should go ahead or be stopped.

The evaluability assessment should be undertaken early in the programme cycle – when the programme is being designed but has not yet become operational, and when something can be done to remedy any weaknesses.

An evaluability assessment includes but is not limited to the following:

- Review of programme documentation.
- Discussion with the main stakeholders.
- Analysis of the programme.

Research design and methodological approach

Once there is a framework in place for an evaluation, consideration can then be given to the research design. The process of developing a logic model starts to addresses key questions such as what should be measured and can offer a significant amount of guidance in respect to choosing indicators. Answers to these questions are finalised during research design.

What to measure

This is key information you will need in order to understand and measure impact; this could be underpinned by a theoretical framework, the intended learning outcome of the programme or wider strategic aims. It is important that some consideration is given to how different aims or approaches interact; it would be unjust to evaluate the impact of a programme against strategic aims if the course was designed or commissioned in isolation of these aims. Discovering this might, however, be key learning. A programme or intervention should be assessed fairly and, therefore, there should be a reasonable expectation of some measure of impact or inter-relatedness between the impacts being measured and the specific course or programme.

Choosing indicators

Once the decision has been made as to what to measure, consideration must be given to how to measure these essentially abstract concepts, such as self-awareness or confidence, and the level of impact expected, such as individual, team or organisational.

For example, if organisational impact is the focus of the evaluation we must ensure our indicators allow us to capture this in respect to the organisation as a whole and not just the impact of the programme on the individual undertaking the programme.

Identifying the indicators can also be revealing if undertaken early in programme development. If the intended learning outcomes do not align with the intended impacts, this can be identified early in the process and addressed.

Effective indicator selection is essential in guiding how to measure impact and how to analyse outputs.

How to measure

How to measure impact is substantively dependent on what we are looking to measure and the indicators selected to measure specific impacts, it will also determine our population of respondents. Consideration must be given to what is practical within the context of the evaluation. Often we consider the impact on clients, patients, or service users and ideally, this would be the population we would sample in order to obtain a measure of this impact, however, this could present significant ethical and logistical issues and may not be appropriate or within the scope of the project.

The relative strengths and weaknesses of different methods should be assessed in line with the intended outputs, if the evaluation is looking to measure statistically significant change then the constructs we are measuring will require the data to be constructed in a specific manner to meet the requirements of the particular method being utilised. Similarly, if the evaluation is looking for a detailed exploration of certain indicators a qualitative approach is required. Indeed, an evaluation may be looking for both and therefore a mixed methodological approach is required.

When considering how to best measure the impact, three unique yet interlinked aspects must be considered.

- What is the appropriate time scale for the evaluation?
- What methods are most appropriate for measuring impact?
- What methods of analysis would be most suitable?

Prior to proceeding with any impact evaluation, we must have a holistic understanding of the specific evaluation requirements and process. This will be bespoke to each evaluation, the underpinning approach depending on the demands and timescale of evaluation. The following key methodological areas must be addressed to ensure the outputs align with the intended purpose of the evaluation.

What is the appropriate time scale for the evaluation?

This section will consider two methodological approaches; Snap-shot studies, and longitudinal studies. The type of methodological approach will be guided, in part, by the evaluation framework, as this will provide guidance as to what impacts are anticipated and over what time period.

Snap-shot

With a snap-shot approach, also known as cross-sectional, data is collected at a specific point in time, providing a snapshot of the variables included in the study. The benefit of this approach is that it allows the comparison of many different variables at the same time.

The advantages of this type of study are that it:

- Obtains the overall picture, as it stands, at the time of the study.
- Is relatively quick and easy to conduct.
- Is able to measure prevalence for all impacts under investigation.
- Is good for descriptive analysis.

Cross-sectional methodologies are often used to assess the prevalence of behaviours, attitudes and opinions. They are relatively quick and inexpensive to administer, as they only require one point of contact with respondents. This type of study allows the variance to be explored within a population by providing consistent comparable measures.

The primary weaknesses of this approach, in the context of evaluating impact, are that it does not normally identify cause and effect and can offer little in respect to understanding the long-term impact. It can, however, offer a snapshot, which can form part of a wider impact evaluation and act as a baseline.

Reflective, self-rating questionnaires ask respondents to rate their level of ability in specific areas after completion. For each respondent, this gives a numerical measure of impact in that particular area.

A cross-sectional methodology can aid in understanding what specific constructs have been impacted and to what extent, but can often leave unanswered questions relating to the implications of the impact or how the impact was achieved.

Longitudinal

In a longitudinal approach, data is collected from the same person at two or more points in time.

The advantages of this type of study are:

- It assesses whether change is maintained over time and is embedded into practice.
- Each subject acts as his or her own personal control, providing a point of reference by which impact can be measured.
- Reduces between subject variability and eliminates the cohort effect.

A longitudinal methodology allows the population and behavioural shift to be recorded as it develops, highlighting what works and just as importantly, what does not work. A rolling longitudinal study allows alterations to be made and then assessed on an on-going basis.

This type of study allows comparable data to be obtained from the population or populations who are undergoing some form of change or intervention; allowing the impact of the change or intervention to be measured and compared to create a measure of impact.

A wide range of methodologies can be applied within a longitudinal study, which gives the flexibility to meet the needs of a specific population; the only requirement is ensuring a consistent measurement, which can be analysed to draw a comparison of the data between or among different points in time.

A longitudinal methodology has four key elements, which underpin the timeline of an evaluation:

Scoping: Creating an evaluation framework based on a robust understanding of both the population and the intervention, change or behavioural shift.

Creating a baseline: Collecting measures by which change can be assessed, that meets the key strategic aims developed through the scoping process.

Embedding: Supporting the population to integrate change into their professional practice and build on their baseline measures.

Measuring impact: Assessing development measured against consistent base-line measures to be assessed and verified, and to what extent the change has been embedded.

A key advantage of a longitudinal approach is that it allows additional data sources to be developed over time, this development can be imperative to the embedding process. The assessment process ensures that the individual not only understood what was taught but can also apply it at the right level.

> *Assignments provide crucial progression of learning, practising and demonstrating understanding and application. Implicitly it is an important feature of the learning journey.*

> (Holroyd and Brown, 2014: 19)

Pre and post intervention questionnaires allow the same numerical measure to be obtained and is technically a form of longitudinal study. However, this is rather lim-ited for it depends on a like-for-like comparison of responses collected at two distinct points in time from a single respondent.

What methods?

There are two main methods that can be employed when evaluating programmes; qualitative and quantitative.

Qualitative research is a naturalistic, interpretative approach concerned with under-standing the meanings that people attach to actions, decisions, beliefs and values within their social world, and understanding the mental mapping process that respondents use to make sense of and interpret the world around them (Ritchie and Lewis, 2003).

Qualitative research can be used to:

- Gain an understanding of underlying reasons and motivations.
- Provide insights.
- Uncover prevalent trends in thought and opinion.

Quantitative research is a positivist, numerically based approach concerned with the application of results to a wider population, hypothesis generation/testing and meas-uring the frequency in occurrence of behaviours, attitudes and opinions. This is not limited to variables that have a physical measurement, such as distance or time, but can be employed to measure abstract concepts.

Quantitative research can be used to:

- Quantify data and generalise results from a sample to the population.
- Measure the incidence of various views and opinions.

  Quantitative research is good at providing information in breadth, from a large number of units, but when we want to explore a problem or concept in depth, quantitative methods can be too shallow.

(Creswell, 2009)

A mix of research methods employing quantitative and qualitative approaches can be adopted, examples of which are included in Table 10.5. The strength of this approach is that the most appropriate method can be employed for each individual data stream. For example, capturing the taught learning by means of a questionnaire offers little opportunity to explore any issues or trends the analysis of the data may highlight, but provides a robust measure in relation to the learning an individual has

Table 10.5 Qualitative and quantitative approaches

Qualitative	Quantitative
• Unstructured Interviews	• Audits
• Qualitative Questionnaire Responses	• Quantitative Questionnaire Responses
• Focus Groups	• Random Control Trials
• Case Studies	• Systematic Observations
• Third Party Testimonies	• Online Polls and Surveys
• Content/Assignment Analysis	• Structured Interviews

undertaken. To assess the impact of this learning over a longer period of time, a secondary data stream is required and, therefore, a qualitative methodology, such as interviews, may allow an opportunity not only to provide context to the quantitative analysis, but can be utilised to gain a measure of the long-term impact of the learning on practice.

A mixed methodological approach requires both quantitative and qualitative data to be integrated to provide a comprehensive understanding of impact as a cohesive concept. Therefore, consideration should be given as to how individual data sources interact in order to allow a robust measure of impact to be distilled.

Analysing impact

One area that is frequently overlooked is the method of analysis used to verify impact. Consideration must be given in the early developmental stages of a methodology as to how the data will function once collated. This is particularly true with respect to statistical testing and, therefore, it is essential to identify any specific testing prior to data collection to ensure the appropriate data structure can be embedded within the tools and instruments used. If a qualitative approach is undertaken, consideration must be given as to how responses will be handled and analysed, as well as the practicalities of sample size, transcription and respondent engagement. If care is not taken it is easy to end up with data that is difficult or disproportionately costly to analyse. Careful consideration needs to be given as to how the data will be recorded, analysed and subsequently presented. Considering this at the planning stage will almost inevitably affect how the data is gathered. This is an aspect of impact evaluation where it is often helpful to ask for advice from someone with a research background. It may well be necessary to use particular statistical techniques and software such as Statistical Package for Social Sciences (SPSS).

Example of impact evaluation

Below is an example of a mixed methodological approach we have used to evaluate one of our most popular programmes.

IPOP (Improving Personal and Organisational Performance)

Table 10.6 below illustrates a mixed methodological approach taken to evaluating the impact of the IPOP unit undertaken by the National Centre of Post-Qualifying Social Work and Professional Practice at Bournemouth University. The table illustrates how each level has been operationalised into methodical functions, which can be mapped against both outcomes and the levels of impact specified by Holroyd and Brown, 2014, seen earlier in this chapter.

The framework for the evaluation of the IPOP unit was initially developed using a theoretical approach and has since undergone further development using an activities

Table 10.6 IPOP impact evaluation

Levels	Methodology	Outcomes
Level 1 Learners' reaction to the development	Pre and post questionnaire comparison	Provides both information about the course delivery and the student-rated impact.
Level 2 Learning attained	Pre and post questionnaire comparison Assignment analysis	Demonstrating whether the students understood and can apply the learning. An accompanying third-party testimony and telephone interviews provided verification of the real practical application.
Level 3 Behavioural change at work	Pre and post questionnaire comparison Assignment analysis Management third party testimony Telephone interviews (at 3 months)	This means that these changes (as specified in Level 2 above) are very likely to have occurred because of the IPOP programme and no other external factors. The assignment and third party testimony demonstrated evidence of behavioural changes at work sustained over time.
Level 4 Impact at team, departmental, organisational level	Assignment analysis Management third party testimony Telephone interviews (at 3 months)	The telephone interviews provided a further opportunity to explore wider impact in terms of team, departmental and organisational.
Level 5 Impact on users and carers	Assignment analysis Management third party testimony Telephone interviews (at 3 months)	Actual examples within the assignments provided evidence of impact on services and users of services.

Field (2012) Adapted from Kirkpatrick (1959), Brown (1996) and Carpenter (2005)

approach. It should be noted that when working in an ever-changing sector such as health and social care, development is essential with regards to both the unit content and the evaluation framework. This development process also gives the opportunity to re-align the content with national or organisation strategic aims to ensure the unit provides the best return on investment with regards to both the social and financial implications of undertaking the process.

The above example demonstrates how methodological approaches can be aligned with unique aspects of the framework. Quantitative methodologies were employed to collect baseline and comparative data to allow testing for significant differences, and qualitative methodologies were utilised to collect a more intricate insight into the long-term impacts. To address long-term impacts a longitudinal approach has been taken. This can help ensure that the learning is embedded into practice. In the case of the IPOP evaluation, it is supported by a formal assessment process, which acts as further evidence of the level of learning that the participant has achieved and the impact of the learning on practice.

Impact evaluation – planning checklist

The following questions can be used to plan an evaluation:

1. What is the context for evaluation (new programme, established programme or pilot programme)?

2. If using a logic model – which approach will you use (theory, activities or outcomes)?

3. What levels of evaluation are you evaluating (reaction, learning, behavioural, impact at team, departmental level, impact at users and carer level)?

4. Is it possible to evaluate the programme in a reliable and credible fashion? (evaluability assessment)

5. What do you intend to measure?

6. Which indicators do you intend to use?

7. What is the appropriate timescale (snap-shot or longitudinal)?

8. Are you planning to use a quantitative, qualitative or mixed method approach?

9. How do you intend to analyse the data?

Key learning points

- Impact evaluations must be undertaken in consultation with all key stakeholders and with a clear focus on strategic aims and outcomes.

- Developing an evaluation framework to assess impact is essential to ensure evaluations are robust.

- Research methodologies should be selected in line with the logic model/evaluation framework and should not lead the process.

- Consideration should be given to outputs, specifically, how any data will be analysed, within the design phase of an impact evaluation.

An effective impact evaluation, therefore, 'provides the details to communicate the explicit benefit of planned development; not simply that the individual understood what was taught but could actually apply it at the right level' (Holroyd, 2014: 15).

Chapter 11

Further key theoretical perspectives

Keith Brown

CHAPTER OUTCOMES

As a result of completing this chapter you will:

- Understand how leadership and management have developed over the years and current thinking.

- Have broadened your understanding of what might constitute effective leadership and management and supervision in health and social care.

- Understand how you lead and manage.

- Have a sense of broad areas for future personal development.

Introduction

The serious and detailed study of people in organisations is relatively recent. Before F.W. Taylor (1911) burst upon the scene with his concept of 'scientific management' in the early years of the twentieth century there was little coherent management thought of any kind. Business was generally in the hands of individual entrepreneurs who saw little need for management theory to assist them in their pursuit of commercial self-interest. Taylor was not an industrial psychologist but his work was based on certain assumptions about man's nature and motivations, and it is probably fair to state that these represented the general view of people in organisations at that time. Although Taylor's assumptions are perhaps psychologically naïve, they are by no means altogether misconceived. They are based on the predominance of the financial incentive and on the 'rationality' of man's response to it (Taylor, 1911).

The most influential refutation of the simple view of industrial man came from Elton Mayo's Hawthorne experiments in Chicago in the 1920s (Mayo, 1933). These lengthy and impressive studies produced telling evidence of complex motivations other than those of a financial nature and demonstrated the importance of group pressures in determining individual behaviour.

Following Hawthorne, the study of groups became paramount and for a period one might have wondered if the individual still existed. In the last three decades the related disciplines referenced by the term 'behavioural sciences' have contributed much to our knowledge of human behaviour in organisations. Emphasis has been placed on a changing concept of man's essential nature (viewpoints expressed broadly by McGregor's (1961) Theory X and Theory Y– see below) and on the needs, drives and motivations that explain man's often apparently irrational behaviour. Not all of this work is as scientific as its generic title would suggest and some conclusions from the evidence appear more idealistic than objective. Nonetheless, it is supported by an impressive amount of research and is undoubtedly leading us towards a clearer understanding of how people work and react within organisations (Mullins, 2007).

We will explore each of these approaches and their application to the management of health and social care before concluding with a review of some key leadership theories.

Scientific management

The theory of scientific management, as developed by F.W. Taylor in the early 1900s (Taylor, 1911) contained two basic assumptions about people which likely represented the general view of management at the time and which have subsequently governed much of the use of incentives in organisations with both beneficial and damaging results. The first assumption was that mankind's incentive to work, his goal and purpose, was financial reward. In order to achieve this goal, he apparently applied to his task some abstraction of sensory and muscular processes that the task demanded and either left at home or put into a state of suspended animation all other aspects of his personality – aims, aspirations, social needs, etc. The second implied assumption was that man was 'rational' in pursuit of this objective. Taylor believed that the deliberate restriction of output by workers, which deeply incensed him, resulted from inadequate management practices and from fear of unemployment. He was convinced that if standards of a 'fair day's work' and 'a fair day's pay' were systematically established and the financial reward was associated with increased output, then workers would produce to the extent of their capabilities. Among theorists, the simple scientific management view of man has long been discredited; yet among practising managers, observation suggests it remains a widely held view (Mullins, 2007).

REFLECTION POINT 11.1

In professional practice in health and social care, it is often suggested that we should be eclectic in our use of theory – we should make use of theory and perspectives to help us best understand a particular situation. The same applies to management – we perhaps need to build a repertoire of theoretical viewpoints we can draw on in helping us analyse and understand leadership and management problems (hence this chapter). Also, if later theorists have taken a different approach it does not mean that earlier work was invalid, rather it is still part of the domain of the discipline and it is better to perhaps see it as augmented or complimented rather than completely outdated or replaced.

- *Can you think of situations where Taylor's concern that managers should analyse tasks, determine the best ways of carrying them out and then ensure that workers follow their instructions is still valid?*

- *Can you think of situations where ensuring outputs are related to financial reward might be important?*

Elton Mayo and the Hawthorne experiments

The Hawthorne experiments, which refuted so dramatically many of the tacit assumptions held in organisations, were conducted between 1927 and 1932 at the Hawthorne works of the Western Electric Company in Chicago (Mayo, 1933). The National Academy of Sciences started the investigations to study the relationship between worker efficiency and workshop illumination and was conducted by means of a control group and an experimental group. The groups were involved in the assembly of telephone relays (a small, intricate mechanism comprising about 40 parts). At the outset, the lighting for the experimental group was improved, with the expected result that the output from the group increased. Unexpectedly, however, the output from the control group also increased. The experimental group's lighting was then reduced and output again increased. It became apparent that some unknown factor, other than the quality of the illumination, was complicating an apparently straightforward investigation. Further changes were therefore introduced, relating to rest pauses, the length of the working day, free lunches, etc. Each was continued for a period of four to 12 weeks. The only change which did not occasion an increase in output was the introduction of six short rest pauses, which apparently upset the workers' rhythm. Finally, all improvements and alterations were removed and conditions were returned to what they had been at the outset of the experiment. Under these conditions, output reached its highest level at any time in the experiment. Medical examinations showed no signs of cumulative fatigue and absenteeism had fallen by 80 per cent. It also showed that each worker in the group had used their own working method and had varied it from time to time to avoid monotony.

Subsequently, the researchers at Hawthorne conducted further investigations into the operation of blank wiring (attaching wires to switches for parts of telephone equipment). This was an investigation into the operation of group pressures, conducted by an observer and an interviewer, and which did not involve the alteration of working conditions. This part of the investigation showed the power of an informal leader and the influence of the values and customs of the group. It was apparent that, to all but one of the group, adherence to group norms of production was a more powerful motivation than a financial incentive.

What had started out as a simple enquiry into the effects of illumination had developed into a demonstration of motives more complex and subtle than anyone had expected. A programme of interviews, introduced as part of the investigation, added to the information available. Some of the conclusions to be drawn from Mayo's (1933) work have been summarised as follows.

- Work is a group activity.
- The social world of the adult is primarily patterned about work activity.
- The need for recognition, security and sense of belonging is more important in determining workers' morale and productivity than the physical conditions under which they work.
- A complaint is not necessarily an objective recital of fact; it is commonly a symptom manifesting disturbance of an individual's status position in the group.
- A worker's attitudes and effectiveness are conditioned by social demands both from inside and outside the workplace.
- Informal groups within the workplace exercise strong social control over the work habits and attitudes of the individual worker.

Put another way, there was more than enough evidence from these experiments to highlight the psychological naïvety of Taylor's theories. Emphasis had also been shifted from the individual to the group as the proper unit of study.

REFLECTION POINT **11.2**

- *Do you agree with the conclusions of Mayo's work as above?*
- *How does this accord with the current emphasis on individual supervision?*
- *If informal groups are so important in determining people's behaviour how can you seek to influence them?*

The needs hierarchy

Another widely held view of motivation is that mankind is always directed towards the satisfaction of some need and that these needs can be hierarchically arranged. As long as the lower ones are not met, they will act as motivators of behaviour but, once they have been satisfied, the individual will be motivated by the attempt to satisfy the next highest level of needs. These needs have been differently described and the number of levels is regarded by different authorities as anything from three to seven. The hierarchy described here is that propounded by A.H. Maslow (1943) and subsequently supported in largely the same form by a series of writers (e.g. Cooke et al, 2005; Mook, 1987).

The first level is that of physiological needs – hunger, thirst, sexual desire, etc. (Figure 11.1). It is recognised that these needs cannot always be clearly isolated: a meal with company, for example, may meet social was well as physiological needs 'A person lacking food, safety, love and esteem, would probably hunger for food more strongly than for

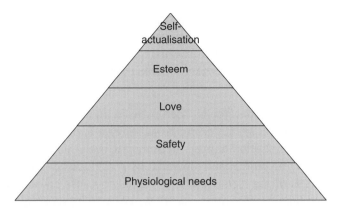

Figure 11.1 Maslow's (1943) hierarchy of needs

anything else' (Maslow, 1943: 373). Man lives for bread alone when there is no bread, but when his stomach is filled, other and 'higher' level needs emerge and become the motivators of behaviour. And when these, in turn, are satisfied, again new needs emerge and so on. Thus 'gratification becomes as important a concept as deprivation in motivation theory' because it releases a person from one need and permits the emergence of another (Maslow, 1943: 375).

The second level of need is the need for safety. Needs for safety are seen at their most easily observable in children, who desire orderliness, consistency, stability; and in normal healthy adults in situations when their safety is, in fact, endangered. As is the case with physiological needs, the normal adult in our society is largely satisfied in his safety needs and frequently, therefore, they are not functioning as active motivators. 'Safety', of course, is used to imply more than just freedom from physical danger and the concept of 'security' may indicate better what is intended.

The third level of the needs hierarchy is love. These are quite simply the needs of love and affection and a sense of belonging.

The fourth level is the need for esteem. These can be classified into two types.

- The need for achievement, competence, adequacy, self-respect, etc.
- The need for recognition from others, reputation, prestige, appreciation, etc.

Satisfaction of these needs produces feelings of confidence, usefulness, worth; thwarting them gives rise to feelings of inferiority and helplessness.

The final level of need is the need for self-actualisation. Maslow describes this as the 'desire to become more and more what one is; to become everything that one is capable of becoming' (Maslow 1943: 382). This need will manifest itself in very different forms in different people according to aptitudes and capabilities. Generally, this need will not emerge clearly until the previous four are satisfied, i.e. one might expect the most creative behaviour from the most satisfied people.

The role in motivation of curiosity, learning and experimenting, etc. has not been discussed and it is suggested that the desire to know and understand can be seen as a need in itself (apart from the role that the cognitive processes play in the satisfaction of other needs). These, however, do not fit easily into the hierarchy and, indeed, interestingly appear to form themselves into a hierarchy, for instance, 'the desire to know, to understand, to systematise, to organise, to analyse, to look for relations and meanings' (Maslow, 1943: 385).

The hierarchy of needs should not be seen as fixed and rigid in all cases. There are individual exceptions in whom, for example, self-esteem appears more important than love, or where self-actualisation appears to dominate everything. In certain cases, levels of aspiration may be permanently lowered by continuous deprivation. There may be apparent reversals of the hierarchical order simply because needs which have been satisfied for a long time become undervalued; we cease to be aware of their propensity until we are again deprived of satisfaction. It should also be noted that this hierarchy is not always manifested in behaviour. Behaviour has many other determinants.

It should not be assumed that the levels are so clear cut that each has to be 100 per cent satisfied before the next emerges. Most people will be partially satisfied and partially unsatisfied in all their basic needs. The hierarchy of needs, as described by Maslow, McGregor and others is not specifically applicable to work situations but its relevance to organisations in a modern affluent society is easy to see. It is likely that the factors which motivate modern 'organisational' man are higher on this scale than much management practice has yet to realise.

REFLECTION POINT 11.3

Thinking of the team you lead or to which you belong:

- *Where do members appear to be on Maslow's hierarchy?*
- *What do you do, or observe others doing in response to their needs and motivate them?*
- *What are your needs and how will these be met?*

Theory X and Theory Y

Douglas McGregor first put forward his concepts of Theory X and Theory Y in 1957 and subsequently developed them in his book *The Human Side of Enterprise* (1961). Theory X represents traditional assumptions made by management about people in organisations and is used in determining managerial behaviour towards people.

- The average human being has an inherent dislike of work and will avoid it if he can.
- Because of this human characteristic of dislike of work, most people must be coerced, controlled, directed, and threatened with punishment to get them to put forth adequate effort towards the achievement of organisational objectives.
- The average human being prefers to be directed, wishes to avoid responsibility, has relatively little ambition and wants security above all (McGregor, 1961).

McGregor cites this as a view of people in organisations, which materially influences large areas of management activity. His claim, however, is that while this theory accounts for some organisational behaviour (otherwise it would not have persisted) there are many observed aspects of behaviour that are not consistent with this viewpoint. Therefore, he proposes Theory Y. It is not suggested that all employees are described by Theory Y or that none would be described by Theory X, but that Theory Y represents a more realistic description of workers in general. The assumptions of Theory Y are:

- The expenditure of physical and mental effort in work is as natural as play or rest.

- External control and the threat of punishment are not the only means for bringing about effort towards organisational objectives. Mankind will exercise self-direction and self-control in the service of objectives to which s/he is committed.

- Commitment to objectives is a function of the rewards associated with their achievement.

- The average human being learns under proper conditions not only to accept but also to seek responsibility.

- The capacity to exercise a relatively high degree of imagination, ingenuity and creativity in the solution of organisational problems is widely, not narrowly, distributed in the population.

- Under the conditions of modern organisational life, the intellectual potentialities of the average human being are only partly utilised.

(McGregor, 1961)

The trend of modern behavioural science research is to confirm Theory Y as a more competent set of assumptions about human nature than Theory X. Observation suggests, however than many of the research findings of recent years have yet to be accepted by practising managers. There have been in many cases misunderstandings, sometimes leading to unduly extravagant claims and distortions by acolytes of their own particular master's message. It is difficult to conduct scientifically controlled research into any but the most peripheral areas of behaviour; consequently, the way remains open for dissension. Behaviour is largely learned and the behaviour of people in organisations can illustrate what they have learned from their experience. In other words, management action based on given assumptions about people will tend to elicit a response, which is in line with those assumptions, thereby confirming initial beliefs. For example, it would be difficult to observe manifestations of Theory Y in an organisation whose management philosophy was based on a belief in Theory X.

McGregor also anticipates, in essence, Herzberg *et al.*'s (1959) 'motivation-hygiene' theory, emphasising the futility of providing ever-increasing means to satisfy lower level needs, when these have ceased to operate as predominant motivators, and the need for people to derive some satisfaction of their higher level needs from the work which they do. He claims that the major rewards provided by management yield satisfaction only when the individual is away from the job. Put another way, it is not

Table 11.1 Man's attitude to work (adapted from McGregor, 1961)

Theory X	Theory Y
1. Man dislikes work and will avoid it if he can.	1. Work is necessary to man's psychological growth.
2. Man must be forced or bribed to put in the right effort.	2. Man wants to be interested in his work and, under the right conditions, he can enjoy it.
3. Man would rather be directed than accept responsibility, which he avoids.	3. Man will direct himself towards accepted targets.
4. Man is motivated mainly by money.	4. Man will seek, and accept responsibility, under the right conditions.
5. Man is motivated by anxiety about his security.	5. The discipline a man imposes on himself is more effective, and can be more severe than any imposed on him.
6. Most men have little creativity – except when getting round management rules!	6. Under the right conditions, many are motivated by the desire to realise their own potential.
	7. Creativity and ingenuity are widely distributed and grossly underused.

surprising that many wage earners perceive work as a form of punishment – the price for various kinds of satisfaction away from the job. Herzberg *et al.* (1959) also found that the factors acting as positive motivators to work were always those connected directly with the job; while the 'hygiene' factors, the potential 'dissatisfiers' (matters which may demotivate but will never motivate) are those concerning the circumstances that surround the job.

REFLECTION POINT **11.4**

McGregor's Theory X can be seen to be based on a Taylorist view of humanity and Theory Y on more humanistic perspectives such as Maslow's.

- *Is the management culture of your organisation based on Theory X or Theory Y?*

- *Is your team culture based on Theory X or Theory Y?*

- *If they are different what problems does this create for you and how do you manage them?*

- *What problems might there be in a Theory X organisation in providing a Theory Y-type service to people who use services?*

Herzberg

Herzberg (1966, 1987); *et al.* (1959) set out to understand what it was that gave people satisfaction at work, with the assumption that this would reveal what motivated them to work harder. He and others conducted many interviews of accountants and engineers – asking them to describe times when they were dissatisfied and times when they were highly satisfied. Analysis of these interviews showed that these two emotional states were caused by two different sets of conditions. The things that were largely responsible for dissatisfaction, if they were absent or inadequate, were:

- Pay.
- Relationship with a peer, job security.
- Status.
- Company policy.
- Working conditions.
- Relationship with the boss.

(Herzberg *et al.*, 1959)

They termed these hygiene factors. This rather odd term was taken from the analogy that just as clean water can help prevent disease, but not cure it, improving these factors would not satisfy people. Once we feel 'secure' in our jobs, making us 'more secure' will not result in improved motivation.

Herzberg *et al.* (1959) cite the extreme motivating psychological factors as:

- Interesting work.
- Significant achievement, personal growth.
- Responsibility for worthwhile activities.
- Advancement.

The key to meeting these needs was to give people additional responsibility, greater opportunity to use their talents, and more control over their jobs. These ideas were termed 'job enrichment'.

REFLECTION POINT **11.5**

Look at Herzberg's 'hygiene' factors and the motivating factors above.

- *Do you agree with the distinction between hygiene and motivating factors?*
- *What motivates you?*
- *What do you think motivates your team and what evidence have you got for this?*
- *What are the implications of what motivates you and your team for your leadership and management practice?*

169

The impact of the group

Prior to the Hawthorne experiments, the general tendency (though not universal) had been to concentrate on the individual as the unit of study in organisational psychology. Following Mayo's (1933) revelations there developed an awareness of the impact of the group on organisational behaviour and knowledge of group processes and group influences continues to be developed.

An important distinction is made between 'primary' and 'secondary' groups. The former are small groups of individuals in face-to-face relationships e.g. the family and workplace and the secondary category comprises such groups as the company, the nation etc., which include the primary groups within them, and which are too large for all members to have personal relationships with all other members. Primary and secondary groups should be seen as opposite ends of a continuum with a vague area in the middle. For the student of organisational behaviour, the important group is the primary group. Primary groups are crucial in determining an individual's personal attributes, their views, their values and their attitudes. They are one of the fundamental sources of discipline and self-control. It is fair to state that an individual's deepest feelings relate to primary groups; secondary groups are too remote.

A study of American flyers during the Second World War showed clearly that an individual's first loyalty was to his crew, then to his squadron, then a group of squadrons and finally to the particular Air Forces of which s/he was a part. Feelings for the US Army were less strong, for the allied armies still less and so on. Loyalty to the people of the allied nations was barely measurable. The same pattern of diminishing strength of loyalty from the workplace to the organisation could be found in any large organisation, and its applications are clear. Essentially, it implies that an organisation will be at a disadvantage in trying to influence group workings in a way that is not compatible with their values.

Primary groups develop norms, standards or group values, and the nature of a group imposes powerful pressure on individuals to conform to the standards of the group. The mere fact that members of a group have similar attitudes does not necessarily mean that similarity is caused by group membership. People with similar attitudes tend to be attracted to one another. People receive their main social satisfaction from relationships with those who hold similar attitudes, and such people have the most influence on their subsequent attitudes. There is a complex interaction process at work. To refer to the hierarchy of needs, one could say that the need for love and esteem tends to be satisfied through membership of primary groups, whereas they tend not to be satisfied through secondary groups. The individual's need to retain his primary group membership, and the consequent pressure on him to conform to its values, is one of the most fundamental and important facts of organisational life. The primary groups within organisations are potent forces for either the furtherance or the obstruction of organisational objectives. One of the problems of high labour turnover is that it gives little opportunity for primary groupings to arise and makes problems of morale, discipline and control much more difficult.

REFLECTION POINT **11.6**

- *Can you think of situations where the influence of primary working groups has under-mined or come into conflict with the organisation and its objectives?*

- *What impact can belonging to different primary working groups have on the multidis-ciplinary team and service quality?*

- *Which primary groups most influence your leadership and management?*

Individuals within groups will occupy different 'roles' and have a different status. They will, in other words, have a position in any group to which they belong and there will be an appropriate pattern of behaviour associated with that position. A person who belongs to several groups may have a quite different status in each. Status can originate from a variety of sources. The importance of status to the individual should not be underestimated – from the point of view of the social psychologist, the need of the individual for status and function is the most significant of his traits, and if this need remains unsatisfied, nothing else can compensate for its lack. Status is relative. It concerns the position of one person in relation to another, and raising the status of one necessarily reduces the status of the other. Its nature may be 'functional' or 'non-functional', which is to say that it can be based on skill, competence or hierarchical position. The former is likely to cause fewer difficulties for the group because it is less exclusive and once acquired is less easily lost. Status is not necessarily associated with promotion (recognition of craftsmanship or functional worth may serve that purposefully) but the relationship between status and conformity to group values has important implications. Homans (1951) has postulated that the higher the rank of a person within a group, the more nearly his activities conform to the norms of the group and vice versa. The group, in fact, confers prestige on those who conform. The low ranking member has less to lose and therefore feels less pressure to conform.

Primary groups and secondary groups tend to make different 'role' demands on the individual. Secondary groups generally require more specific and predictable role behaviour, which the individual may find less natural and less easy to sustain. His ability to meet the demands of the role will vary according to his level of adjustment. Children, for example, will find it difficult to sustain secondary roles: i.e. to behave as they are expected to behave in a social setting outside the immediate family. Because of the personal nature of the relationships, status in primary groups is easily identified; it is less easily seen in secondary groups because of the greater complexity or the communications, hence the need for external signs or 'status symbols'.

Jennings (1960) has distinguished between what he calls the 'socio-group' and the 'psyche-group' and Moreno (1960) with his quaintly titled technique of 'sociometry' has studied the same aspects of group structure. The socio-group is an association which is formed for work or for the accomplishment of some objective; the psyche-group is formed purely for the member's satisfaction in the group activities, with no purpose external to itself. These two types should be regarded as opposite ends of a continuum: real groups will inevitably fall somewhere in between. As Homans (1951) puts it, any group will have an external system, which is task-centred and an internal system, which is group-centred. An appreciation of these two structures within a group can facilitate the organisation of the group for maximum effectiveness. It should not, for example, be assumed that personal friendships and preferences (the psyche-group structure) is necessarily a good indicator of preferred working relationships (the socio-group structure).

The pattern of primary groups within organisations is commonly referred to as the 'informal' structure of organisations, contrasting with the 'formal' structure portrayed on the organisation chart. The importance of this structure, for anyone wishing to understand organisation behaviour, cannot be overestimated. Whether the formal and informal aspects of organisations should be seen as so sharply contrasted is another matter. That they are is perhaps an unhappy reflection on the way in which formal organisations have been designed.

Leadership theories

The following theories: group thinking; action-centred leadership; the decision-making continuum; situational leadership; and transformational leadership are also offered as significant leadership theories which impact on the leadership, management and supervision of staff in health and social care. The aim is to provide a very brief insight into these influential theories and for you to consider their impact on health and social care.

Group thinking

'How could we have been so stupid?' asked President John F. Kennedy, after he and a group of close advisers had blundered into the Bay of Pigs invasion. Stupidity was certainly not the explanation. The group who made the decision was one of the greatest collections of intellectual talent in the history of American government. Irving Janis describes the blunder as a result of 'group-think'.

Group-think occurs when too high a price is placed on the harmony and morale of the group, so that loyalty to the group's previous policies, or to the group consensus, overrides the conscience of each member. 'Concurrence-seeking' drives out the realistic appraisal of alternatives. No bickering or conflict is allowed to spoil the cosy 'we-feeling' of the group. Even the cleverest, most high-minded and well-intentioned of people, can have a blind spot. Janis (1972) identifies eight symptoms.

- Invulnerability – cohesive groups become over-optimistic and can take extraordinary risks without realising the dangers, mainly because there is no discordant warning voice.

- Rationale – cohesive groups are quick to find rationalisations to explain away evidence that does not fit their policies.

- Morality – there is a tendency to be blind to the moral or ethical implications of a policy. 'How could so many good men be wicked?' is the feeling.

- Stereotypes – victims of group-think quickly get into the habit of stereotyping their enemies or other people and do not notice discordant evidence.

- Pressure – if anyone starts to voice doubts the group exerts subtle pressures to keep the person quiet; they are allowed to express doubts but not to press them.

- Self-censorship – members of the group are careful not to discuss their feelings or their doubts outside the group, in order not to disturb the group cosiness.

- Unanimity – unanimity is important so once a decision has been reached any divergent views are carefully screened out in people's minds.

- Mindguards – victims of group-think set themselves up as bodyguards to the decision. 'He needs all the support we can give him'. The doctrine of collective responsibility is invoked to stifle dissent outside the group.

REFLECTION POINT 11.7

- *Can you think of cases nationally where 'group-think' may have been a contributory factor in service breakdowns or problems?*

- *Can you think of team situations or care planning group scenarios from your own experience where 'group-think' might have led to unhelpful outcomes for people who use services?*

- *What can you and your team do to avoid 'group-think' undermining practice?*

Action-centred leadership

Professor John Adair (1979) used his research in both the armed forces and organisations to identify what successful leaders actually do. He then developed this functional model using the three circles concept (Figure 11.2).

A leader is *a person who is appointed to achieve results with and through other people*. Whether or not these results are achieved and how much a leader needs to influence others in order to gain them, depends on varying factors. These include the nature of the task in question, the skills and needs (both technical and personal) of the individuals concerned, and the way they integrate as a team. Efficient leadership therefore requires flexibility and an awareness of these different requirements in order to strike an effective balance for the particular job in hand. This balancing act is shown by Adair's overlapping three circles.

TASK: Ensuring that the task is achieved.

INDIVIDUAL: Satisfying the requirements of individuals within the team.

TEAM: Nurturing and motivating the team as a whole.

Obviously, these needs sometimes conflict with each other and one area will often require more attention than others. The trick is to achieve a long-term balance between

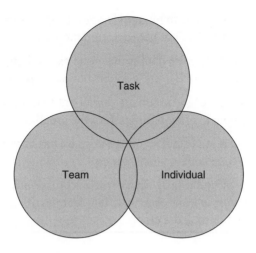

Figure 11.2 The three circles concept (Adair, 1979)

all three and ensure that any imbalances are resolved comparatively quickly. In this way, if one individual demands a heavy input of time and energy for a while, the others will know that their requirements are also being looked after and will be met within the foreseeable future.

Adair's theory can be seen as integrating a number of key perspectives in leadership and management. For instance, in emphasising the management of the task it can be seen to be responding to Taylorist preoccupations, in emphasising the importance of the team it responds to the findings of the Hawthorne experiments and the importance of group life, in looking to the needs of the individual it could be seen to also embrace Maslow and self-actualisation. In noting the importance of leaders giving time to individuals and responding to individual needs it also accords very well with health and social care's culture that emphasises the importance of individual supervision. In fact, our supervisory practice can be held up as an exemplar of what Adair meant by the effective leadership of individuals. The challenge for health and social care leaders is perhaps ensuring this primacy of supervision is balanced by giving attention to team development and task management. The three dimensions of the model, therefore, offer us an important point of reference.

REFLECTION POINT *11.8*

- *Looking at your use of time, is it balanced across the three areas e.g. are you equally methodical and investing as much in unit and business planning, care planning and review and team building and development as in supervision? Do you have improvement plans for each of these areas of activity?*

- *Where are your strengths and weaknesses? In which of the three domains do you need to target your continuing professional development (CPD) as a manager and leader?*

Situational leadership

The theory of situational leadership (Hersey and Blanchard, 1988) suggests that the type of leadership adopted should ideally be dependent on a subordinate's 'maturity' – a term used to describe a team member's degree of competence and commitment in tackling a particular task or role. They identified four categories of leadership style, which could be applied (Figure 11.3):

Directing: the subordinate has little experience of the task in question but high enthusiasm and confidence. S/he needs showing/telling what to do but requires little support while carrying it out.

Coaching: the subordinate is more experienced but is also taking on more demanding tasks and so feels less confident. S/he needs showing/telling what to do but requires little support while carrying it out.

Supporting: the subordinate is well experienced at his/her job but for a variety of reasons (being stale, unchallenged, stressed) lacks motivation. S/he needs high support from the leader while resolving the task/role in hand.

Delegating: the subordinate has all the technical and people skills required for the job, is experienced at it and highly motivated. S/he can be left to happily get on with it.

Because roles within a team are often dynamic, a subordinate's level of 'maturity' will fluctuate according to how assured s/he is at different tasks. Someone who is 'mature' in a long-standing job will be 'immature' when taking on new responsibility. Their leader can then offer technical or emotional support as appropriate until s/he grows in experience and confidence in that particular job. This type of leadership demands flexibility from a leader and an accurate assessment of their subordinates.

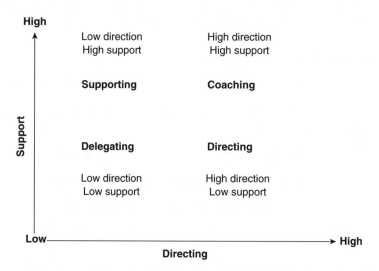

Figure 11.3 Situational leadership (Hersey and Blanchard, 1988)

REFLECTION POINT **11.9**

Take time here to reflect on some of the questions raised by their Hersey and Blanchard's theory.

- *Have you got a clear picture of your team's individual abilities and performance or are there some you need to get to know better?*

- *Can you think of situations when a new responsibility, change or service development meant a mature staff member needed more support and guidance?*

There may be more challenges to a leader in being 'flexible' than Hersey and Blanchard's theory might suggest. The idea of levels of maturity is very similar to Tuckman's (1965) stages of group development. This raises an interesting point, for part of Tuckman's schema involved a period of 'storming' when the power of a leader is challenged. As a team moves into storming, if it is to continue to mature, the leader must give them space to take some control and contribute, rather than reacting negatively and asserting their authority. Can you think of situations when your team has 'stormed'? Did your response allow them to contribute and take some control or did you respond by using your power to assert your authority and put them in their place?

The decision-making continuum

Leadership styles vary according to the characteristics of the leader concerned, the nature of the organisation s/he works in and the needs and expectations of their subordinates. Tannenbaum and Schmidt attempted to define different styles of leadership by looking at the level of participation subordinates have in the decision-making process. This varies according to their level of competence, training requirements and the nature of the task. The decision-making continuum is divided into seven styles:

- Tells: Makes a decision and announces it.

- Sells: Persuades subordinates of the wisdom of their decision – in effect 'selling' it.

- Explains: Presents decision with the background that led to the decision, then invites discussion to build understanding.

- Tests: Presents tentative decision then invites alternative suggestions.

- Selects: Presents problem, invites suggestions then makes a decision.

- Consults: Defines limits, then reaches a decision with subordinates.

- Joins: Defines limits, then abides by the decision reached by subordinates.

The continuum reads from left to right. At the farthest left (Tells) decisions are made using the authority of the manager with little or no subordinate involvement or freedom. Moving to the right the categories rely progressively less on the authority of the manager with progressively more freedom granted to subordinates. At the far right of the continuum subordinates make decisions within limits set by the manager with which the later then abides (Joins).

REFLECTION POINT **11.10**

This model is similar to and complements Hersey and Blanchard's situational leadership theory. Even when theories are similar like this they are still useful as they can offer slightly different perspectives that can cast a new light on situations and help our thinking. For instance, Tannenbaum and Schmidt's continuum can pose questions such as.

- *Can you see in your practice that, as appropriate, you use the range of approaches outlined in the continuum according to the needs of the staff member?*

- *The participation agenda suggests that we should 'join' with people who use services in making decisions. What will this demand from you and your team?*

Transformational leadership

A more recent leadership model is 'transformational leadership'. Transformational leadership is contrasted with 'transactional leadership' (Bass, 1985; Bass and Riggio, 2006). Transactional leadership is leadership by appointed managers using their legitimate authority, based on the contract of employment, to pursue organisational goals and motivating employees to achieve these goals using organisational reward systems. Transactional leadership is therefore closely associated with managerialism while, in contrast, transformational leadership focuses on changing and improving services and is not necessarily invested in appointed managers.

Transformational leadership can be seen as crucial to the achievement of the government's agenda to transform services (DH, 2008a). For instance, the Principles of Social Care Management (SfC/Topss, 2004) in Appendix 5 emphasises the importance of inspiring staff and the Leadership Qualities Framework (DH, 2009a) in Appendix 6 is a leadership model for all staff in the NHS, not just those in management positions.

So, transformational leadership inspires followers, challenges established processes in organisations and services and enables others to bring positive changes. Transformational leadership is dependent on personal effectiveness. This is combined with a vision of how services could best be delivered or improved that is shared with colleagues and which inspires them (Kouzes and Posner, 2007). Transformational leadership is therefore not confined to appointed managers and is not dependent on authority, but rather engages teams in service development and improvement on a voluntary basis. It may also be founded upon and dependent on self-awareness (Hock, 2000).

Current thinking

Over the last 10 years or so the context for leadership has significantly changed, causing us to rethink what we understand about who leaders are and what leadership entails. The historic focus on individual leadership is giving way to the idea of collective leadership within and between organisations. Shifts in the relationship between the state, service users, patients and citizens mean sharing responsibility, power and risk more equally and in new ways. Leadership is recognised as being more widely dispersed with a focus on contributions or behaviours rather than roles. If leadership is less about what an individual can do on their own and more about how they work with others suggests that leadership is primarily a social process, dependent on interaction, with success depending on the ability of each individual to relate successfully to a wide range of people. Such relational ability requires leaders to be able to flex behaviour according to context, the matter in hand and the people involved. This flexibility is needed both when planning how to interact and when adjusting behaviour as an interaction takes place. Flexibility demands a capacity to read a situation and the people involved, developing or adjusting approaches so that intended outcomes are realised. The foundation for this ability is self-awareness – the knowledge a leader has of their own preferences, abilities and attitudes, the capacity to understand how they personally are reacting to a situation and how this might positively or adversely affect a situation. This theme was and explored in Chapter 4 of this text.

While no single theory dominates current thinking about leadership and management a number remain influential such as transformational leadership, situational leadership and emotional intelligence. Theory of a sort is also seen in sector or professional frameworks that articulate what it is believed constitutes good leadership. These frameworks tend to have a competence or behavioural focus and frequently drive recruitment, performance appraisal and leadership development within organisations. The Leadership Qualities Framework (LQF) produced by Skills for Care and the Health Care Leadership Model are two such frameworks to which other organisation specific ones can be added. With all of these frameworks, particularly organisation designed versions, questions need to be asked about the research underpinning their design and whether they anticipate what leadership will need to look like in the future. In addition to established theory and frameworks, other ideas about leadership are emerging concerning for example collaborative and whole system leadership.

At Bournemouth University, we are particularly concerned about the ability of individuals to exercise good professional and leadership judgement when under significant pressure. If fewer staff are handling greater caseloads at a time when investment in leadership and management development and support is relatively low these staff need greater resilience, resourcefulness and capacity to function healthily. In addition to helping managers develop behaviours and skills related to relevant traditional and emerging theory we believe that investment in self-leadership is required which we define as being:

> *the ability to bring out the best in individuals in any circumstances for the ultimate outcome of providing better services.*

(Holroyd, 2015: 24)

Self-leadership is introduced in Chapter 3 or this text and is explored in depth within 'Self-Leadership and Personal Resilience in Health and Social Care', a key text within the Post Qualifying Social Work Leadership and Management Handbook series, published by Sage Publications Ltd.

REFLECTION POINT **11.11**

Looking back over this text.

- *Do you think your personal effectiveness has improved through the different perspectives offered by this book and the developmental opportunities it has offered you?*

- *Which theories or perspectives might be worth revisiting to see if you can make them more meaningful?*

- *What aspects of your personal effectiveness will you try and improve in the future to enhance your leadership?*

- *How will you encourage and support others to lead and develop services?*

Key learning points

- The study of people in organisations has developed from the first naïve assumptions of scientific management to become a sophisticated and complex field.

- The importance of the group has been stressed in more than one study. The trend of current investigation and theory is undoubtedly away from 'rational economic' man-kind, towards a concept of mankind to whom work is a natural, essential part of social life, seeking satisfaction of their 'higher' not 'lower' needs.

- There can be little doubt that we are working towards a more soundly based under-standing of organisational behaviour but perhaps at times theorising could owe more to the writers' idealistic vision of human nature than to their scientific findings. Our health and social care value base will make some theories more attractive to us than others.

- As we are concerned with individuals in particular situations it is arguable that we need a repertoire of perspectives and our theoretical understanding of organisational behaviour should be the basis upon which as managers and leaders we fashion an understanding and approach for each separate situation.

- Our understanding of leadership is constantly shifting. Currently, there is interest in dis-persed leadership and the capacity of individuals to work effectively with a diverse set of collaborators.

- The challenge of working in today's environment demands high levels of resourceful-ness and resilience, the capacity to make sound decisions when under pressure for which we argue self-leadership is required.

References and bibliography

Adair, J. (1979) *Action Centred Leadership*. Aldershot: Gower.

Adass (2016), *Adass Budget Survey 2016*. Available online at: www.adass.org.uk/media/5379/adass-budget-survey-report-2016.pdf. p18.

Age UK, Later Life in the United Kingdom - June 2016, Age UK (2016), www.ageuk.org.uk/Documents/EN-GB/Factsheets/Later_Life...

Alimo-Metcalfe, B. and Alban-Metcalfe, J. (2011) The 'need to get more for less': a new model of 'engaging leadership' and evidence of its effect on team productivity, and staff morale and wellbeing at work, in *Management Articles of the Year*, June 2012, Chartered Management Institute (CMI): 6–12.

Alimo-Metcalf, B. and Alban-Metcalf, R. J. (2001) The Development of a New Transformational Leadership Questionnaire. *Journal of Occupational and Organizational Psychology*, Vol. 74, No.1, pp1–27.

Alltimes, G. and Varnam, R. (2012) *Integration: a report from the NHS Future Forum*. Department of Health, London. Available on: www.institute.nhs.uk/images/documents/Commissioning/Future%20Forum%20-%20Integration%20report%202012.pdf.

Armendariz, N., Kalergis, K. and Garza, J. (2009) An evaluation of the need for self-care programs in agencies serving adult and child victims of interpersonal violence in Texas. Texas: Institute on Domestic Violence and Sexual Assault. Available online at: http://www.ncdsv.org/images/UTSW-IDVSA_SelfCareReport_09-09.pdf.

Armitage, G. D., Suter, E., Oelke, N. D. and Adair, C. E. (2009) Health systems integration: state of the evidence. *International Journal of Integrated Care*, 9. Available on: www.ncbi.nlm.nih.gov/pmc/articles/PMC2707589/pdf/ijic2009-200982.pdf. [accessed 18/1/16]

Archer, D. and Cameron, A. (2013) *Collaborative Leadership: Building Relationships, Handling Conflict and Sharing Control*. Abingdon: Routledge Press.

Avolio, B. J. and Gardner, W. L. (2005) Authentic Leadership Development: Getting to the Root of Positive Forms of Leadership. *Leadership Quarterly*, Vol.16, No.3, pp315–338.

Bandura, A. (2000) Cultivate self-efficacy for personal and organisational effectiveness, in Locke, E.A. (ed.) *Handbook of Principles of Organisational Behaviour*. Oxford: Blackwell, p126.

Banks, S. (1998). *The Missing Link*. USA: Lone Pine Publishing.

Barling, J., Christie, A. and Hoption, C. (2011) Leadership, in Zeldeck, S. *Handbook of Industrial and Organisational Psychology* (1st edition), Washington, DC: American Psychological Association.

Barnett, R. (1997) *Higher Education: A Critical Business,* Buckingham: Society for Research into Higher Education and the Open University Press.

Bass, B. M. (1985) *Leadership and Performance Beyond Expectations*. New York: Free Press.

Bass, B. M. and Riggio, R.E. (2006) *Transformational Leadership*. London: Lawrence Erlbaum.

BASW, UK Supervision Policy, 2011, BASW, www.basw.co.uk/resource/?id=467, 17th April 2016.

Bateson, B. (1979) *Mind and Nature: A Necessary Unity*. New York: E. P. Dutton, p3.

Bean, J. and Hussey, L. (1996) *Managing the Devolved Budget*. London: HB Publications.

Beaumont, B. and Walker, H. (1985) *Working with Offenders*. London: Palgrave Macmillan, p9.

Bee, M. (2016) *It's Tough at the Top*. Professional Social Work, p14.

Bennis, W. (2009) *On Becoming a Leader*. Philadelphia, PA: Basic Books, Perseus Group.

Better Care Fund (2015) Guidance for the Operationalisation of the BCF in 2015–16 Available on: https://www.england.nhs.uk/wp-content/uploads/2015/03/bcf-operationalisation-guidance-1516.pdf [Accessed 18/01/16]

Bilson, A., Ross, S. (1999) *Social Work Management and Practice-Systems Principles*. London: Jessica Kingsley Publishers, p20.

Bion, W. (1994) *In Jon Sokes's Chapter: The unconscious at work in groups and teams: Contributions from the work of Wilfred Bion*. In: Obholzer, A. and Zagier Roberts, V. (edn) (1994) The Unconscious at Work: Individual and Organizational Stress in the Human Services. London: Routledge.

Blom-Cooper, L. (1985) Report into the Death of Jasmin Beckford. London: H.M.S.O., p68–9.

Bommelje, R. (2013) *Listening Pays: Achieve Significance Through the Power of Listening*. Orlando, FL: HCI Printing and Publishing.

Brandes, D. (1981) *Gamesters Handbook*. UK : Nelson Thornes.

Brookfield, S. (1987) *Developing Critical Thinkers*. Milton Keynes: Open University Press.

Brown, B. (2012). *Daring Greatly: How the Courage to Be Vulnerable Transforms the Way We Live, Love, Parent and Lead*. UK: Portfolio Penguin.

Brown, K. (1996) Planning And Evaluation In Training: Some Thoughts On 'How To Evaluate'. Paper presented at the National Association of Training Officers in Personal Social Services Annual Conference, 1996.

Brown, K., McCloskey, C., Galpin, D., Keen, S. and Immins, T. (2008) Evaluating the Impact of Post-Qualifying Social Work Education. *Social Work Education*, Vol.27 No.8, pp853–67.

Burns, J. M. (1978) *Leadership*. New York: Harper and Row.

Butler Sloss, E. (1987) Report into the Child Abuse Crisis. p3360.

Byars, L. (1992) *Concepts of Strategic Management: Formulation and Implementation* (3rd revised edition). London: Longman Higher Education.

Cameron, A., Lart, R., Bostock, L. and Coomber, C. (2012) Factors that promote and hinder joint and integrated working between health and social care services. *SCIE Res Briefing, 41*, p.24.

Caplan, J. (2003) *Coaching for the Future*. London: CIPD.

Carmi, E. and Walker-Hall, N. (2015) *Serious Case Review Family A*. Kingston LSCB, Available on: http://kingstonandrichmondlscb.org.uk/media/upload/fck/file/SCR/Family%20A%20Serious%20Case%20Review%20Report%20November%202015.pdf.

Carpenter, J. (2005) Evaluation Outcomes in Social Work Education Scottish Institute for Excellence in Social Work Education and Social Care Institute for Excelence, Dundee. Available on: www.scie.org.uk/publications/misc/evalreport.pdf

Carpenter, J., Webb, C., Bostock, L. and Coomber, C. (2012) Effective Supervision in Social Work and Social Care SCIE Briefing 43, SCIE, Available on: www.scie.org.uk/publications/briefings/files/briefing43.pdf

Carpenter, J. (2011) Evaluating Social Work Education: A Review of Outcomes, Measures and Research Designs and Practicalities. *Social Work Education*, Vol.30, No.2, pp122–40.

Carroll, M. (2014) *Effective Supervision for the Helping Professions*. London: Sage.

Cebglobal, www.cebglobal.com/shl/us/solutions/products/docs/OPQ32%20Leadership%20Report%20English%20International.pdf.

Centre for Development Impact, How we define impact evaluation, 2016. Available on: http://cdimpact.org/about/what-we-do/how-we-define -impact-evaluation

Chiller, P. and Crisp, B. R. (2012) Professional Supervision: A Workforce Retention Strategy for Social Work? *Australian Social Work,* Vol.65, No.2, pp232–42.

CIPD (2015) Developing the Next Generation: Today's Young People, Tomorrows Workforce, Research Paper published by the Chartered Institute of Personnel and Development, London.

CIPD (2010) Real-World Coaching Evaluation. A Guide for Practitioners. London: Chartered Institute of Personnel and Development.

Clutterbuck, D. (2004) *Everyone Needs a Mentor* (3rd edition). London:CIPD.

Clyde, J.J. (1992) Report of the Inquiry into the Removal of Children from Orkney in February 1991. Edinburgh: H.M.S.O., p2-363.

Community Care, Available on: www.communitycare.co.uk/2016/03/21/lack-reflective-supervision-hindered-action-baby-death-case/.

Considine, T., Hollingdale, P. and Neville, R. (2015) Social Work, Pastoral Care and Resilience, *Pastoral Care in Education*, Vol.33 No.4, pp214–19.

Cooke, B., Mills, A. J., Kelley, E. S. (2005) Situating Maslow in Cold War America: A Recontextualization of Management Theory. *Group and Organization Management*, Vol. 30, No. 2, pp129–50.

Covey, S. R. (2004) *The 7 Habits of Highly Effective People: Powerful Lessons for Personal Change*. London: Simon Schuster UK Ltd.

Creswell, J. W. (2009) Research Design: Qualitative, Quantitative, and Mixed Methods Approaches. London: Sage p 7.

Deal, T. and Kennedy, A. (1982) *Corporate Cultures: The Rites and Rituals of Corporate Life*. New York: Addison-Wesley.

De Mello, A. (1990). *Awareness*, Zondervan. UK: Fount paperbacks.

DH (Department of Health) (2008a) Transforming Social Care (DH Local Authority Circular). Available on: www.dh.gov.uk/en/Publicationsandstatistics/Lettersandcirculars/LocalAuthorityCirculars/ DH_081934

DH (Department of Health) (2009a) The Leadership Qualities Framework. London: DH. Available on: http://www.nhsleadershipqualities.nhs.uk/ [Accessed 17 February 2009]

DH (Department of Health) and HM Treasury (2015) *Department of Health's Settlement at the Spending Review*. Available online at: https://www.gov.uk/government/news/department-of-healths-settlement-at-the-spending-review-2015

Donovan, T. (2016) Lack of Reflective Supervision Hindered Action In Baby Death Case. Available on: http://www.communitycare.co.uk/2016/03/21/lack-reflective-supervision-hindered-action-baby-death-case/

Draper, J. and Clark, E. (2007) Evaluating the Impact of Continuing Professional Education on Healthcare Practice: The Rhetoric and the Reality. *Nurse Education Today*, 27(6) pp515-517.

Dudley, D. (2010) Everyday leadership. Available on: www.ted.com/talks/drew_dudley_everyday_leadership.

Dunn, P., Mckenna, H., and Murray, R., (2016) *Deficits in the NHS 2016*. London: Kings Fund. Available online at: www.kingsfund.org.uk/sites/files/kf/field/field_publication_file/Deficits_in_the_NHS_Kings_Fund_July_2016_1.pdf p1.

Eisenberg, N., Smith, C. L. and Spinrad, T. L. (2011) *Effortful Control: Relations with Emotion Regulation, Adjustment, and Socialization in Childhood*, in Vohs, K. D. and Baumeister, R. F. (eds) *Handbook of Self-Regulation: Research, Theory and Application* (2nd Edition). UK: Guilford Press.

Ellis, P. and Bach, S. (2015) *Leadership, Management and Team Working in Nursing* (2nd edition). London: Sage.

European Observatory on Health Systems and Policies (2012) Health Systems and the Financial Crisis, Vol. 18 No. 1.

Farb, N. A. S., Anderson, A. K. and Segal, Z. V. (2012) The Mindful Brain and Emotion Regulation in Mood Disorders. *Canadian Journal of Psychiatry*, Vol.57, No.2, pp70–77.

Field, R. (2012) *Planning and Budgeting Skills for Health and Social Work Managers*. London: Sage.

Field, R. (2012) Why Evaluate CPD in Social Work and Social Care? The importance of measuring impact. The National Centre for Post-Qualifying Social Work and Professional Practice.

Field, R. and Oliver J. (2013) *Effective Commissioning in Health and Social Care*. London: Sage.

Field, R. and Miller (2016 in press).

Fillingham, D. and Weir, B. (2014) *System Leadership Lessons and Learning from AQuA's Integrated Care Discovery Communities*, London: The King's Fund.

Fook, J. and Gardner, F. (2007) *Practising Critical Reflection*. Maidenhead: OUP.

Frontier Economics (2012) Enablers and barriers to integrated care and implications for Monitor, A report prepared for Monitor by Frontier Economics: London. Available on: www.gov.uk/government/uploads/system/uploads/attachment_data/file/287800/Enablers_and_barriers_to_integrated_care_report_June_2012.pdf.

Ganz, M. (2011) Public Narrative, Collective Action, and Power found in Odugbemi, S. and Lee, T. (eds) *Accountability Through Public Opinion from Inertia to Public Action*. Washington: World Bank. Available online at: http://siteresources.worldbank.org/EXTGOVACC/Resources/Accountabilitybookweb.pdf

Gawande, J. (2014) The Century of the System, Lecture 2 of the Future Of Medicine Series, Reith Lectures 2014, transcription downloads.bbc.co.uk/radio4/open-book/2014_reith_lecture2...

Glei, J. K. (2013) *Manage Your Day-To-Day: Build Your Routine, Find Your Focus and Sharpen Your Creative Mind*. Las Vegas, AZ: Amazon Publishing.

Goleman,D. (1998) *Working with Emotional Intelligence*. London: Bloomsbury.

Goleman, D. (2003) *The New Leaders.* London: Little, Brown.

Goleman, D., Boyatziz, R. and McKee, A. (2013) *Primal Leadership: Unleashing the Power of Emotional Intelligence*. Boston, MA: Harvard Business Review Press.

Goodwin, N., Sonola, L., Thiel, V. and Kodner, D. (2013) Co-ordinated Care for People with Complex Chronic Conditions. *Key Lessons and Markers for Success.* London: The King's Fund.

Grint, K. (2010) *Leadership: A Very Short Introduction*. Oxford: Oxford University Press.

Hafford-Letchfield, T. (2007) *Practising Quality Assurance in Social Care*. Exeter: Learning Matters.

Ham, C., McKenna, H. and Dunn, P. (2016) Tackling the Growing Crisis in the NHS: An agenda for action, The King's Fund.

Ham, C. and Walsh, N. (2013) Making Integrated Care Happen at Scale and Pace: Lessons From Experience. London: The King's Fund. Available on: www.kingsfund.org.uk/publications/making-integrated-carehappen-scale-and-pace

Hawkins, P. and Shohet, R. (2006) Supervision In The Helping Professions (3rd edition). Maidenhead: Open University Press.

Hawkins, P. and Shohet, R. (2012) *Supervision in the Helping Professions* (4th edition). McGraw Hill: Berkshire.

Heffernan, M. (2011) *Wilful Blindness: Why We Ignore The Obvious At Our Peril*. UK: Simon and Schuster.

Heller, J. (1974) *Something Happened*. London: Vintage Books, p5.

Hersey, P. and Blanchard, K. H. (1993) *Management of Organisational Behaviour: Utilising Human Resources (*6th edition). London: Prentice Hall.

Hersey, P. and Blanchard, K. H. (1988) *Management of Organisational Behaviour: Utilising Human Resources*. New Jersey: Prentice Hall.

Hersey, P. and Blanchard, K. H. (1969) Life-Cycle Theory of Leadership. *Training and Development Journal*, Vol.23, pp26–34.

Herzberg, F. (1966) The Work and the Nature of Man. Cleveland, OH: The World Publishing Company.

Herzberg, F. (1987) One More Time: How Do You Motivate Employees? Harvard Business Review, 65(5), pp109–120

Herzberg, F., Mausner, B. and Snyderman, B. B. (1959) *The Motivation to Work*. New York: John Wiley & Sons.

HM Treasury (2011) *The Magenta Book: Guidance for Evaluation*, London, HM Treasury.

Hock, D. (2000). The Art of Chaordic Leadership. *Leader to Leader*, Vol.15 (Winter) pp20–26. Available on wwww.leadertoleader.org/knowledgecentre/journal.aspx?articleid=62

Holroyd, J. (2015). *Self-Leadership and Personal Resilience in Health and Social Care, Post Qualifying Social Work Leadership and Management Handbooks*. London: Sage.

Holroyd, J. and Brown, K. (2011) *Leadership and Management Development for Social Work and Social Care – Creating Leadership Pathways of Progression*; Birmingham: Learn to Care.

Holroyd, J. and Brown, K. (2014) Evaluating the Impact of Learning and Staff Development Programmes: An Example of the Behaviour and Practice Change of Leadership Programme Through the Analysis of Written Assignments. The National Centre for Post-Qualifying Social Work and Professional Practice.

Holroyd, J. and Brown, K. (2014) *Self Leadership: Building Personal Resilience and Relationships that work within Health and Social Care*, Bournemouth: Learn to Care.

Holroyd, J. and Field, R. (2012) *Performance Coaching Skills for Social Work*. London: Sage.

Homans, C. G. (1951) The Human Group. London: Routledge & Kegan Paul.

Howe, K. and Gray, I. (2013) *Effective Supervison in Social Work*. London: Sage.

Ibarra H. (2012) 'Is "command and control" the new leadership model?'. Blog. *Harvard Business Review* website. Available on: http://blogs.hbr.org/2012/02/is-command-and-collaborate-the/

Janis, I. (1971) Groupthink Among Policy Makers, in Sanford, N. and Comstock, C. (eds) *Sanctions for Evil*. San Francisco: Jossey-Bass. Available on: www.er.uqam.ca/nobel/d101000/ JanisGroupthinkPolicyMakers.pdf

Janis, I. (1972) Victims of Groupthink: A Psychological Study of Foreign Policy Decisions and Fiascoes. Boston, MA: Houghton Mifflin.

Jennings, E. E. (1960) *An Anatomy of Leadership: Princes, Heroes and Supermen*. New York: Harper.

Johnson, G., Whittington, R., Scholes, K., Angwin, D., and Regner, P. (2014) *Exploring Corporate Strategy* (10th edition). Harlow: Pearson.

Johnson-Lenz, P.T. (2009) *Six Habits of Highly Resilient Organisations*. Available online at: http://www. peopleandplace.net/perspectives, p120.

Kahneman, D. (2011) *Thinking Fast and Slow*, Allen Lane an imprint of Penguin Books, London.

Kanter, R. M. (2013) *Surprises Are the New Normal; Resilience is the New Skill*, Harvard Business Review Blog Available on: https://hbr.org/2013/07/surprises-are-the-new-normal-r.html.

Keats, J. (1817. Negative Capability, in Hebron, S. (ND) *John Keats and Negative Capability* www.bl.uk/ romantics-and-victorians/articles/john-keats-and-negative-capability.

Keen, S., Brown, K., Holroyd, J. and Rosenorn-Lanng, E. (2013) Evaluating the Impact of The IPOP (Improving Personal And Organisational Performance) Programme: An Introductory Leadership and Management Development Module for Social Work Managers. *Social Work and Social Sciences Review*, Vol.17, No.1, pp64–82.

Keirsey, D. and Bates, M. (1984) *Please Understand Me* (5th edition). Del Mar, CA: Prometheus Nemesis.

W. K. Kellogg Foundation Evaluation Handbook (2004) www.wkkf.org/-/media/pdfs/evaluationhandbook.ashx.

W. K. Kellogg Foundation (2004) Logic Model Development Guide. Battle Creek, MI: W. W. K. Kellogg Foundation. Available at www.wkkf.org/Pubs/Tools/Evaluation/ Pub3669.pdf.

Kierney, B. (1992) Report of the Inquiry into Child Care Policies in Fife. Edinburgh: H.M.S.O., p1-779.

Kirkpatrick, D. L. (1959) Techniques for Evaluating Training Programs. *Journal of the American Society of Training and Development*, Vol. 33, No. 11, pp3–9.

Kline, N. (2009) *More Time to Think: A Way of Being in the World*. London: Fisher King Publishing.

Knight, S. (2002) *NLP at Work* (2nd edition). London: Nicholas Brealey Publishing.

Kolb, D. (1984) *Experiential Learning as a Source of Learning and Development*. Prentice Hall: London.

Kouzes, J. M. and Posner, B. Z. (2002) *The Leadership Challenge* (3rd edition). San Francisco, CA: Wiley.

Kouzes, J. M. and Posner, B. Z. (2007) *The Leadership Challenge*. San Francisco, CA: Jossey-Bass.

Laming, W.H. (2009) *The Protection of Children in England: A Progress Report*. London: Crown Copyright, p1-401.

Leadership Academy www.leadershipacademy.nhs.uk/resources/healthcare-leadership-model/

Lencioni, P. (2005) Overcoming the Five Dysfunctions of a Team: A Field Guide For Leaders, Managers, and Facilitators. Chichester: John Wiley & Sons.

Lencioni, P. (2016) *The Ideal Team Player: How to Recognise and Cultivate the Three Essential Virtues*. Jossey-Bass. A John Wiley & Sons Inc. imprint.

Loehr, J. and Schwartz, T. (2003) *The Power of Full Engagement*. New York: Free Press, p7.

McBain, R., Ghobadian, A., Switzer, J., Wilton, P., Woodman, P. and Pearson, G. (2012) *The Business Benefits of Management and Leadership Development*. London: Chartered Management Institute.

McGonigal, K. (2013) How To Make Stress Your Friend. Available on: www.ted.com/talks/kelly_mcgonigal_how_to_make_stress_your_friend.

McGregor, D. (1961) *The Human Side of Enterprise*. NY: McGraw Hill.

McPherson, L., Frederico, M. and McNamara, P. (2016) Safety as a Fifth Dimension in Supervision: Stories from the Frontline. *Australian Social Work*, Vol.69, No.1, pp67–79, DOI: 10.1080/0312407X.2015.1024265

Manchester City Council (2013a). Living longer, living better: an integrated care blueprint. Paper presented to health and wellbeing board, March. Available on: www.manchester.gov.uk/meetings/ meeting/1886/health_and_wellbeing_board.

Manchester City Council (2013b). Living longer, living better: strategic outline case. Paper presented to health and wellbeing board, June. Available on: www.manchester.gov.uk/meetings/meeting/2058/ health_and_wellbeing_board.

Marshak, J. (2006) *Covert Processes at Work Managing the Five Hidden Dimensions of Organizational Change*. San Francisco, CA: Berrett-Koehler Publishers.

Marshall Ganz (2011) *Public Narrative, Collective Action, and Power* in S. Odugbemi and T. Lee (eds) Accountability through Public Opinion: From Inertia to Public Action. Washington: The International Bank for Reconstruction and Development and World Bank Publications. Available online at: http://siteresources.worldbank.org/EXTGOVACC/Resources/Accountabilitybookweb.pdf

Maslach, C., Schaufeli, W., Leiter, M. (2001) *Job Burnout. Annual Rev. Psychol. (53) 397–422 p409.*

Maslow, A. N. (1943) A Theory of Human Motivation. *Psychological Review*, Vol.50 No.4, pp370–96.

Mayo, G. E. (1933) *The Human Problem of an Industrialized Civilization*. London: Macmillan.

MBTI (2007) Step 1 Report Booklet, CPP Incorporated.

Mendelow, A. (1991) *Proposed Model On Stakeholder Ranking*. Paper presented at the Second International Conference on Information Systems, Cambridge, MA.

Mook, D.G. (1987) Motivation: The Organization of Action. New York: Norton.

Moreno, J. L. (1960) *The Sociometry Reader*. Glencoe, NY: Free Press.

Morrison, T. (2005) *Supervision in Social Care*. London: Pavilion.

Mullins, I. (2007) *Management and Organisational Behaviour* (8th edition). Harlow: Prentice Hall.

Mumford, M. D. (2010) *Leadership 101: The Psych 101 Series*, New York: Springer Publishing Company.

National Voices (2013) *A Narrative for Person-Centred Coordinated Care*, NHS England Publication Gateway Reference Number: 00076 Available on: www.england.nhs.uk/wp-content/uploads/2013/05/nv-narrative-cc.pdf.

Neck, C. P. and Manz, C. C. (2010) *Mastering Self-Leadership: Empowering Yourself for Personal Excellence* (5th edition). Upper Saddle River, NJ: Prentice Hall.

Neff, K. (2011) *Self-Compassion: Stop Beating Yourself Up and Leave Insecurity Behind*. London: Hodder and Stoughton.

Neill, M. (2013) *The Inside Out Revolution*. London: Hay House.

NHS Confederation (2014) *The 2015 Challenge Declaration*. London: NHS Confederation.

NHS England, National Voices, Think Local, Act Personal, A Narrative for Person-Centred Coordinated Care, NHS England Publications, 2013.

NHS England, Our 2016/17 Business Plan, 2016, www.england.nhs.uk/.../2016/03/bus-plan-16.pdf

NHS Leadership Academy, Health Care Leadership Model, NHS Leadership Academy.

Northouse, P. G. (2010) *Leadership: Theory and Practice* (5th edition). London: Sage.

Northouse P. G. (2013) *Leadership: Theory and Practice* (6th edition). London: Sage (Kindle version).

Nuffield Trust, Health Foundation and King's Fund (2015) *The Spending Review: what does it mean for health and social care?* Available online at: www.kingsfund.org.uk/sites/files/kf/field/field_publication_file/Spending-Review- Nuffield-Health-Kings- Fund-December- 2015_0.pdf.

O'Connor, J. and Seymour, J. (2003) *Introducing NLP.* London: Thorsons.

Oliver, M. (2003) The Journey, in Housden, R. *Ten Poems to Change Your Life*. London: Hodder and Stoughton.

Olivier, S., Burls, T., Fenge, L.A., Brown, K. (Apr 2016) *Safeguarding Adults and Mass Marketing Fraud – Perspectives from the Police, Trading Standards and the Voluntary Sector* Journal of Social Welfare and Family Law 38(2):140–151 02

Pavlovich, K., and Krahnke, K. (2014) *Organizing Through Empathy*, Routledge Studies in Management, Organizations, and Society, Routledge Taylor and Francis Group New York and London. (Kindle version)

Pransky, J. (2011) *Somebody Should Have Told Us! (Simple Truths for Living Well) The Mind–Spirit Connection* (3rd edition). British Columbia, Canada: CCB Publishing.

Ramachandran, V. S. (2011) *The Tell-Tale Brain: Unlocking the Mystery of Human Nature*. Windmill Books (Kindle version).

Reinhold, R. (2010) *Personality Pathways: Exploring Personality Type and its Applications*, Available on www.personalitypathways.

Ritchie J. and Lewis J. (eds) (2003) *Qualitative Research Practice: A Guide for Social Science Students and Researchers*. London: Sage.

Rock, D. (2007) *Quiet Leadership: Six steps to Transforming Performance at Work: Help people to think better – Don't tell them what to do*. HarperCollins e-books.

Rogers, J. (2004) *Coaching Skills*. Maidenhead: Open University Press, p48.

Rousseau, D.M. (1989) Psychological and Implied Contracts in Organisations. *Employee Responsibilities and Rights Journal,* (2) p121-139.

Rousseau, D.M. (1989) *Psychological and Implied Contracts in Organisations- Understanding Written and Unwritten Agreements*. CA: Sage.

Royles, D. (2013). Francis report will be biggest leadership the NHS has seen. Available on: www.the guardian.com/healthcare-network/2013/jan/24/francis-report-leadership-challenge-nhs.

Ruch, G. (2007) Reflective Practice in Contemporary Child Care Social Work; The role of containment. *British Journal of Social Work*, Vol.37, No. 4 pp659–80.

Rutter, L. and Brown, K. (2015) *Critical Thinking and Professional Judgement for Social Work* (4th edition). London: Sage p60.

Senge, P. (1990) *The Fifth Discipline: The Art and Practice of the Learning Organization*. London: Century Business.

SCIE (2012) Factors that promote and hinder joint and integrated working between health and social care services, SCIE Research Briefing 41.

Shannon, E. A. and Van Dam, P. (2013) Developing Positive Leadership in Health and Human Services, SA. *Journal of Industrial Psychology*, Vol.39, No.2. Available on: www.scielo.org.za/scielo.php?pid=S2071-07632013000200012&script=sci_arttext&tlng=pt.

Siegel, D. J. (2010) *The Mindful Therapist: A Clinician's Guide to Mindsight and Neural Integration*. New York: W.W. Norton & Company Inc.

Sinek, S. (2009) *Start With Why: How Great Leaders Inspire Everyone to Take Action*. New York: Penguin Group.

Skills for Care, Leadership Qualities Framework, Skills for Care, www.skillsforcare.org.uk.

Snyder, S. (2013) Why is Resilience so Hard, *Harvard Business Review Blog* Available on: https://hbr.org/2013/11/why-is-resilience-so-hard&cm_sp=Article-_-Links-_-End%20of%20Page%20Recirculation

Social Care Institute for Excellence (SCIE) (2015) Co-Production in Social Care: What it is and How To Do It, Available on: http://www.scie.org.uk/publications/guides/guide51/what-is-coproduction/principles-of-coproduction.asp

Social Work Reform Partners (2014) The Standards for Employers of Social Workers in England, Available on: www.local.gov.uk/workforce

Stokes, J. (1994). The Unconscious at Work in Groups and Teams: Contributions from the work of Wilfred Bion, in: Obholzer, A. and Zagier Roberts, V. (eds) (1994) *The Unconscious at Work, Individual and Organizational Stress in The Human Services*. London: Routledge.

Tannerbaum, R. and Schmidt. W. H. (1973) How to Choose a Leaderhip Pattern. *Harvard Business Review*, Vol.51, No.3, pp162–80.

Taylor, F. W. (1911) *Principles of Scientific Management*. New York & London: Harper & Brothers.

The King's Fund (2011) The Future of Leadership and Management in the NHS. No More Heroes. Report from the King's Fund commission on Leadership and management in the NHS. The King's Fund: London.

The King's Fund and Centre for Creative Leadership (2014a). Developing Collective Leadership for Health Care, The King's Fund.

The King's Fund and Centre for Creative Leadership (2014b). Delivering a Collective Leadership Strategy for Health Care, The King's Fund.

The Leadership Qualities Framework for Adult Social Care (2013). The Leadership Qualities Framework for Adult Social Care – Leadership starts with me, National Skills Academy Social Care, London.

Thorpe, R., Gold, J. and Lawler, J. (2011) Locating Distributed Leadership. *International Journal of Management Reviews*, Vol. 13, pp239–250. British Academy of Management and Blackwell Publishing Ltd.

Timmins, N. and Ham, C. (2013) The Quest for Integrated Health and Social Care: A Case Study in Canterbury, New Zealand. London: The King's Fund. Available at: www.kingsfund.org.uk/publications/questintegrated-health-and-social-care.

Torres, R. (2013) What it Takes to be a Great Leader www.ted.com/talks/roselinde_torres_what_it_takes_to_be_a_great_leader. www.local.gov.uk/documents/10180/6188796/The_standards..., 17th April 2016

Tuckman, B. W. (1965) Developmental Sequence in Small Groups. *Psychological Bulletin*, 63, pp384–9.

Wenger, E., 1998. *Communities of practice: Learning, meaning, and identity*. Cambridge University Press.

West, M., Eckert, R., Steward, K. and Pasmore, B. (2014). Developing Collective Leadership for Health Care. London: The King's Fund/Centre for Creative Leadership. Available at: www.kingsfund.org.uk/ publications/developing-collective-leadership-health-care

Whitmore, J. (2010) *Coaching for Performance: Growing Human Potential And Purpose. The Principles and Practice of Coaching and Leadership* (4th Edition). London: Nicholas Brearley.

Wonnacott, J. (2012) *Mastering Social Work Supervision*. London: Jessica Kingsley.

Zacarro, S. J. (2007) Trait-Based Perspectives of Leadership. *American Psychologist*, Vol.62, No.1:pp6–16.

Zheltoukhova, K. (2014). Leadership – Easier Said Than Done: Research Report. London: Chartered Institute of Personnel Development.

Index